THE NEW CAMBRIDGE SHAKESPEARE

FOUNDING GENERAL EDITOR
Philip Brockbank

GENERAL EDITOR
Brian Gibbons, *Professor of English Literature, University of Zürich*

ASSOCIATE GENERAL EDITORS
A.R. Braunmuller, *Professor of English, University of California, Los Angeles*
Robin Hood, *Senior Lecturer in English, University of York*

THE FIRST PART OF KING HENRY VI

Shakespeare's plays about the reign of Henry VI, written at the beginning of his career, were for a long time undervalued. This was because of doubts about their authorship and because of the difficulties of determining their theatrical provenance. Recently, however, a series of outstanding productions by the Royal Shakespeare Company and others has demonstrated their theatrical vitality, their conventions have been better understood in the light of new critical methods, and their innovative and sceptical questioning of Elizabethan orthodoxies has been understood in the light of revisionist readings of the history of Shakespeare's own times. The Wars of the Roses haunted the Elizabethans, as is shown by the number of authors who wrote about them. Shakespeare's account was the most ambitious, the most dramatically innovative, and politically the most radical.

This, the first major edition for over twenty-five years, takes account of recent discoveries concerning Shakespeare's early career, and the statistical tests that have been devised to determine problems of authorship, and pays particular attention to recent theatrical history, relating readings generated by modern performances to new ideologically positioned accounts of the history and politics of Shakespeare's age.

The First Part of King Henry VI, which gives us Shakespeare's portrait of Joan of Arc, stands revealed both as a successful venture in its own exploratory style, and as a necessary account of key events in the Hundred Years War without which the Wars of the Roses, anatomised in the next two plays, cannot be understood.

THE NEW CAMBRIDGE SHAKESPEARE

THE FIRST PART OF KING HENRY VI

Edited by
MICHAEL HATTAWAY
Professor of English Literature, University of Sheffield

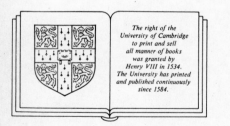

The right of the
University of Cambridge
to print and sell
all manner of books
was granted by
Henry VIII in 1534.
The University has printed
and published continuously
since 1584.

CAMBRIDGE UNIVERSITY PRESS

Cambridge
New York   Port Chester
Melbourne   Sydney

Published by the Press Syndicate of the University of Cambridge
The Pitt Building, Trumpington Street, Cambridge CB2 1RP
40 West 20th Street, New York, NY 10011, USA
10 Stamford Road, Oakleigh, Melbourne 3166, Australia

First published 1990

Printed in Great Britain at the University Press, Cambridge

British Library cataloguing in publication data

Shakespeare, William, *1564–1616*
The first part of King Henry VI. – (The New Cambridge Shakespeare)
I. Title   II. Hattaway, Michael
822.3'3

Library of Congress cataloguing in publication data

Shakespeare, William, 1564–1616.
The first part of King Henry VI.
(The New Cambridge Shakespeare)
Bibliography.
1. Henry VI, King of England, 1421–1471 – Drama.
I. Hattaway, Michael.   II. Series: Shakespeare, William,
1564–1616.   Works.   1984.   Cambridge University Press.
PR2814.A2H38   1990   822.3'3   89-9940

ISBN 0 521 22754 2   hard covers
ISBN 0 521 29634 X   paperback

THE NEW CAMBRIDGE SHAKESPEARE

The *New Cambridge Shakespeare* succeeds *The New Shakespeare* which began publication in 1921 under the general editorship of Sir Arthur Quiller-Couch and John Dover Wilson, and was completed in the 1960s, with the assistance of G. I. Duthie, Alice Walker, Peter Ure and J. C. Maxwell. *The New Shakespeare* itself followed upon *The Cambridge Shakespeare*, 1863–6, edited by W. G. Clark, J. Glover and W. A. Wright.

The New Shakespeare won high esteem both for its scholarship and for its design, but shifts of critical taste and insight, recent Shakespearean research, and a changing sense of what is important in our understanding of the plays, have made it necessary to re-edit and redesign, not merely to revise, the series.

The *New Cambridge Shakespeare* aims to be of value to a new generation of playgoers and readers who wish to enjoy fuller access to Shakespeare's poetic and dramatic art. While offering ample academic guidance, it reflects current critical interests and is more attentive than some earlier editions have been to the realisation of the plays on the stage, and to their social and cultural settings. The text of each play has been freshly edited, with textual data made available to those users who wish to know why and how one published text differs from another. Although modernised, the edition conserves forms that appear to be expressive and characteristically Shakespearean, and it does not attempt to disguise the fact that the plays were written in a language other than that of our own time.

Illustrations are usually integrated into the critical and historical discussion of the play and include some reconstructions of early performances by C. Walter Hodges. Some editors have also made use of the advice and experience of Maurice Daniels, for many years a member of the Royal Shakespeare Company.

Each volume is addressed to the needs and problems of a particular text, and each therefore differs in style and emphasis from others in the series.

PHILIP BROCKBANK
General Editor

CONTENTS

ILLUSTRATIONS

Illustrations 4, 7 and 11 are reproduced by permission of the British Library; illustration 1 by permission of the Folger Shakespeare Library; illustrations 2, 6, 12 and 13, from The Tom Holte Photographic Collection, by permission of the Shakespeare Centre Library, Stratford-upon-Avon; illustrations 9, 14, 15 and 16 by permission of Joe Cocks Photography.

PREFACE

Editing the *Henry VI* plays has been a prolonged and, usually, a rewarding challenge. As texts for editors they are comparatively unexplored, for it is only in the last quarter of a century that their particular qualities have been perceived. It is not to academic colleagues that we owe this revaluation but to directors and actors who have liberated them not only from the condescension of scholars who doubted their authorship but from critics who, by pointing to stylistic imperfections in his earlier works, wanted to prove that Shakespeare was human.

If we forget for the moment about the author, and concentrate on the texts, taking cognisance of their self-delighting pageantry, oratory, and theatricality, their outsize characters, and if we relate our attention to the recently rewritten political and social history of the 1590s, the plays stand revealed as not only telling an epic story, quite remarkable for its scope and ambitions, but offering a prolonged interrogation of the nature of government and the motives of governors. These plays have probably suffered more than most from bardolatry, from preconceptions concerning what ought to be the main interests of 'England's national poet'. We might simply want to remind ourselves at this point that Shakespeare wrote them before he was thirty.

It is in the theatre indeed that the value and dramatic potential of these texts has been demonstrated. In the decades since the last major editions, those of John Dover Wilson (New Shakespeare, 1952) and Andrew S. Cairncross (Arden, 1962), Stratford and London have seen major productions of versions of this history cycle (1964 and 1977), a shortened version went on a national tour (1987–8), and another shortened version appeared at Stratford in late 1988. Reviews of these productions have turned into some of the most perceptive critical appraisals of the Henry VI plays.

These two editions, along with that of Norman Sanders (New Penguin, 1981), created major advances in our knowledge of the texts. To Wilson and Sanders I owe a debt for their major work on the lexical problems of the text, although I have been surprised by how much there was still to do. Now it is possible and necessary for the problems of authorship, theatrical provenance, and textual transmission to be placed in perspective, and for an editor to address himself to the literary, theatrical, and cultural values of his chosen plays. This has been the major work for me. (My Cambridge predecessor, J. Dover Wilson, completed his work on what he considered to be 'one of the worst plays in the canon. . . [and] one of the most debatable' (p. ix) with relief. His introduction is devoted entirely to problems of authorship and composition and of provenance, as well as to possible topical allusions, and has nothing to say about the play's qualities. I share his relief, but not his lack of enthusiasm.) To Cairncross, I offer thanks for his passion for the plays, his conviction that they were by Shakespeare and composed after the order of the chronicle sequence they dramatise, and for challenging theories about the textual dimensions, which, however, I am afraid I am unable for the most part to support. Cairncross's ingenuities are a testimony to his conviction that the plays are worth working on.

The Oxford edition of Shakespeare and the accompanying *William Shakespeare: A Textual Companion* appeared when my work was well advanced. Although I could not agree with many of the revisions made in the Oxford version of this text, I have been creatively provoked by the emendations therein and by the information in the *Companion*.

To Philip Brockbank, who died two weeks before I could send him the final proofs, I am grateful for much encouragement and the loan of his PhD thesis, which not only records pioneering work on the sources of the sequence but generated a series of articles which were really the first to treat the plays as a major achievement. These stood virtually alone and certainly unchallenged for a critical generation and form a central part of his literary memorial.

Librarians at the Universities of Kent, Sheffield, and Texas, the British Library, the London Library, and the Shakespeare Centre in Stratford have been consistently helpful. Dr Pamela Mason guided me towards some of the pictorial archives, and Professor Dominique Goy-Blanquet argued the toss with me over the meaning of the play and directed me to useful French material. Professor Brian Gibbons, my General Editor, was perceptive, courteous both when critical and encouraging, and unfailingly prompt to respond to what I sent him. Professor Patrick Collinson introduced me to the new wave of political, religious, and social historians of the period. Thanks to Sarah Stanton of CUP for her patience and sage suggestions, to Paul Chipchase, who copy-edited my typescript with exemplary care and insight, and to Dr Carol Chillington Rutter for sharpening up a draft of my introduction and for sharing her knowledge of Terry Hands's 1977 production. To Professor Gary Taylor for generously sending me a copy of his 'Shakespeare and others: the authorship of *1 Henry VI*' in advance of its publication. C. Walter Hodges defined the terms of his dialogue with his editor: my notes often serve to illuminate his drawings.

Sue, Ben, Rafe and Max suffered sometimes in silence when Daddy went upstairs to work – more often not. But without them this work would have taken even longer to appear.

M. H.

University of Sheffield

ABBREVIATIONS AND CONVENTIONS

Shakespeare's plays, when cited in this edition, are abbreviated in a style modified slightly from that used in the *Harvard Concordance to Shakespeare*. Other editions of Shakespeare are abbreviated under the editor's surname (Cairncross, Dyce) unless they are the work of more than one editor. In such cases, an abbreviated series name is used (Cam., Johnson Var.). When more than one edition by the same editor is cited, later editions are discriminated with a raised figure (Collier²). All quotations from Shakespeare, except those from *1–3 Henry VI*, use the lineation of *The Riverside Shakespeare*, under the general editorship of G. Blakemore Evans.

1. Shakespeare's plays

Ado	*Much Ado About Nothing*
Ant.	*Antony and Cleopatra*
AWW	*All's Well That Ends Well*
AYLI	*As You Like It*
Cor.	*Coriolanus*
Cym.	*Cymbeline*
Err.	*The Comedy of Errors*
Ham.	*Hamlet*
1H4	*The First Part of King Henry the Fourth*
2H4	*The Second Part of King Henry the Fourth*
H5	*King Henry the Fifth*
1H6	*The First Part of King Henry the Sixth*
2H6	*The Second Part of King Henry the Sixth*
3H6	*The Third Part of King Henry the Sixth*
H8	*King Henry the Eighth*
JC	*Julius Caesar*
John	*King John*
LLL	*Love's Labour's Lost*
Lear	*King Lear*
Mac.	*Macbeth*
MM	*Measure for Measure*
MND	*A Midsummer Night's Dream*
MV	*The Merchant of Venice*
Oth.	*Othello*
Per.	*Pericles*
R2	*King Richard the Second*
R3	*King Richard the Third*
Rom.	*Romeo and Juliet*
Shr.	*The Taming of the Shrew*
STM	*Sir Thomas More*
Temp.	*The Tempest*
TGV	*The Two Gentlemen of Verona*

Tim.	*Timon of Athens*
Tit.	*Titus Andronicus*
TN	*Twelfth Night*
TNK	*The Two Noble Kinsmen*
Tro.	*Troilus and Cressida*
Wiv.	*The Merry Wives of Windsor*
WT	*The Winter's Tale*

2. Other works cited and general references

Abbott	E. A. Abbott, *A Shakespearian Grammar*, 1878 edn (references are to numbered paragraphs)
Alexander	*William Shakespeare, The Complete Works*, ed. Peter Alexander, 1951
Arber	E. Arber, *A Transcript of the Registers of the Company of Stationers of London 1554–1640*, 5 vols., 1875–94
Baldwin	T. W. Baldwin, *Shakspere's 'Small Latine & Lesse Greeke'*, 2 vols., 1944
Bell	*Bell's Edition of Shakespeare's Plays*, ed. J. Bell, 9 vols., 1774
Bentley	G. E. Bentley, *The Jacobean and Caroline Stage*, 7 vols., 1941–68
Boswell-Stone	W. G. Boswell-Stone, *Shakespeare's Holinshed: The Chronicle and the Historical Plays Compared*, 1896
Brewer	E. C. Brewer, *The Dictionary of Phrase and Fable*, n.d.
Brockbank	J. P. Brockbank, 'Shakespeare's Historical Myth: A Study of Shakespeare's Adaptations of his Sources in making the Plays of *Henry VI* and *Richard III*', unpublished PhD dissertation, University of Cambridge, 1953
Brooke	*1 Henry VI*, ed. C. F. Tucker Brooke, 1918
Bullough	Geoffrey Bullough, *Narrative and Dramatic Sources of Shakespeare*, 8 vols., 1957–75
Cairncross	*1 Henry VI*, ed. Andrew S. Cairncross, 1962 (Arden)
Cam.	*Works*, ed. William Aldis Wright, 9 vols., 1891–3 (Cambridge Shakespeare)
Capell	*Mr William Shakespeare his Comedies, Histories, and Tragedies*, ed. Edward Capell, 10 vols., 1767–8
Cercignani	F. Cercignani, *Shakespeare's Works and Elizabethan Pronunciation*, 1981
Chambers	E. K. Chambers, *The Elizabethan Stage*, 4 vols., 1923
Collier	*Works*, ed. John P. Collier, 8 vols., 1842–4
Collier[2]	*Works*, ed. John P. Collier, 1853
Collier MS.	Perkins's Second Folio, 1632 (Huntington Library)
Colman	E. A. M. Colman, *The Dramatic Use of Bawdy in Shakespeare*, 1974
conj.	conjecture
Dekker, *ND*	Thomas Dekker, *Non Dramatic Works*, 5 vols., 1884–6
Dent	R. W. Dent, *Shakespeare's Proverbial Language: An Index*, 1981 (references are to numbered proverbs)
DNB	*Dictionary of National Biography*
Dyce	*The Works of William Shakespeare*, ed. Alexander Dyce, 6 vols., 1857
Dyce[2]	*The Works of William Shakespeare*, ed. Alexander Dyce, 9 vols., 1864–7
Eds.	Various editors
ELR	*English Literary Renaissance*

F	*Mr William Shakespeares Comedies, Histories, and Tragedies*, 1623 (First Folio)
F2	*Mr William Shakespeares Comedies, Histories, and Tragedies*, 1632 (Second Folio)
F3	*Mr William Shakespeares Comedies, Histories, and Tragedies*, 1664 (Third Folio)
F4	*Mr William Shakespeares Comedies, Histories, and Tragedies*, 1685 (Fourth Folio)
Fabyan	Robert Fabyan, *The New Chronicles of England and France*, 1516, reprinted 1811
FQ	Edmund Spenser, *The Faerie Queene*, ed. A. C. Hamilton, 1977
Grafton	Richard Grafton, *A Chronicle at Large of the History of The Affayres of England*, 1569, reprinted in 2 vols., 1809
Hall	Edward Hall, *The Union of the...Families of Lancastre and York*, 1548, reprinted 1809 (page references are to the 1809 edn)
Halliwell	*The Complete Works of Shakespeare*, ed. James O. Halliwell, 16 vols., 1853–65
Hanmer	*The Works of Shakespear*, ed. Thomas Hanmer, 6 vols., 1743–4
Harlow	C. G. Harlow, 'The authorship of *1 Henry VI*', *SEL* 5 (1965), 269–81
Hart	*1 Henry VI*, ed. H. C. Hart, 1909 (Arden)
Hattaway	Michael Hattaway, *Elizabethan Popular Theatre*, 1982
Henslowe	*Henslowe's Diary*, ed. R. A. Foakes and R. T. Rickert, 1961
Holinshed	Raphael Holinshed, *Chronicles of England, Scotland, and Ireland*, 2nd edn, 1587; reprinted in 6 vols., 1808 (unless otherwise specified, page references are to the 1808 edn)
Hudson	*The Complete Works of William Shakespeare*, ed. Henry N. Hudson, 11 vols., 1851–6
Hulme	Hilda M. Hulme, *Explorations in Shakespeare's Language*, 1962
Irving	*The Works of William Shakespeare*, ed. Henry Irving and Frank A. Marshall, 8 vols., 1888–90
Johnson	*The Plays of William Shakespeare*, ed. Samuel Johnson, 8 vols., 1765
Johnson Var.	*The Plays of William Shakespeare*, ed. Samuel Johnson and George Steevens, 10 vols., 1773
Keightley	*The Plays of Shakespeare*, ed. Thomas Keightley, 6 vols., 1864
Kittredge	*The Complete Works of Shakespeare*, ed. George Lyman Kittredge, 1936
Kökeritz	Helge Kökeritz, *Shakespeare's Pronunciation*, 1953
Long	John H. Long, *Shakespeare's Use of Music: The Histories and Tragedies*, 1971
Mahood	M. M. Mahood, *Shakespeare's Wordplay*, 1957
Malone	*The Plays and Poems of William Shakespeare*, ed. Edmond Malone, 10 vols., 1790
Mason	John Monck Mason, *Comments on...Shakespeare's Plays*, 1785
Metamorphoses	Ovid, *Metamorphoses*, trans. Arthur Golding (1567), ed. J. F. Nims, 1965
Mirror	*The Mirror for Magistrates*, ed. Lily B. Campbell, 1938
Munro	*The London Shakespeare*, ed. John Munro, 6 vols., 1958
Nashe	Thomas Nashe, *Works*, ed. R. B. McKerrow, 5 vols., 1904–10, rev. F. P. Wilson, 1958

Neilson	*The Complete Dramatic and Poetic Works of William Shakespeare*, ed. William Alan Neilson, 1906
Noble	Richmond Noble, *Shakespeare's Biblical Knowledge*, 1935
NQ	*Notes and Queries*
OED	*Oxford English Dictionary*
Onions	C. T. Onions, *A Shakespeare Glossary*, rev. Robert D. Eagleson, 1986
Oxford	*William Shakespeare: The Complete Works*, ed. Stanley Wells and Gary Taylor, 1986
Partridge	Eric Partridge, *Shakespeare's Bawdy*, 1968 edn
PBSA	*Papers of the Bibliographical Society of America*
Plutarch	*The Lives of the Noble Grecians and Romanes*, trans. Thomas North, 1579, 8 vols., 1928 edn
PMLA	*Publications of the Modern Language Association of America*
Pope	*The Works of Shakespear*, ed. Alexander Pope, 6 vols., 1723–5
PQ	*Philological Quarterly*
Reed	*The Plays of William Shakespeare*, [ed. Isaac Reed,] 10 vols., 1785
RES	*Review of English Studies*
Riverside	*The Riverside Shakespeare*, ed. G. Blakemore Evans, 1974
Rowe	*The Works of Mr William Shakespear*, ed. Nicholas Rowe, 6 vols., 1709
Rowe[2]	*The Works of Mr William Shakespear*, ed. Nicholas Rowe, 3rd edn, 8 vols., 1714
Sanders	*1 Henry VI*, ed. Norman Sanders, 1981 (New Penguin)
SB	*Studies in Bibliography*
Schmidt	Alexander Schmidt, *Shakespeare-Lexicon*, 1886 edn
Scott-Giles	C. W. Scott-Giles, *Shakespeare's Heraldry*, 1950
SD	stage direction
SEL	*Studies in English Literature*
Seymour	E. H. Seymour, *Remarks...upon the Plays of Shakespeare*, 2 vols., 1805
SH	speech heading
Shakespeare's England	*Shakespeare's England: An Account of the Life and Manners of his Age*, ed. Sidney Lee and C. T. Onions, 2 vols., 1916
Singer	*The Dramatic Works of William Shakespeare*, ed. Samuel Weller Singer, 10 vols., 1826
Singer[2]	*The Dramatic Works of William Shakespeare*, ed. Samuel Weller Singer, 10 vols., 1856
Sisson	*Works*, ed. C. J. Sisson, 1954
Sisson, *New Readings*	C. J. Sisson, *New Readings in Shakespeare*, 2 vols., 1956
SQ	*Shakespeare Quarterly*
S. St.	*Shakespeare Studies*
S. Sur.	*Shakespeare Survey*
Staunton	*The Plays of William Shakespeare*, ed. Howard Staunton, 3 vols., 1858–60
Steevens	*The Plays of William Shakespeare*, ed. George Steevens and Isaac Reed, 4th edn, 15 vols., 1793
Stow	John Stow, *The Survey of London*, 1603 edn, reprinted in Everyman Library, n.d.
subst.	substantively

Theobald	*The Works of Shakespeare*, ed. Lewis Theobald, 7 vols., 1733
Thomas	K. V. Thomas, *Religion and the Decline of Magic*, 1971
Thomson	W. H. Thomson, *Shakespeare's Characters: A Historical Dictionary*, 1951
Tilley	M. P. Tilley, *A Dictionary of the Proverbs in England in the Sixteenth and Seventeenth Centuries*, 1950 (references are to numbered proverbs)
TLN	Through line numbering
Tyrwhitt	Thomas Tyrwhitt, *Observations and Conjectures upon Some Passages of Shakespeare*, 1766
Vaughan	Henry H. Vaughan, *New Readings and New Renderings of Shakespeare's Tragedies*, 3 vols., 1886
Walker	William S. Walker, *Critical Examination of the Text of Shakespeare*, 3 vols., 1860
Warburton	*The Works of Shakespear*, ed. William Warburton, 8 vols., 1747
Wells and Taylor, *Textual Companion*	Stanley Wells and Gary Taylor, *William Shakespeare: A Textual Companion*, 1987
Williams	Penry Williams, *The Tudor Regime*, 1979
Wilson	*1 Henry VI*, ed. J. Dover Wilson, 1952 (New Shakespeare)

Unless otherwise specified, biblical quotations are given in the Geneva version (1560).

INTRODUCTION

Henry VI: the reign and the plays

Rather than describing the 'transgressions against history'[1] that Shakespeare was guilty of in his Henry VI plays – his account, that is, of the period from the funeral of Henry V in 1422 to the battle of Tewkesbury in 1471 – or rehearsing arguments over what parts of the text Shakespeare may or may not have written,[2] let us first consider what might have drawn him to this complicated chapter in the history of fifteenth-century England. Complicated it is, and so it was inevitable that its very wealth of incident led the dramatist to begin his career as a writer of history plays by concentrating as much on actions and their outcomes as on personalities and their motives: he could not avoid investigating politics and the secular as well as morality and the theological.

Unlike the reigns of Henry V or Richard III, that of Henry VI was not dominated by the personality of its monarch; Edward IV's rule during the last years of Henry's reign is stark evidence of this. Rather it was a period of war between nations (the Hundred Years War) and within the kingdom (the Wars of the Roses). It was also a time of dynastic strife which manifested itself in both aristocratic factionalism and popular insurrection, a sequence of contests between allegiance to the monarchy and alliance between peers. Shakespeare offered to the playhouse audiences of sixteenth-century London a deliberate rearrangement of historical events into dramatic themes. For this reason, therefore, the plays are best regarded not simply as 'adapted history' or as dramatic biography but as a complex essay on the *politics* of the mid fifteenth century – an essay which, of course, also offers reflections on his own times. For it was only after Shakespeare had in this way learned to convert chronicle into political analysis that he turned to the kind of history that thrusts personality out into the foreground of the action: *Richard II*, *Henry IV* and *Henry V* were written after the *Henry VI* plays and *Richard III*. The great sequence of studies of the history and politics of England was not composed in the order of the chronology of her Plantagenet rulers.

As this introduction will argue, Shakespeare did not slavishly follow 'the Tudor myth', unlike certain of the authors of his sources. 'The Tudor myth' held that God led England through these troubles to fulfil her destiny. Shakespeare suggests frequently, for example, that it is internal dissension, in particular seditious squabbling among the nobility, that damages England's power and authority abroad. The variety of styles found throughout the sequence may not, contrary to much scholarly opinion, be evidence of multiple authorship or revision,

---

[1] Theobald, IV, 390 n.
[2] See pp. 41–3 below.

but of perspectivism, a dramatic cross-examination from differing points of view, embodied in different dramatic styles, of the issues raised and events enacted on the stage. From the theatrical shorthand techniques Shakespeare used to depict the battles between England and France in *Part 1*, through the developing complexities of character in the events of *Part 2* – which is centred around the death of good Duke Humphrey of Gloucester and the rebellion of York – to the opposition of tormented Henry VI and murderous Richard of Gloucester[1] under Edward IV in *Part 3*, Shakespeare demonstrated a quite extraordinary capacity to 'set a form upon that indigest'.[2] The heroical idioms and scenical strutting of *1 Henry VI* disappear from the stage to be replaced by more workaday theatrical registers as Shakespeare traces the wane of England's glory and the mounting ferment of political intrigue.

THE LOSS OF FRANCE AND THE WARS OF THE ROSES

Henry VI came to the throne as a nine-month-old infant in 1422[3] and, while he was a minor, England was ruled through a council, his uncle 'good' Duke Humphrey of Gloucester being protector. During Henry's reign, despite the heroism on the field of battle of John Talbot, first Earl of Shrewsbury, and the overthrow and capture of the champion of the French, Joan, La Pucelle (see *1 Henry VI* 5.3–4), the French territory won back for England by virtue of his heroic father Henry V's victory at Agincourt in 1415 (*Henry V* 4.1–8) had by 1453 been recovered by his maternal uncle, Charles VII of France.

In *1 Henry VI*, Shakespeare moves from the funeral of Henry V through to the marriage of his son. He takes us a through a sequence of battles at Orléans (*1 Henry VI* 1.2 ff.), Rouen, and Bordeaux (*1 Henry VI* 3.2 ff. and 4.2 ff.),[4] leading to a truce which was called at Tours in 1444 (*1 Henry VI* 5.4) and which centred on a politic marriage for Henry (arranged with an eye to his own benefit by the Earl of Suffolk) with Margaret of Anjou, a cousin to King Charles. Although *1 Henry VI* thus ends, unhistorically, with an English triumph, Shakespeare has demonstrated *en route* that the empire has been irremediably weakened and that this was principally caused by internal sedition.

Margaret's coronation in 1445 marks the beginning of *2 Henry VI*, which concentrates largely on the conspiracy between Buckingham, Somerset, and Cardinal Beaufort, Bishop of Winchester, to drive Humphrey of Gloucester from power, and on civil tumult, the Wars of the Roses. These had begun when Henry's cousin

---

[1] Youngest son of York, and later Richard III.
[2] *John* 5.7.26; see Larry Champion, 'The search for dramatic form: *1, 2, 3 Henry VI*', in *Perspectives in Shakespeare's English Histories*, 1980, pp. 12–53.
[3] Ralph Griffiths, *The Reign of King Henry VI*, 1981, offers a modern history of the reign; see also K. B. McFarlane, *England in the Fifteenth Century*, 1982. W. G. Boswell-Stone, *Shakespeare's Holinshed: The Chronicle and the Historical Plays Compared*, 1896, reprints passages from the sources in the order Shakespeare deployed them; Peter Saccio, *Shakespeare's English Kings*, 1977, offers a modern account of the dramatic chronicle provided by Shakespeare.
[4] Rouen in fact was not taken by the French until 1449–50 and the fighting at Bordeaux took place nine years *after* the truce of Tours in 1444.

Richard, third Duke of York, laid claim to the throne. The claim was based on the grounds that York was the maternal great-great-grandson of Lionel, Duke of Clarence, third son of Edward III (1327–77), whereas Henry was great-grandson of John of Gaunt, Duke of Lancaster, the fourth son (see pp. 202–4 below). York chose as his badge a white rose, while the Lancastrians, led by York's enemy Somerset, wore red roses (*1 Henry VI* 2.4). (Henry VI's claim was further weakened by the fact that his grandfather Henry IV – 'Bullingbrook' – was commonly held to have usurped the throne and murdered the childless Richard II in 1400.) Moreover, rebellion broke out in Ireland, and York, who was assigned to put it down, took the opportunity to make his army serve his own ambition (*2 Henry VI* 3.1), winning the first battle of St Albans on 22 May 1455. This is depicted in the final sequence of *2 Henry VI*.

Henry was compelled to acknowledge York as heir apparent to the crown in 1460 (*3 Henry VI* 1.1), but York was defeated and savagely killed at the battle of Wakefield at the end of the year (*3 Henry VI* 1.3–4), a battle in which the barbarous Cliffords played a prominent part on the Lancastrian side. The Yorkists were defeated again at the second battle of St Albans in February 1461 (*3 Henry VI* 2.1),[1] but the Lancastrians then withdrew north while York's eldest son Edward was proclaimed as King Edward IV in London. The next month Edward marched northwards and won the battle of Towton which established him on the throne (*3 Henry VI* 2.3–6), and Henry took refuge in Scotland (his wife and son going into exile in France) until he was captured (*3 Henry VI* 3.1). He was imprisoned in the Tower (*3 Henry VI* 3.1) from 1465 until 1470 when he was restored to the throne by the 'Kingmaker' Earl of Warwick (*3 Henry VI* 4.2 and 4.6). Warwick had been enraged by the news that Edward, 'taking counsel of his own desire',[2] had made an impolitic marriage with the widow Elizabeth, Lady Grey (*3 Henry VI* 3.2), while Warwick was abroad negotiating the hand of a French princess for the new king. In April 1471, after losing the battle of Barnet in which Warwick was killed (*3 Henry VI* 5.2–3), Henry fell into the hands of Edward again, and Queen Margaret was defeated by Edward's younger brother, Richard of Gloucester, at the battle of Tewkesbury the next month (*3 Henry VI* 5.4–5). Henry was recommitted to the Tower, where, on the night of Edward's return, he was murdered (*3 Henry VI* 5.6) – by Gloucester, it is supposed. The sequence ends with a brief appearance by Edward's twelve-year-old son, later Edward V, who also was to be murdered in the Tower by Gloucester, along with his brother Richard.[3]

The reign then was a pattern of disorder, a mirror for Shakespeare's contemporaries of the disasters caused by the type of dynastic strife, centred on personalities and not ideology, which could so easily have broken out upon the

---

[1] The famous scene in which the king sees a father who has killed his son and a son who has killed his father (*3H6* 2.2) is fictitious.

[2] Hall, p. 366.

[3] See *R3* 4.3; Richard III, of course, was to be defeated and killed by Queen Elizabeth's Tudor grandfather, Henry VII, at the battle of Bosworth in 1485, so uniting the white rose with the red.

death of Elizabeth. Francis Bacon was to rejoice at the succession of King James, fearing that without it:

after Queen Elizabeth's decease, there must follow in England nothing but confusions, interreigns, and perturbations of estate, likely far to exceed the ancient calamities of Lancaster and York.[1]

Not only were there 'vertical' divisions between the noble factions: the reign witnessed division between the populace and the élite in the Jack Cade rebellion.[2] In his handling of this event, Shakespeare defined a distinct class consciousness[3] for his rebels, although he was interested also in the way in which political conflagration occurred when the horizontal divisions manifest in popular discontent were exacerbated by aristocratic dissension.[4]

To dramatise all this was massively ambitious, innovative – there were no popular plays on English history before the Armada in 1588 – and potentially radical. On 12 November 1589 the Privy Council instructed the Archbishop of Canterbury, the Lord Mayor of London and the Master of the Revels to inspect the 'books' (that is, the prompt-books) of all the players in the city so that 'matters of divinity and state' might be censored.[5] A dramatic sequence as long as this must also have created distinctive theatrical conventions – as modern revivals have demonstrated. It would have been expensive to perform in sequence without recourse to a standardised repertory style with some uniformity in costumes and with doubling – which may well have made telling political comments on the action. These plays are not vehicles for star performers – although modern actors have amassed great reputations from playing in them.

Political plays fell out of favour in the Jacobean period, and in the eighteenth century the plays disappeared almost completely from the canon of performed works. Perhaps they were too radical and anti-establishment; the female characters, moreover, were not objects of sentiment but seekers after power.[6] For the nineteenth century, they were unsuited for performance on naturalistic stages – and perhaps their anatomy of empire was too strong. In our own times critics have found them disappointingly based on narrative rather than significant struc-

---

[1] *The Beginning of the History of Great Britain*, in Bacon's *Works*, ed. Spedding, Ellis and Heath, 15 vols., 1857–74, VI, 276–7.

[2] See *2H6* 4.2–3, 5–9.

[3] On this notion in the period, see J. A. Sharpe, *Early Modern England: A Social History, 1550–1760*, 1987, p. 121; see also Michael Hattaway, 'Rebellion, class consciousness, and Shakespeare's *2 Henry VI*', *Cahiers Élisabéthains* 33 (1988), 13–22.

[4] For an account of the military power of aristocratic magnates in the 1590s see Sharpe, *Early Modern England*, p. 160.

[5] Chambers, IV, 306.

[6] So we read in the introduction to Bell's *Edition of Shakespeare's Plays*, 9 vols., 1774: 'National transactions, however important they may be in their nature and consequences, are not likely to have a very popular effect, as they tend chiefly to indulge political reflection, but have very little to gratify taste. Such pieces as this are also very barren of female characters and affecting circumstances, without which the drama is too defective. Shakespeare has herein adhered to facts, and maintained just preservation of character, without producing one striking scene: it is not therefore to be recommended for representation' (VII, 89).

ture, lacking both psychologically complex characters and the kinds of verbal density that Shakespeare was to attain in his later plays. The account of a modern actor's excited encounter in rehearsal with Molière, who in some respects is like the early Shakespeare, might sum up the disabling preconceptions actors and readers have brought to these texts in our time:

There's no poetry, no sub-text, just a very basic situation, like sit-com. [Our director] says, 'All there is is what is there, but that happens to be brilliant.' He says the French find Shakespeare [i.e. the later Shakespeare] difficult for the opposite reason. Why is he so oblique, they cry in Gallic confusion, why doesn't he just say what he means?[1]

Antony Sher, who wrote these lines, was to play a notable Richard III a few months later.

The decay of empire[2]

In the second speech of *1 Henry VI*, Humphrey, Duke of Gloucester, delivers in praise of his dead brother, King Henry V, an oration that constitutes a dramatic prologue to the sequence:

> England ne'er had a king until his time:
> Virtue he had, deserving to command;
> His brandished sword did blind men with his beams,
> His arms spread wider than a dragon's wings;
> His sparkling eyes, replete with wrathful fire,
> More dazzled and drove back his enemies
> Than midday sun fierce bent against their faces.
> What should I say? His deeds exceed all speech:
> He ne'er lift up his hand but conquerèd.   (1.1.8–16)

Henry V in fact will haunt the ensuing action: like the Ghost in *Hamlet*, he is a presence whose honour, prowess, and acquisition of empire throw into contrast the attacks of fatalism and debilitating piety suffered by his contemplative son.[3] What is remarkable about the speech, however, and indeed about the whole play, is its particular style. Henry V is presented not as a man but as a rhetorical construct fashioned out of hyperbole, as a heroic image or heraldic icon, and the speech takes its place in an extremely formal scene in which the mourners, clad in wailing robes (1.1.86; see illustration 1), enter to a dead march and range themselves about a stark theatrical image, the coffin of the late monarch. This stands in the centre of the stage as an emblem of fame and also establishes an image that

---

[1] Antony Sher, *Year of the King*, 1985, p. 46.
[2] Judith Hinchcliffe, *King Henry VI, Parts 1, 2, and 3*, Garland Shakespeare Bibliographies, 1986, provides an annotated survey of criticism. For a bibliographical essay see Edward Berry, 'Twentieth-century Shakespeare criticism: the histories' in Stanley Wells (ed.), *The Cambridge Companion to Shakespeare Studies*, 1986, pp. 249–56. Elizabethan theories of empire may be pursued in Frances A. Yates, *Astraea: The Imperial Theme in the Sixteenth Century*, 1975.
[3] Hall titles his section on Henry VI 'The Troublous Season of King Henry the Sixth' (p. 114). This comes after 'The Victorious Acts of King Henry the Fifth' (p. 46).

1   The funeral of Sir Philip Sidney, from Thomas Lant's *Sequitur Celebritas et Pompa Funeris* (1587)

seems to have been displaced in a discomforting way from the end of a tragedy or tragical history. 'Unhappy the land that is in need of heroes.'[1]

The speech is similar to the Pyrrhus speech in *Hamlet* (2.2.450 ff.).[2] That is obviously epic in mode, perhaps serving to set the dramatic qualities (and thus the political realities) of the surrounding play into relief. But the Pyrrhus speech also feels deliberately archaic, offering glimpses of an antecedent culture in which enterprises of revenge were not overlaid by the scruples of a more sophisticated society.[3] Both passages offer a degree of 'defamiliarisation'[4] (are written in such a way as to draw attention to their textual strategies) and thereby stand as preliminary measures of the play's other styles – and other realities – rather than as assertions. In the *Hamlet* passage, Shakespeare, it may be argued, was saying hail and farewell to the manner and achievement of his earlier work. In this, our earlier text, the iconic style serves as a way of evoking a mythic past and thereby measuring the present.

For archaism need not imply primitivism. The play is far more sophisticated than Maurice Morgann's dismissal of it as 'that Drum-and-trumpet Thing'[5] would imply. Even at this stage in his career, Shakespeare was working with deliberate artistry and forging a dramatic narrative that accommodated the straggling chronicles of his sources into tough-minded historical, historiographical, and con-

[1] Bertolt Brecht, *The Life of Galileo*, scene 13, in *Plays*, 1961, I, 320.
[2] See Michael Hattaway, *Hamlet: The Critics Debate*, 1987, pp. 88 ff.
[3] The speech is very similar to the description of the Black Prince in Peele's *The Honour of the Garter*, 1593, sig. B3ᵛ.
[4] See Victor Shklovsky, 'Art as technique', in Lee T. Lemon and Marion J. Reis (eds.), *Russian Formalist Criticism*, 1965, pp. 13 ff. For a general account of the way in which poets of the English Renaissance ceased to 'believe in' their images see Patrick Grant, *Images and Ideas in the Literature of the English Renaissance*, 1979, p. xi.
[5] *An Essay on the Dramatic Character of Sir John Falstaff* (1777) in D. Nichol Smith (ed.), *Eighteenth Century Essays on Shakespeare*, 1963, p. 226.

2   Act 1, Scene 1: the funeral of Henry V, from Peter Hall's production for the Royal Shakespeare Company, 1964

stitutional explorations. It is a young man's play – not because it is crude, but because it is ambitious, not because of the unsatisfactoriness of its form, but because of the diversity of its forms. Although 'history' plays had been written by others before Shakespeare,[1] these tended to be developments of Morality plays devoted to mapping the road to salvation for the common weal rather than that for the individual. Shakespeare invented the history play, which may be defined as a dramatisation of historical narrative that seeks to investigate not only the course of past events but the way in which they had been and were now perceived; to investigate by idealisation (sometimes) and demystification (sometimes) the power structures of its chosen period;[2] and to draw parallels between, and thereby anatomise, past and present political institutions and social realities.[3]

---

[1]   Irving Ribner, *The English History Play in the Age of Shakespeare*, rev. edn, 1965; see also Paul Dean, 'Shakespeare's *Henry VI* trilogy and Elizabethan "romance" histories: the origins of a genre', *SQ* 33 (1982), 34–48. Shakespeare may also have had a hand in the anonymous *The Reign of King Edward III* which was probably written and performed in 1589.

[2]   See J. W. Blanpied, ' "Art and baleful sorcery": the counterconsciousness of *Henry VI Part I*', *SEL* 15 (1975), 213–27; Leonard Tennenhouse, *Power on Display: The Politics of Shakespeare's Genres*, 1986, pp. 6–7; David Scott Kastan, 'Proud majesty made a subject: Shakespeare and the spectacle of rule', *SQ* 37 (1986), 459–75.

[3]   Like Sidney and Spenser, Shakespeare espoused the Aristotelian doctrine that the epic or tragic poet need not feel bound to adhere to actual events or the truth of history. The contrary position had been spelt out in Castelvetro's edition of *The Poetics* (see Geoffrey Shepherd's edition of Sidney's *Apology for Poetry*, 1973, p. 221).

The play may have been written shortly after the defeat of the Armada,[1] when the flush of self-congratulation occasioned by the defeat of the Spanish was to give way to a *fin-de-siècle* awareness of decay which was fed by uncertainty over the problem of determining a successor to Elizabeth and readily evoked by the spectacle of civil war manifest in the Wars of Religion in France. It was composed not very long after the Babington Plot of 1586 that led to the execution of Mary Queen of Scots.[2] It was a time when the Virgin Queen was hiding the ravages of age with make-up and concealing her person in costumes that gave her the profile of a funerary statue: Elizabeth had herself become an icon worshipped as a memorial to a dream of romantic feudalism. (The reality was what has been called 'bastard feudalism', a system by which patronage was based on payment rather than personal loyalties,[3] and fair Eliza had to cope not only with love-lorn 'servants' but with religious opposition, insurrection in Ireland, and rising food prices.) Typological parallels between past and present were constantly alive to the Elizabethans,[4] and Shakespeare chose to match – and sometimes subvert[5] – the symmetries and statuesque ornamentation of the new popular playhouses of Renaissance London (the façades of which so resembled the arches of triumph and fame used in civic pageantry) with an epic narrative inhabited by heroic personages stamped into the collective consciousness of the nation. Personalities are subsumed into themes, characters tend to archetypes, scenes to tableaux, and the verse embroiders around them the great symbols of garden[6] and court, innocence and machination.

STRUCTURE AND STYLE

Shakespeare's archaism is like Spenser's in *The Faerie Queene*, which was being published in the years of the play's composition. As in the allegory of the poet, the art is one of presentation as well as of representation. Narrative in this play, moreover, tends towards montage, a procession of speaking pictures that defines a bold dramatic rhythm. The *liaison des scènes* is figurative rather than causal; it is non-

---

[1] See below, p. 34.

[2] The concern of the queen over aristocratic factionalism of the sort we see emerging in this play was registered in 1585 in the 'Act for provision to be made for the surety of the Queen's most royal person' (27 Eliz. I, c.1) which sought to control the 'Bond of Association', an initiative taken two years earlier by Protestant gentry against those who might support Mary Queen of Scots.

[3] G. R. Elton, *England Under the Tudors*, 1974, p. 3; for an examination of the legal and moral bonds between the monarch and the lords in the trilogy see F. L. Kelly, 'Oaths in Shakespeare's *Henry VI* plays', *SQ* 24 (1973), 357–71.

[4] If we postulate a late date of composition the play may have been prompted by the death in 1590 of George Talbot, sixth Earl of Shrewsbury, and descendant of the first earl, one of the play's central heroic figures. Wilson offers a topical parallel with 'the growing sense of exasperation, anger, and even despair which was felt in London at the impending failure of an invasion of France launched in the autumn of 1591' (pp. xvi ff.).

[5] David Bevington, *Action is Eloquence*, 1984, notes how Joan's capture of the upper stage area in 1.5–6 (the walls of Orléans) constitutes a 'victory tableau [which] is visually and ironically similar to those actually mounted on city gates in Elizabethan victory celebrations' (p. 102).

[6] See James C. Bulman, 'Shakespeare's Georgic histories', *S. Sur.* 38 (1985), 37–47.

Aristotelian in that the action is not end-directed, and the meaning cannot, there-fore, be deduced simply from the play's resolution.[1] The play examines by implicit comparison, for example, the relationships between the various fathers and sons to be found in it: Henry V and Henry VI, the Earl of Cambridge and the Duke of York, Old Talbot and Young Talbot.[2] Other examples of the technique can be seen in the insertion of 1.3 (depicting aristocratic factionalism in England) into the sequences of scenes that depicts the struggles at Orléans between England and France, and in 5.3.30 ff., where York's capture of Joan is immediately fol-lowed by Suffolk's capture of Margaret. The effect of this pattern can be stunning – as it was to R. W. Chambers who, after seeing a performance of the first tetralogy at the Pasadena Playhouse, wrote that to see these plays 'was to realize that Shakespeare began his career with a tetralogy based on recent history, grim, archaic, crude, yet nevertheless such as, for scope, power, patriotism, and sense of doom, had probably no parallel since Aeschylus wrote the trilogy of which *The Persians* is the surviving fragment'.[3]

The structure of the play, then, is processional as a series of characters, events, and images is presented successively to the audience – rather in the manner in which the pageants of the mystery plays passed in order before the spectators as they stood in the streets or squares of a medieval town. Indeed the opening sequence of Act 2 can be understood only if we recognise its montage technique: the scene opens with the setting of the French watch at Orléans – presumably on the tiring-house balcony. Below the English enter in a procession. They are bearing scaling-ladders and also sounding a dead march on their muffled drums: Salisbury has been killed and they are grimly mustering for revenge. These two images tell us all we need to know about the opposing armies. (In like manner a film director in a western might cut from shots of one camp to another.) We do not read the scene naturalistically, for then we should assume that the French would 'hear' the English drums and be thereby warned before they are eventually attacked.[4]

1 Henry VI was written for and, in my opinion, demands to be acted upon a stage which makes no attempt to create scenic illusion. The play is as much about the present – Shakespeare's present and our own – as it is about the beginning of the Wars of the Roses. *Scenery* depicting any kind of late-medieval 'reality' therefore would be not only inappropriate but would hinder the fluid groupings that the fast

---

[1] Compare Clifford Leech, *Shakespeare: The Chronicles*, 1962, p. 14: '[*1 Henry VI*] is a fairly shapeless piece of writing, beginning with some pomp and indeed impressiveness...but soon falling into an anecdotal kind of drama in which incidents are presented in turn for the sake of immediate dramatic effect rather than for their contribution to a total pattern'.

[2] See Ronald S. Berman, 'Fathers and sons in the *Henry VI* plays', *SQ* 13 (1962), 487–97.

[3] *Man's Unconquerable Mind*, 1939, p. 254.

[4] Working from this premise Dover Wilson removed the dead march from the stage direction on the assumption that it had been caught from a prompter's note at the opening of 2.2 (Wilson, p. 138). See Textual Analysis, pp. 189–90 below; for an overall account of this technique in the trilogy see B. Hodgdon, 'Shakespeare's directorial eye: a look at the early history plays', in S. Homan (ed.), *Shake-speare's 'More than Words can Witness'*, 1980, pp. 115–29.

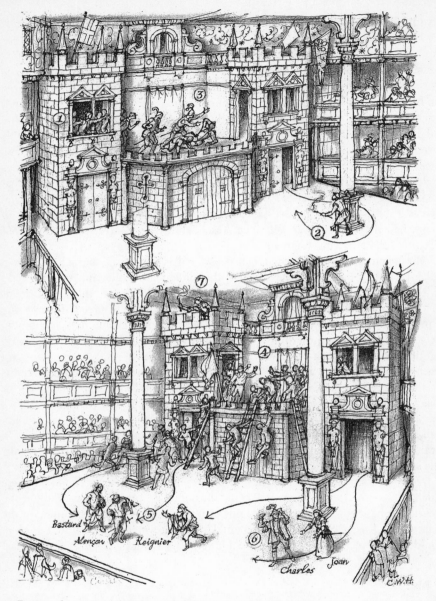

3 Devices for staging the siege of Orléans in a London playhouse *c.* 1593: a conjectural reconstruction by C. Walter Hodges

Act 1, Scene 4: (1) *Salisbury*: Here, through this grate, I count each one, / And view the Frenchmen how they fortify... (2) *Enter the Boy with a linstock* (3) *Here they shoot, and Salisbury [and Gargrave] fall down*

Act 2, Scene 1: (4) *The French [Sentinels] leap o'er the walls in their shirts* (5) *Enter several ways [below]* BASTARD, ALENÇON, REIGNIER, *half ready and half unready* (6) *Charles*: Is this thy cunning, thou deceitful dame?

Act 3, Scene 2: (7) *Enter [LA]* PUCELLE *on the top, thrusting out a torch burning*

pace of the action demands. A historical period might well, however, be defined by costumes and properties – in Shakespeare's time actors would have used Elizabethan and not Plantagenet costumes with possibly a few details of dress or some properties to suggest the period in which the play was set.[1] Among Shakespeare's early plays, *1 Henry VI* makes use in a comparatively large number of scenes of the playing space 'aloft'[2] – an indication of how much the play is concerned with the relative power of its protagonists, power which can be suggested and defined by their theatrical dominance. A director's use, moreover, of the permanent features of an Elizabethan or modern stage – all that is required is an upper playing area and some large doors at the back of the stage to serve as town gates – can help establish a unity for the action by 'quoting' theatrical images, groupings, or players' gestures.[3] It might well be felt, for example, that Gloucester's 'siege' of 'The Tower of London' in 1.3 is placed by design immediately before the scene in which the Gunner and his Boy wreak such havoc upon the English who are besieging Orléans by shooting down Salisbury and his fellows as they stand on another set of 'walls'.

The non-representational stage did not, of course, demand consistently non-naturalistic acting. Stately declamation alternates with racy colloquialism, scenic ritual with the possibility of sardonic direct address to the audience. As J. W. Blanpied wrote:

1 Henry VI does *not* in fact rest contentedly with its stiff spectacular dramatic accomplishment, its too-easy manipulation of history, its Senecan postures and Heroick Song. The curious sense of original life beneath all the brassy opacity is the play's dis-ease by which it pre-empts and embodies our live discomfort.[4]

As a preliminary account of the play's structure we might notice how its theme is brought out by a dramatic pattern defined by a series of death or funeral scenes: 1.1 portrays the funeral of Henry V, 2.2 the funeral of Salisbury, 2.5 the death of Mortimer, 3.2 the death of Bedford, 4.5–6 the death of Talbot – all survivors from a vanishing chivalric world, warriors, and defenders of the integrity of the realm.[5] Scenes of pageantry, battle, and movement are juxtaposed with scenes of stasis containing only one or two people – often the manipulating politicians. Dramatic interest is frequently created by reversing the audience's expectations and disrupting the ceremonies in which these images appear.[6] Ceremonies thus become a paradoxical demonstration of the stability and instability of rule. In this sequence,

---

[1] Hattaway, pp. 86–8.
[2] In 1.6, 2.1, 3.2 (on two occasions), 4.2, and 5.3.
[3] See Hattaway, chaps. 1–3.
[4] Blanpied, 'Counterconsciousness', p. 215.
[5] Henry V is presented not only as a titanic figure but as a biblical hero, a latter-day David (see 1.1.31 n.). The coronation pageant of Elizabeth had presented her as a Deborah 'consulting with her estates for the restoration of good government in Israel' (Williams, p. 365).
[6] See Hereward T. Price on the motif of the interrupted ceremony in *Construction in Shakespeare*, 1951; also Roger Warren, '"Contrarieties agree": an aspect of dramatic technique in *Henry VI*', *S. Sur.* 37 (1984), 75–83.

too, theatrical images or 'gests'[1] are repeated – the pattern of the interrupted funeral of Henry V is quoted when Sir John Fastolf bursts in on the coronation of Henry VI in 4.1. (The action is further punctuated by choric utterances from Exeter and Lucy at 3.1, 4.1, 4.3, and 5.1.)

Shakespeare's verse in this period is also marked by symmetries, by a fondness for rhetorical patterns of parallelism, repetition, and antithesis.[2] This is apparent not only in formal speeches (like Gloucester's encomium quoted above, in Warwick's early intervention in the quarrel between Plantagenet and Somerset in the rose-plucking scene (2.4.11 ff.), in the formalised wooing of Margaret by Suffolk in 5.3), but in briskly-paced action scenes like the opening of 1.5. We find variations on the same idea – copiousness, as it was called by the rhetoricians – and a large number of maxims and proverbs. Like the scenes, the lines draw attention to their own strategies and thereby to the theatricality of politics. They can also achieve a kind of self-delight in their heraldic stiffness. There is a much higher proportion of end-stopped lines than in the later plays, but, to my ear, the possibility of more enjambment than is signalled by the punctuation of some modern editors. The characteristic manner of this early (and very Marlovian)[3] style emerges in the following speech of Joan la Pucelle, where we note a recourse to declamation, to heroic simile and analogy, to a modular use of phrase and clause, and a delight in figures of sound as well as figures of sense:[4]

> Look on thy country, look on fertile France,
> And see the cities and the towns defaced
> By wasting ruin of the cruel foe
> As looks the mother on her lowly babe
> When death doth close his tender-dying eyes.
> See, see the pining malady of France;
> Behold the wounds, the most unnatural wounds
> Which thou thyself hast given her woeful breast.
> O turn thy edgèd sword another way:
> Strike those that hurt and hurt not those that help.
> One drop of blood drawn from thy country's bosom
> Should grieve thee more than streams of foreign gore.
> Return thee therefore with a flood of tears,
> And wash away thy country's stainèd spots.   (*1 Henry VI* 3.3.44–57)

The passage is obviously rhetorical – and its function is rhetorical: to persuade Burgundy to turn his allegiance to the side of the French. The audience is invited

---

[1] Hattaway, p. 3.
[2] For a general analysis of the style of the play see David Riggs, *Shakespeare's Heroical Histories: 'Henry VI' and its Literary Tradition*, 1971; Ronald Watkins, 'The only Shake-scene', *PQ* 54 (1975), 47–67; L. C. Knights, 'Rhetoric and insincerity' and Wolfgang Clemen, 'Some aspects of style in the *Henry VI* plays', in P. Edwards, I-S. Ewbank, G. K. Hunter (eds.), *Shakespeare's Styles: Essays in Honour of Kenneth Muir*, 1980, pp. 1–8 and 9–24; James C. Bulman, *The Heroic Idiom of Shakespearean Tragedy*, 1985, pp. 26–44.
[3] Nicholas Brooke, 'Marlowe as provocative agent in Shakespeare's early plays', *S. Sur.* 14 (1961), 34–44.
[4] For these terms see George Puttenham, *The Arte of English Poesie*, 1589, p. 133.

to see through Joan's strategies, her capacity to be 'copious in exclaims'.[1] We can compare that with the more fluid movement and greater metaphorical density of this speech by Burgundy in *Henry V*:

> ...Why that the naked, poor, and mangled Peace,
> Dear nurse of arts, plenties, and joyful births,
> Should not in this best garden of the world,
> Our fertile France, put up her lovely visage?
> Alas, she hath from France too long been chased,
> And all her husbandry doth lie on heaps,
> Corrupting in it own fertility.
> Her vine, the merry cheerer of the heart,
> Unprunèd dies; her hedges even-pleached,
> Like prisoners wildly overgrown with hair,
> Put forth disordered twigs; her fallow leas
> The darnel, hemlock, and rank femetary
> Doth root upon, while that the coulter rusts
> That should deracinate such savagery;
> The even mead, that erst brought sweetly forth
> The freckled cowslip, burnet, and green clover,
> Wanting the scythe withal, uncorrected, rank,
> Conceives by idleness, and nothing teems
> But hateful docks, rough thistles, kecksies, burs,
> Losing both beauty and utility;
> And all our vineyards, fallows, meads, and hedges,
> Defective in their natures, grow to wildness.   (*Henry V* 5.2.34–55)

To use Clemen's terms, there seems to be a move from 'self-description' to 'self-expression'[2] as Burgundy in the later speech explores his landscape of the mind, moving amongst its particular details. The imagery of *Henry V* serves a heuristic function, serves to explore and investigate thought and emotion. In the earlier play, it may be argued, this function is performed by the strong contrasts in style. The switches from blank verse to couplets, from high astounding terms to colloquialism, are signs of the text's capacity to interrogate reality, to create a variety of perspectives upon the representation. This creates the basic problem for a director: to establish the tone of the play. Sometimes there will be a temptation to use the fustian of the self-proclaimed heroes to expose their pretensions; at other times the heroic idiom makes a simple positive assertion.

THE CAUSES OF DECAY

To return to the play's opening: first we see an anticipatory tiff between Gloucester and the Bishop of Winchester[3] that interrupts the funeral rites and prefigures the civil broils which, despite Bedford's prayer to the ghost of the departed king (1.1.52

---

[1] *R3* 4.4.135.
[2] Clemen, 'Aspects of style', p. 20.
[3] The play is of course contemporary with the Marprelate tracts (1588–9) and their denunciation of worldling bishops. The authors of the Epistle to the Geneva Bible (1560) list papists, worldlings, and ambitious prelates as the main enemies to the 'Temple' or new commonwealth.

ff.), will wrack the realm throughout the trilogy. Later in the play (3.1.72–3, 191 ff., 4.3.47) these broils will be explained through metaphors of disease and predatory animals as society reverts to a more primitive order;[1] here, however, there is established a clear demonstration of naked and graceless rivalry between two political worldlings. Next we hear news and watch the reception of it as messengers enter in succession to announce great loss in France, the coronation of the dauphin, and the capture of the English champion Lord Talbot:

> GLOUCESTER   Is Paris lost? Is Rouen yielded up?
>   If Henry were recalled to life again
>   These news would cause him once more yield the ghost.
> EXETER   How were they lost? What treachery was used?
> MESSENGER   No treachery, but want of men and money.   (1.1.65–9)

Shakespeare's dramatic method may contain archaic elements, but his historiography, as these interruptions reveal, can seem strikingly modern.[2] France was lost, it is claimed, not as the result of treachery or moral failing on the English side, but through 'want of men and money' (1.1.69) – a phrase which, in my view, resonates through the whole sequence. The terse words of the Messenger criticise not only the conduct of the nobility, but their self-deluding fustian style. 'Politics', a demystificatory analysis of the forces that shape events, has interrupted 'history' – at least that kind of history that derives from theology and reads human chronicles as chapters in a book of God.[3] (The bishops' order of 1599 'That no English histories be printed except they be allowed by some of her majesty's privy council'[4] bears witness to the ways contemporaries recognised the potentially subversive nature of history.) This is not to say that we could argue that *Shakespeare* was wholly sceptical concerning a benign providence. Providence is not denied but hidden, the concentration here is 'humanist', on efficient rather than first or final causes.[5]

Indeed Shakespeare's attention seems to have been seized by this kind of explanation, for he moved it into prominence at the beginning of the play and then offered it once more as an explanation for Salisbury's failures in the siege of Orléans in the second scene of the play – 'Nor men nor money hath he to make

---

[1] Shakespeare may be said to have tested the dark realism of Richard Hooker whose *Laws of Ecclesiastical Polity* were to appear in 1593: 'Laws politic, ordained for external order and regiment among men, are never framed as they should be, unless presuming the will of man to be inwardly obstinate, rebellious, and averse from all obedience unto the sacred laws of his nature; in a word, unless presuming man to be in regard to his depraved mind little better than a wild beast' (Book 1, chap. x; Everyman edn, 1907, 1, 188).

[2] Compare the anti-historicist statement of Jean Bodin in 1566: 'human history mostly flows from the will of mankind, which ever vacillates and has no objective' (*Method for the Easy Comprehension of History*, trans. B. Reynolds, 1966, p. 17).

[3] For a general survey see Peter Burke, *The Renaissance Sense of the Past*, 1969.

[4] See Arber, III, 316 ff.

[5] In the terms of a modern Marxist, a pragmatic materialist ideology is *emerging* that will contest not only the *residual* ideology of feudalism but the *dominant* ideology that supported the Tudor regime by means of 'the Tudor myth'. See Raymond Williams, *Marxism and Literature*, 1977, pp. 121–7; Williams's schema is more subtle than the actual account of the plays offered by Paul N. Siegel, *Shakespeare's English and Roman History Plays: A Marxist Approach*, 1986.

war' (1.2.17). (The chroniclers had applied it to another event, the loss of Paris in
1436, some twelve years after the funeral here portrayed;[1] see Appendix 1, p. 197
below.) The Messenger's charge can be read as a bold and important historical
hypothesis: instead of portraying historical events as a Morality drama – as Ralegh,
for example, in his *The History of the World* (1614), was to portray them –
Shakespeare here offers for consideration a pragmatic, secular interpretation of
this precipitating event. Moreover, power would seem to derive – as Machiavelli
had pointed out – not from God, as St Paul had claimed in the Epistle to the
Romans (13.1), but from the actions and reactions of particular personalities to
particular circumstances.[2] The Hundred Years War becomes entangled in the
Wars of the Roses as Shakespeare gives the feuding aristocrats a far more prominent role than they have in the chronicles.

A further insistence on this modern 'common sense' view of historical change
comes from the tone of the Messenger himself: whereas an orthodox Tudor historian or theological propagandist might scrutinise the run of events for divine displeasure, Shakespeare offers, through the words of the Messenger, a commoner's
rebuke for aristocratic factionalism and disregard for the commonweal:

> Amongst the soldiers this is mutterèd:
> That here you maintain several factions
> And, whilst a field should be dispatched and fought,
> You are disputing of your generals...
> Awake, awake, English nobility!
> Let not sloth dim your honours, new begot.
> Cropped are the flower-de-luces in your arms:
> Of England's coat one half is cut away.[3]   (1.1.70–81)

The tone and substance of this rebuke anticipate themes in *2 Henry VI*.

A previous generation of commentators, following in the footsteps of E. M. W.
Tillyard's *Shakespeare's History Plays*, 1944, argued that Shakespeare endorsed 'the
Tudor myth', a religious scheme of history whereby under the eyes of God disaster
unrolled over the kingdom as the consequence of a curse precipitated by the
murder of Richard II. 'With Henry VI the curse is realized and in the dreaded
form of a child being king – "woe to the nation whose king is a child [see 4.1.192
n.]." Not that disaster comes immediately, but the few years of the new king and
later his retiring disposition allow the sin of pride to show itself in various places and
ultimately to ruin the kingdom.'[4] It is surely significant, however, that the centrally

[1] Holinshed, p. 185; Hall, p. 179.
[2] See Richard Tuck, '*Power* and *Authority* in seventeenth-century England', *The Historical Journal* 17
(1974), 43–61.
[3] Compare the French Sentinel's rebuke of his superiors at 2.1.5–7.
[4] Tillyard, *Shakespeare's History Plays*, 1944, p. 60; Tillyard's line is fairly close to that of M. M. Reese,
The Cease of Majesty, 1961. Reese's conviction that the plays depict England under Henry VI lying
under a divine curse enabled him to find only 'strident monotony' in the texts (p. 167). H. A. Kelly,
Divine Providence in the England of Shakespeare's Histories, 1970, finally disposed of Tillyard's
schematic account of the history plays. His view has been followed by John Wilders, *The Lost Garden:
A View of Shakespeare's English and Roman History Plays*, 1978. For a general questioning of the
assumptions of Tillyard and others see Michael McCanles, *Dialectical Criticism and Renaissance
Literature*, 1975.

placed speech of Mortimer (2.5.61 ff.) which surveys the course of English history makes no reference to a providential pattern such as we find, it could be argued, in *Richard III*.[1] From time to time we do hear religious terms, in particular references to 'scourges of God', agents of divine retribution for the sins of this world (2.3.14, 4.2.16, 4.7.77). Joan la Pucelle is said to play this role (1.2.129). But as we watch her political astuteness and ruses on the battlefield it is difficult not to believe that she is simply endowed with the faculties for worldly success. Nor is there a pattern here of hubris and nemesis for individual characters. The deaths of Salisbury and Talbot, for example, are in no ways deserved.[2]

Rather than stressing the theological framework and divinely inspired historiography, therefore, we might argue that Shakespeare was a realist. It was common in the Renaissance to contrast the ideal world of the poet with the realities depicted by the historian. Thus Sidney wrote, 'But the historian, being captivated to the truth of a foolish world, is many times a terror from well-doing, and an encouragement to unbridled wickedness.'[3] Yet if we feel reluctant to concede that Shakespeare was portraying a wholly secular order, we might at least agree, with Coleridge, that, in this kind of drama, fate (or providence) has been at least displaced from its traditional category:

The transitional link between the Epic and the Drama is the Historic Drama. In the Epic poem a pre-announced Fate gradually adjusts and employs the will and the Incidents as instruments...while the Drama places Fate & Will in opposition [to each other, and is] then most perfect when the victory of fate is obtained in consequence of imperfections in the opposing Will, so as to leave a final impression that the Fate itself is but a higher and a more intelligent Will.[4]

A POPULAR DRAMA

Shakespeare's histories were, as we have seen, performed in the popular – in Elizabethan terms, 'public' – playhouses. Although it has been claimed recently that Elizabethan audiences contained a higher proportion of 'privileged' spectators than it used to be thought,[5] it may be argued that Shakespeare was exploring a populist kind of history, a notion of history that would appeal to anyone of any rank who was sceptical of authority or the use of determinism to justify political action. 'In order that a drama may be properly historical, it is necessary that it should be the history of the people to whom it is addressed', said Coleridge, and he went on:

---

[1] This play probably owes more to the Senecan tradition of revenge than to Christian providentialism.
[2] See A. L. French, 'The mills of God and Shakespeare's early history plays', *English Studies* 55 (1974), 313–24.
[3] Sidney, *Apology*, ed. Shepherd, p. 111. Thomas Heywood, *An Apology for Actors* (1612) serves up the idealist view of the history play (see Allan H. Gilbert, *Literary Criticism: Plato to Dryden*, 1962, p. 558). Compare L. C. Knights: 'What Shakespeare gained from the historical writings of his time, though not from these alone, was a conviction that politics and morals cannot be separated without falsification and disaster. That conviction lasted him a lifetime' (*Explorations 3*, 1976, p. 163).
[4] S. T. Coleridge (on *R2*) in *Lectures 1808–1819 on Literature*, ed. R. A. Foakes, 2 vols., 1987, I, 283.
[5] Ann Jennalie Cook, *The Privileged Playgoers of Shakespeare's London*, 1981; her thesis is disputed by Andrew Gurr, *Playgoing in Shakespeare's London*, 1987.

In this mode, the unity resulting from succession is destroyed, but is supplied by a unity of a higher order, which connects the events by reference to the workers, gives a reason for them in the motives, and presents men in their causative character.[1]

Bringing characters from 'history' onto the stage was itself a political act, a report to a wider audience of what had been private to court circles or concealed by the ordering imposed on the chronicles which were his sources. Shakespeare was concerned not to dramatise a transcendent doctrine of order but to portray 'men in their causative character'. His interest was therefore political: his focus was on the nature, origins, and transfer of power as he traced in the play the *changing* relationships between monarchy, aristocracy, and commoners or the bourgeoisie[2] – thereby registering a change in the conception of kingship from that of a mystic office, endowed with divine rights, to a more limited power that operated within a corporate community.[3] To certain ages and to certain audiences, however, such kinds of drama, as we have seen, appeared not only unappealing but dangerous. An introduction from our own period deploys a subtle kind of critical censorship, suppressing the politics by *moralising* the play:

In its present form the play might well be called the Tragedy of Talbot. His career is the framework of the structure. The scheme is the struggle of Talbot and Joan in which he represents the forces of England and righteousness, she the forces of demonic malice.[4]

Plays of this kind are, accordingly, unlikely to be built around a hero or avatar: John Dover Wilson's assumption that a play must have a hero and that the hero must be Talbot resulted in a misleading theory not only of the nature and quality of the drama but of its compositional genesis.[5] Talbot is rather a victim – of the aspiring and contriving York who is prepared to let Talbot die so that Somerset will take the blame (4.3.31–3). In this play the title role of the king was probably taken by a boy player, an index of the power the noble politicians of the court would have had, and of the way the play is not just concerned with a central personality.

Nor are these plays likely to invoke the sense of an ending that we associate with the history of heroes. That is appropriate to tragedy: *1 Henry VI*, like the political play it is, is open-ended, suggesting that although this part of the story is over, the play of politics goes on.

To return to the first scene: the process of demystification is carried further in the epic narrative of Talbot's stand against the French delivered by the Third Messenger (1.1.108 ff.). What is notable here is the way in which the heroic style contrasts with unheroic action. Talbot met defeat not in chivalric combat but when

[1] Coleridge, *Lectures and Notes on Shakspere*, ed. T. Ashe, 1908, p. 252.
[2] Paul N. Siegel points out (p. 77) how Winchester appeals to the Mayor of London and the citizens by evoking their desire for order and relief from high taxes. He names Gloucester as one that 'still motions war and never peace, / O'ercharging your free purses with large fines' (1.3.63–4).
[3] See Robert Eccleshall, *Order and Reason in Politics: Theories of Absolute and Limited Monarchy in Early Modern England*, 1978.
[4] Kittredge, p. 665.
[5] Wilson, pp. ix–xiii.

4   A battle scene from Holinshed's *Chronicles*: compare 'A base Walloon...Thrust Talbot with a spear into the back' (1.1.137–8)

'a base Walloon' (1.1.137) stabbed him in the back (see illustration 4). Three scenes later Salisbury, a surviving titanic hero from the reign of Henry V, is sniped down by a cannon fired by a boy. Battles are no longer fought with lance and bow, instruments of the gentle arts of hunt and war, but are trials of strength won by guerrilla tactics within towns, fought with weapons of Renaissance technology. This first scene ends with a confirmation for the audience of pervading *Realpolitik*: Winchester confides to the audience his intent to kidnap the king and thus becomes a stage villain in the play of politics. This is the first of a series of Senecan prophecies that runs through the play,[1] but here power lies not with the gods but with the prophets.[2]

HE THAT PLAYS THE KING

The delay before King Henry actually appears on stage is probably deliberate. Before he enters in 3.1 an audience has seen battles won and lost as well as civil broils unleashed by political rivalry. In this scene, moreover, more than sixty lines pass before the king speaks. It all signifies the comparative powerlessness of a monarchy compelled to rule not through servants but through barons who, as Machiavelli noted, 'hold their positions not by favour of the ruler but by antiquity of blood'.[3] Power, of course, as Machiavelli was equally aware, derives not only from the constitution of the state but from the personality of the ruler.

[1] See W. Clemen, *Shakespeare's Dramatic Art*, 1972, pp. 18–25.
[2] For the popular uses of prophecy in the period see Simon Shepherd, *Marlowe and the Politics of Elizabethan Theatre*, 1986, pp. 122–31.
[3] *The Prince*, chap. iv.

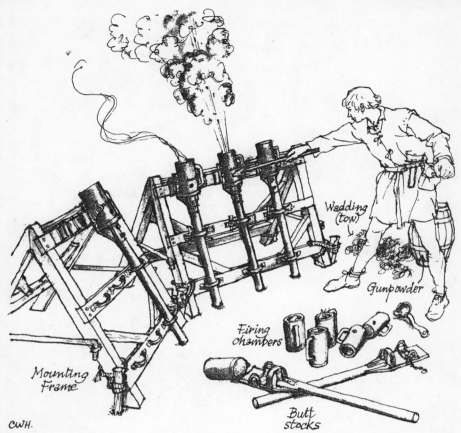

5 Act 2, Scene 3: *a peal of ordnance*. Apparatus for producing the noise of gunfire in the theatre: a conjectural arrangement, by C. Walter Hodges. The firing chambers, as used for breech-loading artillery in the Elizabethan period, are shown here separated from the gun barrels and mounted on portable frames, to be fired on open ground behind the theatre

What, then, can we make of the personality of the boy king in this play? The text, like so many others, is open to interpretation:

> Uncles of Gloucester and of Winchester,
> The special watchmen of our English weal,
> I would prevail, if prayers might prevail,
> To join your hearts in love and amity.
> O, what a scandal is it to our crown,
> That two such noble peers as ye should jar!
> Believe me, lords, my tender years can tell
> Civil dissension is a viperous worm
> That gnaws the bowels of the commonwealth.
>
> (3.1.65–73)

Later in the scene we see Henry trying the power of his 'sighs and tears' (108) to

6   David Warner as Henry VI in Peter Hall's 1964 production

make peace between his uncles. Compared with his father he seems indeed pious
and effete, but these and other lines also invite a player to assert at least a moral
authority.[1] Later in the scene his action of acceding to Plantagenet's request to be
restored to his title may be impulsive – but may equally be construed as politic: it is
better to have York's loyalty than his hatred, even if events prove that the duke was
a man unlikely to observe his monarch's admonition to 'be true' (162). Henry may
be compared in this scene to Richard II who intervened in the duel between
Mowbray and Bullingbrook so that he could banish both:[2] Mowbray because he
knew too much, Bullingbrook because he wanted too much. As so often in his
political plays, Shakespeare is demonstrating the way in which political ideals
cannot be separated from individual aspirations.[3] In 4.1 equally, Henry shows
himself capable of firm and judicious decisions, quelling the strife between Vernon
and Basset on the grounds that internecine squabbling among the English will
weaken their standing with the French. His donning of the red Lancastrian rose
(4.1.152) may be impolitic, may be disingenuous, but is the only way to maintain
his own claim to the throne by possession against York's possible claim by right.

JOAN OF ARC

The play's second scene adds a thematic density to the historical moment defined
in the first. In it we see a battle between French and English forces and a sequence
in which Joan of Arc finds out Charles, the true king. Joan, or 'Pucelle' as the text
designates her, has been at the centre of a lot of critical writing about the play.
Earlier commentators were disturbed by Shakespeare's unchivalrous treatment
of the 'holy maid'; later ones, as we have seen, saw her as a figure in a historical
allegory, a witch who had put a hex on the powers of England, God's scourge
working to punish the crimes of past and present, in particular the original sin of
the Lancastrians, the deposition and murder of Richard II.[4] Such arguments raise
the problem of the 'belief' of the dramatist in the matter of his plays: the second
interpretation in particular leads us to infer that even if Shakespeare (like Reginald
Scot, whose sceptical book on witchcraft had appeared a few years before the play
was written)[5] did not actually believe in the power of witches, he felt that through
Joan a pattern of divine intervention could be perceived.

---

[1] Rowe's reductive description of Henry's character has hardened into received opinion: 'His manners
are every where exactly the same with the story; one finds him still described with simplicity, passive
sanctity, want of courage, weakness of mind, and easy submission to the governance of an imperious
wife or prevailing faction' ('Some Account of the Life etc. of Mr William Shakespeare', in D. Nichol
Smith (ed.), *Eighteenth Century Essays on Shakespeare*, 1963, p. 16). Compare William Hazlitt's
description of 'the effeminacy...of an indolent good-natured mind, naturally averse to the turmoils
of ambition and the cares of greatness, and who wishes to pass his time in monkish indolence and
contemplation' (*Characters of Shakespeare's Plays*, in *The Complete Works of William Hazlitt*, ed. P. P.
Howe, 21 vols., 1930–4, IV, 294).
[2] *R2* 1.3.12 ff.
[3] See Wilders, *The Lost Garden*.
[4] This is the view of Tillyard, *History Plays*, pp. 164 ff.; it is robustly countered by A. L. French, 'Joan
of Arc and *Henry VI*', *English Studies* 49 (1968), 425–9.
[5] *The Discoverie of Witchcraft*, 1584.

7 Joan of Arc, La Pucelle, from André Thévet's *Pourtraits et vies des hommes illustres* (1584)

On stage, however, the scene does not give rise to either of these comparatively simple responses. To begin with, it is no more 'realistic' than the first, which means that we need not explore Shakespeare's intentions concerning the reality of Joan *au pied de la lettre*. It is cast in the mode of a folk game: after a short theatrical battle with alarums sounding and 'four or five most vile and ragged foils . . . disposed in brawl ridiculous' where the French are stunningly defeated, Joan appears and is invited to treat with Reignier who plays Charles's part. She rapidly dismisses this impostor and vanquishes the dauphin in a sword-fight – male critics are apt to categorise the sequence as an image of disorder – then moves aside to persuade him to her cause – thus creating an equivocal tableau for the prurient French nobles. All this takes place in fifty lines of text. As for her fight with Talbot in 1.5, there is simply no way of telling from the text whether Shakespeare intended her to overcome her antagonist by magic or by sheer martial art.[1]

Although the story of Joan was probably less deeply imprinted in the popular consciousness than it is today, Shakespeare seems to have taken it for granted that its outlines were known and to have written the scenes in which Pucelle appears in a stylised way – with a deliberate naïvety, in fact, rather like the sequence between Titania and Bottom. Just as that sequence raises no question about whether Shakespeare believed in fairies, so this raises no question about whether Joan was or was not a witch. Rather it plays its part in the structure of the play; it appeals to folk memories concerning the finding of the true king, the stuff of so many romances and fairy-tales. The thunder and lightning that appear in the stage direction at 1.4.96 need not be read as a providential sign, but merely amplify this archetypal action by theatrical art. In terms familiar to critics of Shakespeare, we notice that in Reignier, who takes Charles's place on the throne, we are presented with a preliminary figure of the player king, one of the great Shakespearean archetypes[2] and one that helps to establish our awareness of the pathos that attends Henry VI who, as the play demonstrates, exercises only the shadow of power as his 'substance' is usurped by the 'protectors' of the realm. At the end of the play, after another defeat, Charles too will be reduced to that state:

> Must he be then as shadow of himself?
> Adorn his temples with a coronet,
> And yet, in substance and authority,
> Retain but privilege of a private man?   (5.4.133–6)

What, though, of Joan's personality? Is she more than a figure in the game of politics? Her lines

> And whereas I was black and swart before
> With those clear rays which she [the Virgin] infused on me,
> That beauty am I blest with, which you may see   (1.2.84–6)

suggest that the boy player who originally took her part was rigged out in a dazzling blond head-piece. Joan becomes, accordingly, a Venerian[3] figure, a sexual lure for

---

[1] See Alan C. Dessen, *Elizabethan Stage Conventions and Modern Interpreters*, 1984, pp. 112–13; in a recent production by Michael Bogdanov the scene was accompanied by mysterious flute music coming from nowhere.

[2] See Appendix C, 'The player king before Shakespeare', in Emrys Jones, *The Origins of Shakespeare*, 1977; and Williams, pp. 360 ff.

[3] Lisa Jardine, *Still Harping on Daughters*, 1983, notes how the chroniclers classify her as an 'Amazon/virago...[a] "rejection of her sex"...a...man-woman, an outsider and a sensationalised freak' (p. 105); see also Catherine Belsey, *The Subject of Tragedy*, 1985, pp. 183–4; Marilyn L. Williamson, '"When men are rul'd by women": Shakespeare's first tetralogy', *S. St.* 19 (1987), 41–60; Gabriele Bernhard Jackson, 'Topical ideology: witches, Amazons, and Shakespeare's Joan of Arc', *ELR* 18 (1988), 40–65.

Charles – who promptly takes the bait – so reinforcing the English audience's prejudices about the sexual depravity of the French. Before their eyes Mars is seduced by Venus – the identifications are made by allusions to these deities at the opening and close of the scene (1.2.1 and 1.2.144). The scene's second encounter between Charles and Joan is an erotic 'buckle' (1.2.95), a sexual as well as a martial combat, a figure for the contention between male and female that is an *obbligato* to the confrontations between England and France, Lancaster and York throughout the trilogy.

Once again, however, we are being drawn into allegory. Might we not consider here the impression a modern actress might make on the part? Joan is not only a sex-object but a woman, and a woman who boldly usurps male dominance by physical strength, the occasional use of Marlovian rhetoric (1.2.72–92, 129), and simple guile. Her irreverence for the rituals of authority is matched by the racy vigour of her speech. Her ruse to lead soldiers into Rouen disguised as 'the vulgar sort of market-men' (3.2.4) arouses the audience's delight in the skill and energy of the trickster. Individual ingenuity can subvert corporate authority, and Joan pulls off this coup not by metaphysical aid but by politic contrivance. She is also given, as we have seen, a moving plea for peace (3.3.44 ff.). La Pucelle is, simply, a born populist leader.

In 5.3, however, Shakespeare shows Joan conjuring the fiends who, in a scene like that in which Hercules leaves Antony,[1] show that they are deserting her. We might, allegorically again, be reminded of the folk plays of devils who can turn into seeming angels and, applying the lesson to Joan herself,[2] consider that the paragon of beauty was like the false Helen who burnt the topless towers of Ilium. But, more realistically, we might also remember that in a society where women exercised so little political power, resort to witchcraft was 'generally believed to be a method of bettering one's condition when all else had failed'.[3] The scene, in other words, appearing as it does so late in the play, cannot be taken as an unequivocal manifestation of the diabolic power of Joan. She turns to witchcraft only in despair, and there is no evidence earlier in the text to support the English view that her victories were won through supernatural agency. In any case, like Faustus who seizes the advantage of his conjuring scene by imperiously dismissing the devil the moment he emerges from the stage trap, Joan dismisses her fiends with a bravura obscenity (see 5.3.23 n.). In the male world of Mars that is the only gesture left to her.

It was the final appearance of Joan in 5.4 that most disturbed those nineteenth-century commentators who had been seduced by an idealised and virginal vision of the Maid of Orleans. Here she is shown denying her father, asserting she is pregnant, and claiming any French potentate who might save her as the father of her child. (In the preface to his *Saint Joan* George Bernard Shaw called the scene

[1] *Ant.* 4.3.
[2] J. P. Brockbank, 'The frame of disorder – *Henry VI*', in J. R. Brown and B. Harris (eds.), *Early Shakespeare*, 1961.
[3] Thomas, p. 623.

8   Act 5, Scene 3: the conjuring scene, by C. Walter Hodges. *Joan*: O hold me not with silence over-long... *They hang their heads*

'scurrilous'.[1]) One reading of the scene would make her a politician treating with politicians, deploying any plea, true or not, to the end of saving her life. She is then haled off unrepentant. Carol Rutter describes[2] how in the 1977 Royal Shakespeare Company production[3] Charlotte Cornwell, 'in a manic swivel that scattered the circling English and made York yelp, marked each of their faces with spit on her fingers. She left cackling.'

Another reading of the scene would register the way her despair overgrows her cunning – and it may be that Shakespeare was rather lamely going along with Holinshed's anti-French sentiment when the latter was following Monstrelet, who called her 'a damnable sorcerer suborned by Satan'.[4] In a man's world, moreover,

[1]   See Edwin Wilson (ed.), *Shaw on Shakespeare*, 1961, p. 103.
[2]   Privately.
[3]   See p. 49 below.
[4]   Holinshed, p. 172. Dominique Goy-Blanquet, *Le roi mis à nu: l'histoire d'Henri VI de Hall à Shake-speare*, 1986, pp. 86 ff., argues that the contradictoriness of the character derives from Shakespeare's imperfect amalgamation of the views of Hall and Holinshed.

9   Charlotte Cornwell as Joan la Pucelle in Terry Hands's 1977 production

it is all too easy for pride to convert to guilt. She could, as she squirms away from
the stake that awaits her – unlike the Protestant martyrs graphically described in
Foxe's *Acts and Monuments* – remind us of Cressida kissed and pawed 'in general'
by a circle of sexually chauvinist Greeks.[1] Joan here is a woman alone surrounded
by warriors who had come to destroy her country and for whom she could be only
'Puzel or Pucelle', whore or virgin.[2] In a review of a 1963 production Alan Brien
described 'a shifty Joan of Arc...man-handled to the stake by the thuggish
barons'.[3] She had tried the liberation of her patrimony, her sex, and her self, and
these idols lie shattered. In such a situation the price of 'virtue' is simply too high.
She may also have served as a sacrifice to male insecurity for, immediately after
she is led off to execution, comes the ironic news that the 'states of Christendom'
(5.4.96) have negotiated a peace. Joan may, in fact, be the tragic figure in this play.[4]

Joan is, of course, not the only woman in the play. In 2.3 we encounter the
Countess of Auvergne, another figure of feminine contrivance and, like Joan,
one who would save her country by ensnaring another male imperialist, English
Talbot.[5] (The similarity of the two roles may well have been underscored by
doubling the two parts.) The scene is unhistorical: like the quarrel in the Temple
Garden (2.4, see below), it is emblematic – of the clash between an old-fashioned
honour code and modern political pragmatism. The countess too has resorted to a
form of witchcraft, seeking to control Talbot by image-magic,[6] hanging his
picture in her gallery:

> Long time thy shadow hath been thrall to me,
> For in my gallery thy picture hangs;
> But now the substance shall endure the like,
> And I will chain these legs and arms of thine,
> That hast by tyranny these many years
> Wasted our country, slain our citizens,
> And sent our sons and husbands captivate.   (2.3.35–41)

Again, however, the Herculean vigour of the male breaks through.[7] Talbot's
substance eludes her and, by a show of sheer martial strenth, he subdues her. The
scene ends, as it began, with a hint of sexual equivocation.

The third of the trio of French 'seductresses' is Margaret of Anjou[8] who,
captured by Suffolk, is enthralled by the attractiveness of his person. She makes

---

[1] *Tro.* 4.5.
[2] There is a good discussion of the scene in E. A. M. Colman, *The Dramatic Use of Bawdy in Shake speare*, 1974, pp. 49–53.
[3] Alan Brien, *Sunday Telegraph*, 21 July 1963.
[4] Hers does not seem to be a role which parodies Marlowe's heroic prototype as Riggs argues in *Shakespeare's Heroical Histories*, pp. 104–7.
[5] The scene is analysed by Sigurd Burckhardt, *Shakespearean Meanings*, 1968, pp. 47–77, and by J. A. Riddell, 'Talbot and the Countess of Auvergne', *SQ* 28 (1977), 51–7.
[6] Thomas, pp. 612 ff.
[7] Hercules is presented as a central figure of chastity in Peele's poem *The Praise of Chastity* (1593), lines 57 ff.
[8] See David Bevington, 'The domineering female in *1 Henry VI*', *S. St.* 2 (1966), 51–8.

10 Act 2, Scene 3: Talbot and the Countess of Auvergne, from Knight's Victorian edition of Shakespeare; after the painting by W.Q. Orchardson

her first entrance immediately after the fiends have left Joan: it is as though the female politician has inherited the power of the heroic Joan as a subtler and more dangerous kind of threat to the English cause. Suffolk's greeting suggests some magical ritual gesture as if to tame her power:

> For I will touch thee but with reverent hands.
> I kiss these fingers for eternal peace
> And lay them gently on thy tender side. (5.3.47–9)

(The parallel between the two is further marked by portraying them with their fathers in contiguous scenes, 5.3 and 5.4.) Yet neither Suffolk nor Margaret is prepared to disentangle passions from politics. Suffolk sees his relationship with Margaret as a means of making towards the fountainhead of power. In her turn Margaret, while playing the shadow role of queen, will control the substance of power in the second and third parts of the play.

TALBOT AND ENGLISH NATIONALISM

To these types of subversion Shakespeare opposes a popular antitype, Talbot, champion of the English and figure of Hercules (2.3.18 and 4.7.60).[1] His cheer-

---

[1] Hall calls him an 'English Hector' (p. 227); Shakespeare's mode of characterisation here is well described by Bulman, *The Heroic Idiom*, pp. 28–35; Talbot's central role is described by P. Sahel, 'L'autre des autres: la marginalité dans *1 Henry VI*', in *La Marginalité dans la littérature et la pensée anglaises*, 1983, pp. 21–35.

of the son rejecting the authority of the father as Prince Hal riots and revels in Eastcheap and Aumerle raises arms against the Lancastrian regime, here we see father and son linked in a common cause and vying with each other in martial prowess and the pursuit of honour.[1] The sequence stands as a testimony to all that was lost with the death of Henry V: the decay of empire implies the destruction of family. More generally it stands as an emblem of vanity: 'antic Death' (4.7.18) mocks the state of kings and potentates as they strut and fret to their confusion. 'Right without might is helpless, might without right is tyrannical', said Pascal:[2] death will confound the conflict of the mighty and the righteous that runs through the play. Again, however, we must not consign the scene to the category of the merely emblematic. The couplets leave it open to the players to suggest that, as in the scene from *Richard II*, the characters are here indulging in a species of self-dramatisation.

MYTHS AND POLITICS

Talbot is set against Joan in an earlier montage sequence, the siege of Orléans, the depiction of which runs from 1.2 to 2.2. 1.4 depicts the shooting of Salisbury, and 1.5 Joan's defeat of Talbot. 1.6 opens with some emblematic lines, central to the imaginative construction of the play:

> PUCELLE Advance our waving colours on the walls;
> Rescued is Orléans from the English.
> Thus Joan la Pucelle hath performed her word.
> CHARLES Divinest creature, Astraea's daughter,
> How shall I honour thee for this success?
> Thy promises are like Adonis' gardens
> That one day bloomed and fruitful were the next.   (1.6.1–7)

Charles's exultant hyperboles mark the climax of the rising action of the first act, but the two classical references set the moment in an ironic perspective. Adonis's gardens were originally celebrated as a sort of forcing-bed for herbs (Plato, *Phaedrus* 276b), but soon became a symbol of mutability as in Spenser's elaboration of the myth in *The Faerie Queene* (III, vi, 30 ff.). Like Talbot, Joan will meet death before the end of the play. As for Astraea, she was, as Frances Yates has shown,[3] a central symbol in the cult of Elizabethan imperialism. The goddess of justice and a virgin, she had fled the earth in its iron age:

> All godliness lies under foot. And Lady Astrey, last
> Of heavenly virtues, from this earth (in slaughter drownèd) passed.
> (*Metamorphoses* I, 169–70)

In one of the most famous lines in classical literature, her return as a sign of a new order, a new golden age, was celebrated by Virgil in his paean of praise to Augustus: 'Iam redit et virgo, redeunt Saturnia regna' (*Eclogue* 4.6). These lines were readily

---

[1] See Bulman, *The Heroic Idiom*, pp. 32–3.
[2] *Pensées*, trans. A. J. Krailsheimer, 1966, p. 56.
[3] Yates, *Astraea, passim*.

adapted by Christians who identified Astraea as the Virgin. Now Charles's exclamation is extraordinary: the virgin could have no daughter, or else, blasphemously, he salutes her as a female saviour. Joan here has been turned into a myth, but it is a myth of a false Astraea, the antitype of the order represented by Talbot. From this perspective her vision of the Virgin in the fields[1] (1.2.74 ff.) marks the beginning of the end of pastoral innocence.

In a symmetry characteristic of the play, Shakespeare chooses another secluded and idealised place, the garden of the Temple, in which to set the beginning of the bloody contention between York and Lancaster (2.4) emblematised by the plucking of red and white roses from the tree. It is a brilliant piece of dramatic shorthand as well as being, perhaps, an oblique compliment to England's Astraea, Queen Elizabeth, whose Tudor Rose badge symbolised the union of red rose and white.[2]

What, though, of the *real* political aspects of this scene? It may be argued that, in this London garden, Shakespeare was offering a secularised version of the story of another plucking from a tree, the story of the loss of Eden in Genesis. The origins of the Wars of the Roses – the original sin, as it were – lie here, in the squabbling in the Temple garden, rather than in Bullingbrook's deposition of Richard II a quarter of a century before. It is notable that in this scene brawl grows to faction[3] – it seems that an unspecified affair of honour turns into the occasion for civil war. Moreover Shakespeare, as I have argued, was no mere Tudor propagandist, no unthinking upholder of the 'rule of order', a man who must therefore show the origins of any insurrection in the most unfavourable light. As the scene proceeds, he dramatises the tough moral decisions, those 'cases of truth', confronting those who, like Hamlet, felt that they were serving an illegitimate regime but who knew that rebellion against that regime was itself a wrongful act. The dilemma is insoluble, as is suggested by the lines of Warwick that frame the contention between Somerset and Richard Plantagenet in the garden:

> Between two hawks, which flies the higher pitch,
> Between two dogs, which hath the deeper mouth,
> Between two blades, which bears the better temper,
> Between two horses, which doth bear him best,
> Between two girls, which hath the merriest eye,
> I have perhaps some shallow spirit of judgement;
> But in these nice sharp quillets of the law,
> Good faith, I am no wiser than a daw.   (2.4.11–18)

His jocularity is both a testimony to his equivocation and to embarrassment at the thorniness of the constitutional crisis. Play 'hardens into history', as Blanpied put it.[4] As the scene progresses we register a desperate quality in the protestations of both parties as though the two men are seeking to legitimise actions that are in part

---

[1] Astraea had appeared as a shepherdess in Peele's pageant, the *Descensus Astraeae* of 1591.
[2] Yates, *Astraea*, pp. 50 ff.
[3] Compare 2.4.124–5. The point was made to me privately by Carol Rutter.
[4] Blanpied, 'Counterconsciousness', p. 218.

dictated by a crude will to power. As well as recognising that it is an allegorical scene, therefore, we are aware of what Shakespeare calls the 'dumb significants' (2.4.26)[1] as well as the 'signified': this is a realistic depiction of the triviality of emulous factions.[2] The nobles turn questions of right into questions of might and attempt to solve the succession problem by counting the roses plucked from the tree.

Again we note Shakespeare's montage technique. The rose-plucking is sandwiched between two titanic scenes: Talbot's defeat of the wily Countess of Auvergne, and the death of Mortimer who had chosen politic silence rather than insurrection against Lancastrian rule. It serves as prologue too to 3.1 where Winchester, already established as a Machiavel and suspicious to popular audiences as a seditious Catholic, joins quarrel with the emerging authority of 'Good Duke Humphrey' of Gloucester. (Gloucester is no mere 'roaring-boy', as Dover Wilson branded him; he could not concede that Gloucester's character in *Part 1* matches that of the 'noble gentleman' we see in *Part 2*.[3] Rather he stands as another popular hero alongside Talbot and Joan, the particular enemy of the contriving cardinal.)

> Civil dissension is a viperous worm
> That gnaws the bowels of the commonwealth[4]   (3.1.72–3)

proclaims the king, and his observation is immediately proved true by the inrush of servingmen fighting for their respective masters (see Appendix 1, p. 199 below). Henry manages to enjoin peace upon the factions and moves to settle the claim of Richard Plantagenet by restoring him to his title and rights as Duke of York. But just as the audience had been prepared for Winchester's machinations by his aside to the audience at the end of 1.1, so York's threat – to 'make mine ill th'advantage of my good' (2.5.129) – must undermine their confidence in this constitutional settlement. The parliament sequence in 3.1 ends with a flourish: a modern director might well ponder whether to sound a concord or a discord.

The rest of the play works by further ironical understatement. The 'shadow' of the action is what is done on the stage, the winning and losing of battles, although the audience is by now aware that the substance of power is wielded not by the fighters but by the politicians. After the death of Talbot in Act 4 a new order

---

[1] The modern term is 'signifiers'.

[2] The play takes its place in a sequence of works by various hands that inveigh against the iniquities of civil war when 'Force mastered right, the strongest governed all' (see Marlowe's Lucan, 177). These include Marlowe's translation of the first book of Lucan's *Pharsalia* (entered for publication in 1593) and Thomas Lodge's play *The Wounds of Civil War* (entered 1594). Lodge's play, however, has resort to supernatural intervention for its resolution. Robert Wilson's *The Cobbler's Prophecy* (1590?) delivers a hard attack on the perils of national disunity.

[3] Wilson, p. xii.

[4] D. G. Hale, *The Body Politic*, 1971, notes how imagery of the body permeates Shakespeare's plays while the action questions the applicability of organic analogies to political situations (p. 8); for an exhaustive study of categories of images in the play see C. McG. Kay, 'Traps, slaughter, and chaos: a study of Shakespeare's *Henry VI* plays', *Studies in the Literary Imagination* 5 (1972), 1–26.

emerges. York, regent of France, had betrayed Talbot in order to destroy the reputation of Somerset (see 4.3.31–3), and it is he who emerges to deliver the *coup de grâce* to Joan. At the end of the scene he imposes an unhistorical capitulation upon Charles, and the sequence ends as though the narrative of the wars between France and England is complete. This is not, however, the end of the play. It is as though chronicle subverts narrative, history overcomes art, for Suffolk, as we have seen, having captured Margaret on the battlefield at Angiers, has plans for a betrothal between her and the king to further his own ambitions. The play comes to a poise with the arrangements for these nuptials. It had begun with a funeral, the customary end of tragedy: it ends with arrangements for betrothal, the customary end of comedy. But, as we should now expect, the play of politics interrupts both ceremonies, and it is left to the politician Suffolk to speak the play's epilogue and the prologue to *2 Henry VI*. The speech ironically invokes the romantic archetypes of antiquity and significantly does not close with rhyme:

> Thus Suffolk hath prevailed, and thus he goes
> As did the youthful Paris once to Greece,
> With hope to find the like event in love,
> But prosper better than the Trojan did.
> Margaret shall now be queen, and rule the king:
> But I will rule both her, the king, and realm.   (5.5.103–8)

Date and occasion

1 Henry VI, or a version of it, would seem to have been written and performed by 8 August 1592, the date of entry in the Stationers' Register of Thomas Nashe's *Pierce Penilesse his Supplication to the Divell*.[1] There, in the course of a defence of drama, the author offers a description of theatrical heroism as a 'reproof to these degenerate effeminate days of ours'. He continues:

How would it have joyed brave Talbot (the terror of the French) to think that after he had lain two hundred years in his tomb, he should triumph again on the stage, and have his bones new embalmed with the tears of ten thousand spectators at least (at several times), who, in the tragedian that represents his person, imagine they behold him fresh bleeding.[2]

This would seem to indicate that Nashe had seen, in a public playhouse, a play with Talbot as a central figure. It is reasonable to assume that this was a performance of the text that the compilers of the Folio present to us as being by Shakespeare, because in 1593, when Nashe wrote another pamphlet, *The Terrors of the Night*, he included a number of expressions and images found in that text.[3] (Nashe might well, indeed, have written part of the play himself.[4])

On 2 September of the same year (1592), another pamphleteer and dramatist,

---

[1] Arber, II, 292.
[2] Nashe, I, 212.
[3] See C. G. Harlow, 'A source for Nashe's *Terrors of the Night* and the authorship of *1 Henry VI*', *SEL* 5 (1965), 31–47 and 269–81.
[4] See p. 42 below.

Robert Greene, lay dying.[1] Later that month and shortly after his death another pamphlet was printed, *Greenes Groats-worth of Witte . . . Written before his death and published at his dyeing request*,[2] which contains a famous warning to gentlemen play-makers, the so-called university wits, to distrust the fickle nature of players, especially one:

Yes, trust them not; for there is an upstart crow, beautified with our feathers that, with his 'Tiger's heart wrapped in a player's hide', supposes he is as well able to bombast out a blank verse as the best of you: and being an absolute *Iohannes fac totum*, is in his own conceit the only Shake-scene in a country.[3]   (sig. F1ᵛ)

The reference is obviously to Shakespeare who was, as may be inferred from this mock invective, serving as a player as well as a playwright – the phrase 'beautified with our feathers' means, probably, that he appeared in plays by Greene and his fellows. (The problem is whether Greene was attacking Shakespeare's pride or alleging plagiarism – taking 'beautified with our feathers' to mean the latter.[4]) Moreover, the pastiche of the line from *3 Henry VI*, 'O tiger's heart wrapped in a woman's hide!' (1.4.137), indicates that the third play of the trilogy was at least written by this date, although we cannot surmise at this stage of the argument whether Greene knew the line from reading a manuscript or from hearing it in the playhouse.

As for the *terminus a quo* for the play's composition, there is very little evidence.[5] Now that the opinion of Chambers that Shakespeare made a 'late start' in his writing career has been strongly challenged,[6] it has seemed possible that Shakespeare may have begun to write plays as early as 1584, and that the Henry VI plays may have been written soon after the publication of the second edition of Holinshed's *Chronicles* in 1587. Honigmann is prepared to conjecture that *1 Henry VI* could have been written as early as 1589.[7] I am inclined to believe that the play was written before the other two parts of the sequence at some date between 1589 and 1591, although recent work, based on rare-word tests, suggests that it may have been written after them.[8]

The problem of when exactly *1 Henry VI* was first *performed* and by whom has given rise to a vast amount of enquiry and is intricately bound up with the question of the theatrical genesis of the other two plays in the sequence. The following

---

[1] The date comes from a pamphlet entitled *The Repentance of Robert Greene* (1592), sig. D2ʳ.

[2] Entered in the Stationers' Register 20 September 1592 (Arber, II, 620).

[3] The controversies raised by this passage since Malone are reviewed by D. Allen Carroll, 'Greene's "vpstart crow" passage: a survey of commentary', *Research Opportunities in Renaissance Drama* 28 (1985), 111–27.

[4] We cannot tell whether Greene was alluding to vain or ostentatious crows described in Macrobius, Martial and Aesop or, far less likely, to a thieving crow in Horace's third *Epistle*. See S. Schoenbaum, *William Shakespeare: A Compact Documentary Life*, 1977, pp. 151 ff.

[5] For some circumstantial evidence see 4.7.61–70 n.

[6] See E. A. J. Honigmann, *Shakespeare's Impact on his Contemporaries*, 1982, pp. 70 ff.

[7] *Ibid.*, p. 88. Chambers argued that *1H6* 'was put together in 1592, to exploit an earlier theme which had been successful' in *2* and *3H6* (*William Shakespeare*, 2 vols., 1930, I, 292–3). A. Hammond (ed.), *R3*, 1981, p. 61, argues that *R3* was written in 1591.

[8] See p. 36 below.

account is the most probable: it is based on the premise that Shakespeare wrote the whole of the trilogy and in the order of the events it portrays.[1] (The part of the argument that follows concerning the play's theatrical provenance, however, is not invalidated by a proof that the play was written and performed after *2* and *3 Henry VI.*) It assumes that the Folio texts derive from holographic copy (see the Textual Analysis, p. 190 below) and admits the possibility of some revision. It assumes that Shakespeare wrote the trilogy for performance by Lord Strange's Men.

On 3 March 1592 Philip Henslowe recorded taking £3 16s 8d at a performance at the Rose playhouse of '*harey the vj*' put on by Lord Strange's Men.[2] Ferdinando, Lord Strange, who succeeded his father as fifth Earl of Derby in 1593, was a patron of Shakespeare[3] and a descendant of the Lord Talbot who appears in the play.[4] As we know of no other play about Henry VI, it is reasonable to assume that this note refers to one of the plays from Shakespeare's sequence. Henslowe's entry bears a marginal note 'ne', but it is not certain that this designates a new play rather than one newly licensed by the Master of the Revels[5] – or else substantially revised. (It was unlikely to have been a performance of *2 Henry VI* or *3 Henry VI* since Henslowe regularly registered the first parts of multi-part plays only by their main titles, and indicated parts only for later plays in these sequences.[6]) There is, however, some external evidence to support the very reasonable conjecture that this entry records receipts for a play by Shakespeare. Nashe's *Pierce Penilesse* (which contains the passage about Talbot) is dedicated to Lord Strange, and contains an encomium of Edward Alleyn who at the time was

---

[1] For the debate over authorship see pp. 41–3 below. My findings in respect of chronology are supported by Antony Hammond (ed.), *R3*, 1981, pp. 54–61 (the most recent edition of the play). Wilson centred his contention that *1H6* must have been written after the other two parts of the sequence on two observations: that the six months between March and September offered Shakespeare insufficient time to write and have performed *2H6* and *3H6*, and that Talbot, the 'hero' of *Part 1*, is not mentioned in the latter plays (p. xiii). But this latter observation is predicated on a misleading literary premise, that plays must have heroes and that Talbot is here 'the' hero. It is also unlikely that Shakespeare would have conflated (as he did in *1H6*) two generations of the houses of Warwick and Somerset (see Notes to the List of Characters, p. 63 below). Wells and Taylor also argue that the play was written after *2* and *3H6*: 'Internal evidence has suggested to most editors that *Part One* assumes a familiarity with *Contention* and *Duke of York*, which in turn require no familiarity with *Part One*. Rare vocabulary in the portions most securely attributable to Shakespeare link them most strongly (in order) with *Duke of York* [i.e. *3H6*], *Richard III*, *Titus*, and *Two Gentlemen*' (p. 113). Rare vocabulary tests, however, surely point only to possible near contiguities with, say, *3H6* and *R3*, which could obviously have been as easily written soon *after 1H6* as *before*. The Taylor chronology also rests on the assumption that *2H6* and *3H6* had already been written and *performed* before March 1592.

[2] Henslowe, p. 16; for the company see Chambers, II, 118–27.

[3] E. A. J. Honigmann, *Shakespeare: The 'Lost Years'*, 1985, pp. 59 ff.; Honigmann's findings contest the long-held and influential view that Shakespeare did not have anything to do with Strange's Men before 1594. For this see Peter Alexander, *Shakespeare's 'Henry VI' and 'Richard III'*, 1929, pp. 188 ff.

[4] One of Talbot's titles is 'Lord Strange of Blackmere' (4.7.65).

[5] Henslowe, p. xxx; Honigmann, *Shakespeare's Impact*, pp. 76–7, is extremely sceptical about taking 'ne' to mean 'new'. It could even be that the Privy Council Order of 12 November 1589 cited above (p. 4) made relicensing in 1592 necessary.

[6] See Roslyn L. Knutson, 'Henslowe's naming of parts', *NQ* 228 (1983), 157–60.

the leading player of Lord Strange's Men.[1] The play, moreover, may well have been newly written – or, equally plausibly, revived – for events in the play parallel recent contemporary history: in the period from 1589 to 1591 three forces of English soldiers were sent to France in support of the Huguenot Henry of Navarre.[2] From October 1591 until January 1592 Englishmen under the command of the Earl of Essex participated in another, unsuccessful, siege of Rouen.[3] (It is extremely unlikely, furthermore, that there was a rival Henry VI play performing at the same time of which no record has survived.[4])

After this (first?) performance '*harey the vj*' was performed fourteen more times until 19 June.[5] The comparatively high receipts for these performances compared with those from the plays that are not marked 'ne' in this sequence of the diary could further confirm the conjecture that the play was newly written or of topical interest. (It is worth recording that Strange's Men were performing Greene's *A Looking-Glass for London and England* and *Friar Bacon and Friar Bungay* during this same season,[6] which may explain that author's jealousy. Greene therefore could have known *3 Henry VI*, from which he parodied the 'tiger's heart' line, from performances, from manuscript, or even, if the play was newly written, from rehearsal.)

Unfortunately these inconclusive entries are the only documentary material that would associate Shakespeare with Strange's Men, although Honigmann has recently adduced strong circumstantial evidence that would point to a long association with that company.[7] This helps to dispose of claims, made by those theatre historians who were uneasy about the Henslowe evidence, that there is a stronger probability that at this time Shakespeare was working for the rival Queen's Men with whom Greene also had an association.[8] (A recent advocate of this theory, G. M. Pinciss, argued his case from the presence of verbal similarities between lines of Shakespeare and lines from plays known to have belonged to the Queen's Men.[9] However, an author's knowledge of a company's repertoire does not imply that the author was a member of that company. Then as now, players and playwrights presumably saw each other's offerings.)

Henslowe's season came to an end in June, for on 23 June the Privy Council,

---

[1] Chambers, II, 120.

[2] See 4.7.61 n; for a general account of possible topical interest see Bullough, III, 24–5, who on these grounds argues for composition in autumn 1591 or winter 1591–2.

[3] See J. E. Neale, *Queen Elizabeth I*, 1979 edn, pp. 326 ff.; Bullough, III, 80–6, reprints extracts from the journal kept at the siege by Sir Thomas Coningsby. These historical analogues, however, offer no proof of the chronology of Shakespeare's early works and there is no reason not to postulate, as Honigmann does, a date of composition and performance as early as 1589.

[4] See Hanspeter Born, 'The date of *2, 3 Henry VI*', *SQ* 25 (1974), 323–34, and Peter Alexander's revised opinion, *Shakespeare*, 1964, p. 80.

[5] Henslowe, pp. 16–19.

[6] *Ibid.*, pp. 16–17.

[7] Honigmann, *The 'Lost Years'*, pp. 59–76.

[8] See Pollard's introduction to Alexander, *Shakespeare's 'Henry VI' and 'Richard III'*, pp. 13–21.

[9] 'Shakespeare, Her Majesty's Players, and Pembroke's Men', *S. Sur.* 27 (1974), 129–36.

because of an outbreak of the plague,[1] forbade theatrical performances until Michaelmas[2] of that year, and the players were kept out of their theatres. About July – the documents are undated – Strange's Men, supported by the Watermen of the Bankside (who ferried members of the audience across the Thames), petitioned the Privy Council for leave to return from provincial touring to the Rose: 'forasmuch . . . our company is great, and thereby our charge intolerable in travelling the country, and the continuance thereof will be a mean to bring us to division and separation'.[3] By 29 December, more entries in Henslowe's diary indicate that they were installed in their playhouse again, and the relevant run of entries includes receipts from two more performances of '*harey the vj*' before it ceases on 1 February,[4] all theatrical performances having been again prohibited because of the plague.[5]

The arguments of many scholars who have investigated the problems of the Henry VI sequence have rested on the assumption that it would have been impossible for Strange's Men to have prepared all three plays for performance in the period between February (Henslowe records his first takings from what we may now presume to have been *1 Henry VI* on 3 March) and 2 September, when Greene lay dying. (This is the nub of Dover Wilson's argument[6] and would seem to have been taken over by Cairncross who argues that all of the plays must have been *written* before the first was *performed*.[7]) However, as Bernard Beckerman, working from Henslowe's diaries, pointed out, 'the time between final purchase of the manuscript and the first indication of production extends from three to fifty-one days, the average duration being a little over twenty days'.[8] If the plays had not been written and performed before 1592, this would still allow ample time for the company to have prepared if not performed the whole of the sequence before Greene's death – that is, between March and early September 1592. Shakespeare may well have been finishing *2* and *3 Henry VI* during the spring of that year in preparation for a summer production which had to be cancelled because of the plague.[9]

There is confirmation for both these schedules in the Folio texts, which indicate that the manuscripts from which they derive were at least prepared for performance in a London playhouse rather than for the scantier theatrical resources of a provincial tour. All three parts of the sequence demand that scenes be played

[1] Chambers, IV, 347–8.
[2] *Ibid.*, pp. 310–11.
[3] *Ibid.*, pp. 311–12.
[4] Henslowe, pp. 19–20; the epilogue to *H5* (1599) notes that the Henry VI plays were 'oft' shown on the stage (13).
[5] Chambers, IV, 313.
[6] Wilson, p. xiv.
[7] Cairncross, p. xxxv; this is also the view of Bullough, III, 23–4.
[8] B. Beckerman, *Shakespeare at the Globe*, 1962, p. 10.
[9] This is also the conclusion of Born, 'The date of *2, 3 Henry VI*', pp. 328 ff. It seems legitimate to infer from 3.1.133 that in *1H6* the part of the king was taken by a boy player who would have surrendered his role to an adult for the later plays of the sequence. This might account for the way in which *2H6* and *3H6* were associated as a two-part 'Contention' play.

'aloft'. *1 Henry VI* 1.4.21 (*on the turrets*), 1.6.0, 3.2.40, and 5.3.130 (*on the walls*), 3.2.25 (*on the top*), 4.2.2 (*aloft*); *2 Henry VI* 1.4.12, 4.9.0 (*on the tarras* (= terrace)); *3 Henry VI* 5.1.0 and 5.6.0 (*on the walls*). Two plays contain references to the tiring-house doors that could signify the gates to a city[1] or serve to build up a symmetrical stage image.[2]

But some time in the latter half of 1592 it seems that what Lord Strange's Men had feared did happen: while they were exiled from the Rose it appears that they divided,[3] and one group, under the patronage of the Earl of Pembroke, embarked on a provincial tour that began in October and lasted about ten months until the group had to return to London, pawn their costumes, and sell their playbooks.[4] The name of Pembroke's company is on the title page of the 'bad' quarto of *3 Henry VI*, *The True Tragedy of Richard Duke of York* (1595), on that of *Titus Andronicus* (1594), and *The Taming of a Shrew* (1594) – a bad quarto of *The Taming of the Shrew*[5] – as well as of Marlowe's *Edward II*. *1 Contention* does not bear the name of a company on its title page. The Shakespearean texts all show evidence of having been shortened and adapted for a smaller number of players. The presence of three of his plays in this group would confirm Shakespeare's association with the new company as well as the association with the parent group, Strange's Men – which confirms in turn the preliminary assumption of this argument that '*harey the vj*' was probably *1 Henry VI*. It seems, however, that he was not acting with the new touring group for his name does not figure among those of the six sharers of the company.[6]

Further confirmation that *2 Henry VI* and *3 Henry VI* were written for performance by Strange's Men comes from the appearance of actors' names in speech headings. (There is no way of telling whether these derive from Shakespeare or the book-keeper.) John Holland is named in *2 Henry VI* 4.2 and Sincklo in *3 Henry VI* 3.1. These in all probability were the same J. Holland and John Sincler whose names appear in the 'plot' of *2 Deadly Sins* which Greg conjectures to have been performed by Strange's Men at the Curtain, probably in 1590.[7] A third player is named in *3 Henry VI* 3.1 simply as 'Humphrey'. The only known player of the period with this name is Humphrey Jeffes, whose name occurs frequently in

---

[1] *1H6* 1.3.14 and 28 (*the Tower gates*), 2.1.38 (*Enter several ways* (indicating that each character was to use a different entrance)).

[2] *3H6* 2.5.54 and 73.

[3] Chambers, II, 129; however, Karl P. Wentersdorf, 'The origin and personnel of the Pembroke Company', *Theatre Research International* 5 (1979–80), 45–68, argues that Pembroke's Men had belonged to the Queen's Men.

[4] Chambers, II, 128; Henslowe, p. 280.

[5] See Ann Thompson (ed.), *Shr.*, 1984, pp. 1–3.

[6] See Mary Edmond, 'Pembroke's Men', *RES* 25 (1974), 129–36. Edmond shows that two of the other sharers had earlier associations with Henslowe. See also D. George, 'Shakespeare and Pembroke's Men', *SQ* 32 (1981), 305–23.

[7] W. W. Greg, *Elizabethan Dramatic Documents*, 1931, p. 113; see also B. Morris (ed.), *Shr.*, 1981, pp. 49–50. George Bevis who appears in 4.2 and 4.7 of *2H6* does not appear in this 'plot'. Andrew Gurr notes that 'There is also a "Nicke" in that list who may be the same as the "Nicke" named in the Cade scene in the pirated text of *2 Henry VI* and in *The Taming of the Shrew* (3.1.82)' (*The Shakespearean Stage 1574–1642*, 1970, p. 26).

Henslowe's diary, but only from 1597. Recently W. Schrickx found a record of the date of his birth (23 December 1576) and conjectures that he was abroad from 1592.[1] This small piece of evidence would push back the beginning of the period of composition to some time before that date and confirms the conjecture that although the three plays may all have been written for Strange's Men, only the first part was performed by them for the reasons given above.

The hypothesis that would follow from the above argument would be that *1 Contention* and *The True Tragedy* which are adaptations of *2 Henry VI* and *3 Henry VI*, were designed for the provincial tour. Strange's Men would have retained ownership of the 'books' of these plays but may have allowed some of their ex-members to prepare the abridgements. David George has accumulated a list of fifteen players who could have been included in the 1592 Pembroke company;[2] the number of players required for 2.3 of *1 Contention* is eighteen, the same number as that required for 1.1 of *The True Tragedy*[3] and the quarto version of *Richard III*.[4] (This number allows for only two extras and includes two boys' parts.[5]) It is possible, then, that there were at least three more players in the group who have left no trace. This would have been a larger group than usual: texts like the 1600 quarto of *Henry V* that derive from touring performances can be played by as few as eleven players.[6] But a large company *is* conceivable, given the fact that many players would have been driven out of the metropolis by the plague.

There is, however, some evidence in the stage directions of *1 Contention* which might suggest that the text *recalls* performance in a London playhouse:[7] two doors are stipulated in 1.1, 3.2, and 5.2, there is a possible reference to a discovery space in 3.2, alarms are sounded 'within' in 4.1, and 1.4 demands three levels since Dame Eleanor goes *up to the tower* (1.4.5 SD) and exits *above*, while a spirit *riseth up* (1.4.20 SD), presumably from a cellarage. Likewise *The True Tragedy* seems to demand a tiring-house: two entrances are called for (2.4), a post is sounded *within* (3.3.94 SD) and a functional door is required (*The Mayor opens the door and brings the keys in his hand* (4.7.18 SD)). Other stage directions suggest a stage gallery: 'three suns' appear, presumably lowered from above (2.1.8 SD), and an upper playing area is used in 5.1 which is set *on the walls*. Unless *2* and *3 Henry VI* had in fact been performed at the Rose by June we have to conjecture that the compilers of these texts were players recalling actions worked out in rehearsals – or that the stage directions are the relics of performances designed for halls. The

---

[1] W. Schrickx, 'English actors at the courts of Wolfenbüttel', *S. Sur.* 33 (1980), pp. 153–68.

[2] David George, 'Shakespeare and Pembroke's Men', p. 313.

[3] A. C. Sprague, *Shakespeare's Histories: Plays for the Stage*, 1964, calculated that thirteen players were needed for *1H6* (p. 114).

[4] See A. Hammond (ed.), *R3*, 1981, p. 65.

[5] The arguments of Scott McMillin, 'Casting for Pembroke's Men: the *Henry VI* quartos and *The Taming of A Shrew*', *SQ* 23 (1972), 141–59, must be considered invalid as he inexplicably discounts 'bit' parts, 'defined as roles of [less] than ten lines altogether'. His article does contain, however, useful descriptions of the regrouping of Strange's Men as Pembroke's Men.

[6] See Stanley Wells and Gary Taylor, *Modernising Shakespeare's Text*, 1979, pp. 72 ff.

[7] My arguments are confirmed by William Montgomery's Oxford D.Phil. thesis, '*The Contention of York and Lancaster*: A Critical Edition', 1985; see also Wells and Taylor, *Textual Companion*, p. 176.

recollections of *1 Henry VI* which appear in the text of the second play[1] also allow us to conjecture that this text was compiled while memories of London performances of *Part 1* were still fresh.

The conclusion must be that the whole sequence was *written* some time before March 1592. If they were written late, circumstances probably conspired to prevent the *production* in that season of the second and third parts of the play. The quartos may represent a condensation of Shakespeare texts for performance in one afternoon, either planned but not performed for London, or planned and performed in the provinces.

Authorship

Centuries-long debates over the date and provenance of the play inevitably opened up the question of authorship – and vice versa. Circumstantial or external 'evidence' was adduced to prove that Shakespeare could not have written all of the play, and this was complemented by internal evidence.

None of the three parts of the sequence was named by Francis Meres who listed twelve plays by Shakespeare in 1598.[2] The classic case against Shakespeare's authorship of the whole of *1 Henry VI* and of parts of *2* and *3 Henry VI* was made by Malone, who included in his edition a 'Dissertation on the Three Parts of King Henry VI' (1790). Malone built up his argument on the basis of observations offered earlier by Theobald. His case rested on the large number of classical allusions which he thought more characteristic of Peele or Greene, on the play's 'stately march of versification' characteristic of contemporary tragedy,[3] on its historical inexactitude, and on its 'paucity of regular rhymes'.[4] Peter Alexander's *Shakespeare's 'Henry VI' and 'Richard III'* (1929) won the plays back for Shakespeare,[5] although Dover Wilson's edition of 1952 apportioned particular scenes in the play to various of the 'university wits', Nashe, Peele, and Greene.

Cairncross believed that Shakespeare wrote the whole play, but was forced into sophisticated and unlikely theories concerning the nature of the text which he used to emend what he took to be stylistic faults. But quality of writing can be used neither as a test for authorship, nor, on its own, as a reason for supposing scribal or compositional interference.

Earlier critics generally worked impressionistically, making much use of verbal parallels, distribution of sources,[6] and various *ad hoc* stylistic methods;[7] more re-

[1] A. S. Cairncross (ed.), *2H6*, 1957, pp. 182–5; M. Hattaway (ed.), *2H6* (forthcoming), Appendix 2.
[2] *Palladis Tamia. Wits Treasury* (1598), pp. 281–2.
[3] Boswell's Variorum edn of Malone's *Plays and Poems of William Shakespeare*, 21 vols., 1821, XVIII, 560.
[4] *Ibid.*, p. 568.
[5] In the introduction he supplied for this work, A. W. Pollard notes that he was 'inclined to believe that *1 Henry VI* was originally written by Shakespeare in collaboration with Peele' (p. 25). Alexander's conclusions were supported by Hereward T. Price in his *Construction in Shakespeare*, 1951, and by Leo Kirschbaum, 'The authorship of *1 Henry VI*', *PMLA* 67 (1952), 809–22.
[6] See Bullough, III, pp. 32 ff.
[7] See Marco Mincoff, 'The composition of *Henry VI, Part 1*', *SQ* 16 (1965), 279–87.

cent work has centred on vocabulary, rare words,[1] imagery, structural parallels,[2] metrical evidence, stage directions, stylometry, and, most recently, the study of function words ('but', 'by', 'for', 'no', 'not', 'so', 'that', 'the', 'to', 'with', etc.).[3] The most recent analysis of the authorship of *1 Henry VI*, that of Gary Taylor,[4] is based on vocabulary, spelling, and metrical tests, as well as on scene divisions, and orthographical and linguistic features, and concludes that the play was written collaboratively, proposing the following division of shares:[5]

1.1.1–102	Y? (or X)
1.1.103–51	?
1.1.152–77	Y? (or X)
1.2–1.6 (1.2–1.8)	Thomas Nashe
2.1–2.3	X
2.4	Shakespeare
2.5	X
3.1–3.4 (3.1–3.8)	Y
4.1	X? (or Y)
4.2–4.7.32	Shakespeare
4.7.33–96	mixed? (Shakespeare and Y?)
5.1–5.5 (5.1–5.7)	Y

'The identities of X and Y are unknown, though Y has particular links with *Locrine* . . .and both have strong similarities to the dramatic writings of Robert Greene and George Peele.'[6] However, these findings are not decisively supported by the function-word tests.[7] (One of the cruces in the play, Exeter's surprise at Winchester's elevation to the rank of cardinal (5.1.28 ff.) after the latter had appeared in cardinal's robes in 1.3 may be due to Shakespeare's use of sources rather than revision or multiple authorship.[8] On the strength of their authorial hypothesis the Oxford editors removed all references to Winchester as a cardinal from their text of 1.3.[9])

I do not believe that stylistic analysis is sufficient to prove or disprove authorship, as it is likely that at an early stage in his career Shakespeare was moving freely

---

[1] Eliot Slater's rare-vocabulary test of *Edward III* links this play from the Shakespeare apocrypha very closely with *1H6*. Slater concludes that his tests prove that their findings are compatible with Shakespeare's authorship of *Edward III*. See his *The Problem of 'The Reign of King Edward III'*, 1988.

[2] On construction generally see Price, *Construction in Shakespeare*.

[3] See Wells and Taylor, *Textual Companion*, pp. 80 ff.

[4] Gary Taylor, 'Shakespeare and others: the authorship of *1 Henry VI*', *Medieval and Renaissance Drama in England* (forthcoming); Joachim Thiele, 'Untersuchung der Vermutung J. D. Wilson über den Verfasser des ersten Aktes von Shakespeares "King Henry VI, First Part" mit Hilfe einfacher Textcharakteristiken', *Grunlagenstudien aus Kybernetik und Geisteswissenschaft* 6 (1965), 25–7.

[5] References are to this edition, with the Oxford act and scene numbers in parentheses.

[6] Wells and Taylor, *Textual Companion*, p. 217.

[7] *Ibid.*, pp. 87–8.

[8] See 1.3 headnote in Commentary and 5.1.28–9 n.

[9] See collation at 1.3 passim. On this passage and the Oxford edition generally, see David Bevington, 'Determining the indeterminate', *SQ* 38 (1987), 501–19.

between the various verse registers that were being deployed in the plays in which he was probably acting. Moreover, since none of the other statistical analyses I have read makes an indisputable case for dual or multiple authorship, I do not feel inclined to dispute the implicit claim, made by Heminges and Condell when they included the play in the First Folio, that *1 Henry VI* is Shakespeare's work. And even if it could be proved that the play was in whole or in part not by Shakespeare, should that affect the way in which we read or direct it?

Stage history

After the performances of the play by Strange's Men at the Rose from March 1592 (see p. 36 above) we know of no further performances before the closing of the theatres. The only revival of the play during the Restoration[1] and the eighteenth century was on 13 March 1738 at Covent Garden[2] 'by desire of several Ladies of Quality'[3] during a period that saw productions of many plays that were less well known at the time.[4] It included dances by two Pierrots and a Scots dance.[5]

It was produced by Edmund Kean as part of J. H. Merivale's five-act adaptation, *Richard Duke of York* (1817), a compilation of the three parts of the play performed at Drury Lane (with passages from Chapman and Webster thrown in) from 15 December in that year.[6] This included the Temple garden scene and Kean took the star part of York. Another abridgement of the three parts into three acts was made by Charles Kemble (1775–1854, younger brother to John Philip Kemble) but there is no evidence that it was published or performed in his lifetime.[7]

There were productions in Germany and Austria in the nineteenth century, including a notable version at the Burgtheater in Vienna in 1873 in which Mitterwurzer played Winchester.[8]

In April 1889 it was lavishly produced by G. Osmond Tearle at Stratford. Tearle himself played Talbot, Erskine Lewis the king, and Ellen Cranston Margaret.[9] F. R. Benson produced the three parts of the play at Stratford on 2, 3, and 4 May

---

[1] The production of '*Henry the Sixth, the First Part*' by the Duke's Company at Dorset Garden Theatre in 1681 turns out to be Crowne's expanded adaptation of Acts 1–3 of *2 Henry VI* (John Genest, *Some Account of the English Stage from the Restoration in 1660 to 1830*, 10 vols., 1832, I, 302–4; see also Hazelton Spencer, *Shakespeare Improved*, 1927, pp. 310–13).

[2] The cast is given by C. B. Hogan, *Shakespeare in the Theatre, 1701–1800*, 2 vols., 1952–7, I, 202.

[3] Genest, *English Stage*, III, 555.

[4] George C. D. Odell, *Shakespeare from Betterton to Irving* 2 vols., 1920, I, 227.

[5] A. H. Scouten, *The London Stage*, 1961, Part 3, p. 707.

[6] Charles H. Shattuck, *The Shakespeare Promptbooks*, 1965, p. 154; accounts are given in Genest, *English Stage*, VIII, 636–41, and Odell, *Betterton to Irving*, II, 128–30. It was not well received: see the review in *The Times*, 23 December 1817, and L. L. and C. W. Houtchens (eds.), *Leigh Hunt's Dramatic Criticism*, 1949, pp. 180–2. A contemporary review from *The European Magazine* is reprinted by Gāmini Salgādo, *Eyewitnesses of Shakespeare*, 1975, pp. 86–7.

[7] It is printed in *The Henry Irving Shakespeare*, 8 vols., 1888, III, 201–46.

[8] See E. L. Stahl, *Shakespeare und das Deutsche Theater*, 1947.

[9] The prompt-book is in the Library of the Shakespeare Centre. For the changes Tearle made see Sprague, *Shakespeare's Histories*, p. 112 n.; see also Muriel C. Day and J. C. Trewin, *The Shakespeare Memorial Theatre*, 1932, pp. 69–70.

1906[1] – *3 Henry VI* being revived for the first time. Benson played Talbot and Tita Brand was Joan. The director used a permanent set which could yet be deployed in the service of illusion. An anonymous reviewer wrote: 'There was no changing of scenery, except of portable furniture, the action was continuous, and the auditors were expected to exercise not only their attention but their imagination. "The Players' House" served for all castles and battlements and balconies: the arras and painted cloths for all backgrounds; curtains gave opportunities for concealment, and ordinary exits and entrances allowed a continuous stream of performers to pass over the proscenium.'[2] A week earlier, however, a reviewer remarked: 'The effect of the opening scene was most picturesque, the interior of the old Abbey at Westminster, with its sable mourning draperies, the nobles and their followers around the coffin, the rich costumes, the solemn music – everything, in fact, blended with perfect harmony to give the prevailing sentiment of mournful grandeur due precision.'[3] It was also noted that 'To make it an acting play there has to be a great transposition of scenes, and the text undergoes rather serious mutilation... The historical dramas were only sparsely patronized, with the exception of *Henry V*, and the revival play [*3 Henry VI*] brought the smallest house of the week.'[4]

Robert Atkins produced the play along with the first half of *2 Henry VI* at the Old Vic on 29 January 1923. Ernest Meads played Talbot; Rupert Harvey, York; Guy Martineau, the king; Jane Bacon, Pucelle; and Esther Whitehouse, Margaret.[5] In the United States under the direction of Gilmor Brown the play was performed for the first time at the Pasadena Community Playhouse in California from 25 to 27 July 1935 as part of a season which saw productions of all ten histories,[6] and in 1975 it was produced at the Oregon Shakespeare Festival.[7]

A sequence of notable modern revivals began when, under Sir Barry Jackson, the whole sequence was directed by Douglas Seale at the Birmingham Repertory Theatre from 1951.[8] The sequence was played in London on successive nights at the Old Vic.[9] 'Douglas Seale was a director who knew what a clean thrusting style could do for a crowded chronicle. Hence the ultimate triumph at the Vic in Finlay James's setting of triple Gothic arches.'[10] Jack May played the king and

[1] Benson's interpretative note is given by Sprague, *Shakespeare's Histories*, p. 112, who also notes that the production is reviewed at length in *The Athenaeum*, 12 May 1906.

[2] *Stratford-upon-Avon Herald*, 11 May 1906.

[3] *Ibid.*, 4 May 1906.

[4] *Ibid.*, 11 May 1906.

[5] See *The [London] Shakespeare [League] Journal* 8 (February 1923), 57. The playbill is reprinted in John Parker, *Who's Who in the Theatre*, 1925.

[6] Louis Marder describes a production of the three parts of the sequence condensed by Arthur Lithgow into a single one-act play and performed in August 1952 at Antioch Area Theater, Yellow Springs, Ohio: 'History cycle at Antioch College', *SQ* 4 (1953), 57–8.

[7] See Dessen, *Elizabethan Stage Conventions*, p. 113.

[8] Seale produced *2H6* in 1951, *3H6* in 1952 (22 July), and *1H6* in 1953 (4 July). See Sir Barry Jackson, 'On producing *Henry VI*', *S. Sur.* 6 (1953), 49–52; J. C. Trewin, *Going to Shakespeare*, 1978, p. 20.

[9] The whole sequence was reviewed in *The Times*, 15–17 July 1953.

[10] J. C. Trewin, *Shakespeare on the English Stage, 1900–1964*, 1964, p. 225.

12   Act 4, Scene 1: the coronation of Henry VI in Peter Hall's 1964 production at Stratford-upon-Avon. David Warner as Henry, Nicholas Selby as Winchester

Rosalind Boxall Queen Margaret. In 1957 Seale brought the production again to the Old Vic, where it was played from 16 October with *Parts 1* and *2* condensed into one performance.[1]

Sprague[2] describes an uncut amateur production by the Hovenden Theatre Club in August 1959 that used only ten men and three women and which offered a sympathetic portrait of Joan.

In 1963 John Barton reduced the three plays of the sequence into two, '*Henry VI*' and '*Edward IV*', which were directed for the Royal Shakespeare Company at Stratford by Peter Hall under the joint title of *The Wars of the Roses*.[3] They were revived at Stratford in 1964 as part of the centennial presentation of the complete sequence of history plays. Barton not only cut passages, but added material of his own, usually derived from the chronicles.[4] Fastolf and the Countess of Auvergne disappeared, the performance began with a recitation of Henry V's dying exhorta-

[1]   Little of *1H6* remained. The reviewer in *The Times* felt that the London performances did not match the original ones (17 October 1957).
[2]   Sprague, *Shakespeare's Histories*, pp. 114–16.
[3]   See John Russell Brown, *Shakespeare's Plays in Performance*, 1966, pp. 195–202. A television version of this production was broadcast by the BBC. Barton's text '*Henry VI*' was performed at the Stratford Festival Theatre in Ontario in 1966.
[4]   The text is given in J. Barton and P. Hall, *The Wars of the Roses: adapted for the Royal Shakespeare Company from William Shakespeare's 'Henry VI, Parts I, II, III and Richard III'*, 1970.

tion as recorded in Hall's chronicle, and '*Henry VI*' ended with retribution upon Gloucester's murderers. In the programme, John Barton and Peter Hall wrote: 'We are sure that these early plays produced in an unadapted form would show to a modern audience the force of their political and human meaning.' Bamber Gascoigne noticed that Barton 'introduced, among many other things, one particularly bold invention. Early on he makes Gloucester resign his full Protectorship; power is henceforth to rest in the majority decision of the council, with only the King having the right of veto. So the voice of each councillor becomes important (lines are duly provided), the shifting patterns of power are laid open in a process of voting, and the full dramatic ingredients are provided for Gloucester's own impeachment and Henry's failure to protect him.'[1] The productions won huge critical acclaim, especially for David Warner, who took the part of the king, and Dame Peggy Ashcroft, who played Margaret of Anjou.

The intention, however, seems not to have been to create star vehicles, but to establish a unified company style played on a set that eschewed any kind of historical accuracy or theatrical glamour – the influence of Brecht's notions of history and the theatrical style of his Berliner Ensemble was manifest: 'Hall's policy? To fashion a company that can play together, to and with each other, with only the occasional use of stars with ready-made reputations...Whatever distant historical ends these Kings and nobles may be carrying out, it is their individual actions that are determining the sway of the struggle.'[2] (Not everyone was pleased, however, by the overall conception: 'They begin by seeming to share the common anti-Lancastrian feeling of our day. It is fashionable to scorn Henry V living, and Mr Barton and Mr Hall start their chronicles with a speech...designed to show him unappetizingly dead...The valiant Talbots are so ludicrously miscast that we seek for some Brechtian jeer at physical courage.'[3] David Pryce-Jones missed a sense of doom: 'Now [the barons] are presented merely as the greedy symbols of ambition and power, thwarted by the even greedier symbols of absolutism.'[4]) 'There were even titters of protest at some of the decapitations, but the triumph of the production is the even conversational tone with which the discussions are carried forward and the care to avoid ranting, even in dealing with martial bombast.'[5]

Part of the acclaim won for the production derived from the set: 'It is a hard world – shaped in steel, John Bury, the present designer says. He has told us how he has tried to mark the English court by "thick enclosing walls", the English countryside by trees, and France by the use of copper. All is stern, metallic, and ringing. The stage is wide and bare, a sounding-board for fierce words and fierce deeds.'[6] The stage was backed by steel trellis work, and the 'walls' were great

[1] Bamber Gascoigne, *Observer*, 2 August 1964.
[2] Bernard Levin, *Daily Mail*, 18 July 1963.
[3] Harold Hobson, *Sunday Times*, 21 July 1963.
[4] David Pryce-Jones, *Spectator*, 26 July 1963.
[5] Philip Hope-Wallace, *Guardian*, 18 July 1963.
[6] J. C. Trewin, *Birmingham Post*, 18 July 1963.

triangular structures faced with a pattern of riveted plates, which could be moved like massive city gates. 'We seem to be claustrophobically caught between two swinging metal wings that crush us first from one side then from the other.'[1] Prominent was a large council table which could be thrust out over matching stylised flagstones to the front of the stage, suggesting the domination of lords over monarch. 'The play is admirably produced to show us how behind the scenes decisions are cooked up to be ratified later at this table.'[2] 'The endless succession of sorties and sieges with clanking figures wrestling in half-light actually became restful interludes between the far more dramatic and exciting clashes of ambition and policy.'[3] Also thrust out was a 'push-on-push-off throne and dais ...itself a miniature architectural masterpiece, oddly contemporary yet not without the dignity of history. It would have graced Coventry Cathedral or the Shell Building.'[4]

Instead of historical costumes actors wore uniform greys, blacks, and browns flecked with gold: the barons were 'nicely differentiated but not in a fancy Guthrie fashion'.[5] Instead therefore of appearing as heroes in a divinely appointed saga they were operators within a specific political milieu. Robert Kee wrote of 'the svelte anarchy in which the ambitious and fear-ridden nobles who are the real successors to Henry V operate. This must be exposed from the very first moment, and is in fact here instantaneously conjured up by the sinister and fidgety bickering on their knees of this Winchester (Nicholas Selby) and this Gloucester (Paul Hardwick). It is developed with the fury of Greek tragedy, each man revealing continuously in his eyes a terrible suspicion that in hounding down the others he is hounding down himself.'[6]

David Warner's Henry was hailed as one of the greatest acting performances of the age. 'There is no obvious beauty about him, for, tall as he is, he walks with the slouching gait of a clumsy scholar or farm-hand. Yet his sad, distressed face beneath his fair hair, meeting each new misfortune with an absolute absence of protest or indignation, spreads over the darkest waters of the play a quiet and persistent gold glory.'[7] 'Heavy boots, sloping shoulders, weak but utterly likeable. An unworldly saint in a cesspool of intrigue', wrote Felix Barker.[8] 'W. H. W.' spoke of Warner's 'shambling diffidence behind which there are tortures of conscience'.[9]

'Janet Suzman's Joan La Pucelle [is]...a hell-cat used for political purposes and not the sluttish witch that Shakespeare characteristically invented...The decencies of chivalric warfare observed against the French are abandoned with

---

[1] T. C. Worsley, *Financial Times*, 18 July 1963.
[2] *Ibid.*
[3] Alan Brien, *Sunday Telegraph*, 21 July 1963.
[4] Ken Griffith, *South Wales Evening Argus*, 19 July 1963.
[5] T. C. Worsley, *Financial Times*, 18 July 1963.
[6] Robert Kee, *New Statesman*, 7 August 1964.
[7] Harold Hobson, *Sunday Times*, 21 July 1963.
[8] Felix Barker, *Evening News*, 18 July 1963.
[9] W. H. W., *Birmingham Mail*, 18 July 1963.

13   Janet Suzman as Joan la Pucelle, 1964

eagerness and increasing savagery when the throne is at stake.'[1] When the play was revived in the following year *The Times* noted: 'There are a few alterations in the production itself, of which the most striking is the drum-head trial of Joan of Arc which has been removed from the battlefield to a stately chamber where Warwick and York, goblets in hand, play sarcastically with the wretched girl before sending her to the stake.'[2]

Brewster Mason as Warwick 'adopts a watchfully aloof style in the earlier scenes, and throughout the two plays a half-humorous, half-savage grin which suggests supreme self-confidence characterizes his bearing'.[3] Donald Sinden played York, 'fiery, impetuous, unhampered by too much intelligence but honourable in his own way',[4] and Nicholas Selby gave a 'saurian Bishop of Winchester'.[5]

A French adaptation – of the three Henry VI plays and *Richard III* – was prepared and directed by Denis Llorca in 1978. It was entitled *Kings, ou les adieux à Shakespeare*, comprised three parts, 'L'été', 'L'automne' and 'L'hiver' with a preliminary adaptation of the deposition of Richard II by Bullingbrook – 'Le printemps' – and took the form of a twelve-hour performance that was remarkable for its spectacle and symbolic structure. It was performed at the Maison des Arts André Malraux at Créteil near Paris in May 1979 after being the centrepiece of the festival at Carcassonne the previous summer.[6]

The complete sequence of three plays was directed by Terry Hands at Stratford-upon-Avon for the Royal Shakespeare Company from 12 July 1977.[7] They were staged in conjunction with a revival of Hands's very successful 1975 Stratford production of *Henry V*: Alan Howard played both kings, father and son, to great acclaim. The productions were revived at the Aldwych Theatre in London in April 1978.

The style of production was, like that of *Henry V*, epic in the Brechtian manner. An iron bridge created a gallery, a device that enabled the director, on a 'deep, bare, and threatening'[8] stage, 'to mount an immensely vast production, scene cutting to scene, long-shot to close-up, as in a film scenario . . . After the first scene

[1] David Pryce-Jones, *Spectator*, 26 July 1963.
[2] *The Times*, 30 July 1964.
[3] Charles Graves, *Scotsman*, 31 July 1963.
[4] E. M. A., *Leamington Spa Courier*, 9 July 1983.
[5] B. A. Young, *Punch*, 24 July 1963.
[6] See Marie-Claude Rousseau's account of the discussion on the play at the Société Française Shakespeare (*Actes du congrès*, 1979), and reviews in *Midi Libre*, 18 and 19 July 1979; *La Dépêche du Midi*, 17 July 1978; *Les Nouvelles littéraires*, 20 July 1978; *Le Monde*, 5 August 1978 and 16 May 1979.
[7] The story of the productions is told by Sally Beauman, *The Royal Shakespeare Company*, 1982, pp. 338–42; see also J-M. Maguin, 'Review of Terry Hands' RSC Stratford production of *Henry VI*', *Cahiers Élisabéthains* 12 (1977), 77–80; G. K. Hunter, 'The Royal Shakespeare Company plays *Henry VI*', *Renaissance Drama* 9 (1978), 91–108; G. M. Pearce, 'Review of Terry Hands' RSC London production of *Henry VI*', *Cahiers Élisabéthains* 14 (1978), 107–9; D. Daniell, 'Opening up the text: Shakespeare's Henry VI plays in performance', in J. Redmond (ed.), *Themes in Drama 1: Drama and Society*, 1979; H. D. Swander, 'The rediscovery of *Henry VI*', *SQ* 29 (1978), 146–63; R. Warren, 'Comedies and histories at two Stratfords, 1977', *S. Sur.* 31 (1978), 141–53.
[8] R. Cushman, *Observer*, 17 July 1977.

14 Salisbury and the English at the siege of Orléans (Act 1, Scene 4) in Terry Hands's 1977
production at Stratford-upon-Avon

the bare plank stage is seldom free of guns.'[1] Scenes or 'gests' could be 'quoted',
as Brecht described, in order to bring out the thematic unity of the play: 'The
opening scene shows the angry barons disputing over Henry V's coffin, and is
cleverly paralleled later when they rage in court across the etiolated pallid figure of
his adolescent son.'[2] Irving Wardle wrote: '[Hands] excels in speed and contrast,
fading in and out between Talbot's last battle upstage and wrangling political
disputes in the foreground, revealing the lyrical Margaret crouched behind a
cannon at the moment the captured Pucelle is dragged off, and dividing Farrah's
raked stage with a complex assembly of lighted areas and light curtains.'[3] The
'reading is full of marvellous ideas like the contrast between the skeletal throne
and the full richness of the costumes'.[4] '[Hands] hasn't found an overpowering
single image for the three plays, like the diamond shaped council-table that
dominated [Hall's] *The Wars of the Roses*. But he has...evoked a style that admirably suits chronicle plays. It's based on a minimal setting, roving spotlights,
and a bold frontal style of playing that gives the actors a chance to establish direct
lines of contact with the audience.'[5] Benedict Nightingale claimed that the

[1] B. A. Young, *Financial Times*, 13 July 1977.
[2] John Baker, *Daily Telegraph*, 13 July 1977.
[3] Irving Wardle, *The Times*, 13 July 1977.
[4] *Sunday Times*, 24 April 1978.
[5] Michael Billington, *Guardian*, 17 April 1978.

productions succeeded 'without that editorializing, moralizing touch which has sometimes spoiled promising productions at Stratford'.[1] After the London revival, the critic of the *Financial Times* wrote: 'To my mind this is the best Shakespeare production I have ever seen. There is no scenery, no more than a token growth of grass [in *2 Henry VI*]; but there is a spare yet powerful use of props – cannon mostly in Part 1 where the war is on an international scale, the Throne and the benches of Parliament in the other parts – and there are fine costumes devised so that the wearer is always recognizable.'[2]

'Outstanding...are Helen Mirren's Margaret and Peter McEnery's Suffolk. The battlefield wooing is notable not only in the exceptional speaking of the verse, but in the power lurking behind the restraint...Joan is seen by Charlotte Cornwell at first as a giggling half-wit, and a city girl if ever I heard one. She giggles less as she matures in warfare, but in her captivity she is inclined to peals of hysterical laughter.'[3] 'The first sight of Mr Howard is indeed astounding: not only does he look like a child, hand in hand with his two feuding uncles, his very body seems to have shrunk, as he stands absurdly overloaded in coronation regalia, the image of a man with no desire for authority surrounded by power-ravenous underlings...Emrys James [is] a snarling underdog steadily on the way up, characteristically seen sniffing his white rose in the act of dispatching Joan to the stake...[There is] a memorable duel between...Talbot [David Swift] and... Joan: two national champions, one a grizzled old hunter, the other an unromanticized peasant given to explosions of ecstatic laughter. Both are presented with a realist dignity in honourable contrast to their ignominious allies.'[4]

The BBC's television version of the play was broadcast on 2 January 1983. It was produced by Jonathan Miller and directed by Jane Howell. For this, the other two parts of the plays, and *Richard III*, a constructivist, anti-illusionist set was used, a seemingly circular playing space surrounded by walls and galleries made of old doors and timber. The director 'worked with her designers [Oliver Bayldon and John Peacock] to produce a set suggestive of a brightly coloured playground, with Playcraft props, "dressing up" costumes, and armour inspired by the shoulder pads of American football'.[5] It worked well, far better in my opinion than those productions shot on location or which used an illusionist set.[6] The text was taken at a rattling pace, displaying a Brechtian sense of *Spass* (fun), and the players seemed, as in a pantomime, to relish the simplicity of parts of the verse and scenic construction. Fights often had the lusty style of a comic strip. Talbot (played by

---

[1] Benedict Nightingale, *New Statesman*, 22 July 1977.

[2] B. A. Young, *Financial Times*, 17 April 1978.

[3] B. A. Young, *Financial Times*, 13 July 1977.

[4] Irving Wardle, *The Times*, 13 July 1977.

[5] Robert Hapgood, 'Shakespeare on film and television', in Wells, *Cambridge Companion*, p. 278; see also Henry Fenwick, 'The production', in *The BBC TV Shakespeare: Henry VI Part One*, 1983, pp. 22–3.

[6] See Graham Holderness, 'Radical potentiality and institutional closure: Shakespeare in film and television', in J. Dollimore and A. Sinfield (eds.), *Political Shakespeare*, 1985, pp. 193 ff.; J. C. Bulman and H. R. Coursen (eds.), *Shakespeare on Television*, 1988, pp. 292–6.

15 Act 1, Scene 5: Pucelle (Charlotte Cornwell) and Talbot (David Swift) in Terry Hands's production

Trevor Peacock, who was to play Cade in *2 Henry VI*) and Joan (Brenda Blethyn) were populist figures, un-jingoistic and distrustful of authority, confident of their energy and happy to address the camera directly. Joan was a swanky northern girl, sardonic and childlike, who won power by her personality. She was neither a seductress nor a witch – the fiends of 5.3 were not shown but were figures in her mind. Henry (Peter Benson) was not taken by a boy actor – the same actor took the part through the three plays – but the Gunner's Boy of 1.4 was a lad of about six. In the Temple scene (2.4) jest turned to earnest, the jape of plucking roses from the tree catalysed a bitter political reaction.[1]

In 1986 the English Shakespeare Company under the artistic direction of Michael Pennington and Michael Bogdanov began to mount, for a national tour, seven of Shakespeare's histories under the title of *The Wars of the Roses*. The Henry VI plays were condensed into two texts: *Henry VI: House of Lancaster*, and *Henry VI: House of York*. *1 Henry VI* was shortened to become the first half of the former and received its first performance on 14 December 1987 at the Theatre Royal in Bath. Bogdanov directed and Pennington played Mortimer. The play was performed in a box formed by black screens, and much use was made of recorded classical music. Costumes and a certain amount of weaponry were taken from styles of the First World War, although swords were also occasionally used. Paul Brennen, a tall, thin, and almost totally bald actor, played the king, John Tramper in a scarlet regimental jacket and black eyepatch was Talbot, and Mary Rutherford was a very genteel Joan whose magical power, indicated by the sound of recorded flute music, was able to charm her adversaries to stillness. She died with a petrol-soaked tyre about her body, 'necklaced' in the manner of contemporary killings in South Africa.

The Royal Shakespeare Company produced another adaptation, *The Plant-agenets*, at Stratford in 1988, directed by Adrian Noble and designed by Bob Crowley. The three parts of *Henry VI* were condensed into two plays, '*Henry VI*' and '*The Rise of Edward IV*', in an adaptation of a version by Charles Wood, the plays being performed as a trilogy along with *Richard III*.[2] 'Noble...stages a nine-hour cycle of three plays as a blood-purge of pestilent elements ending in optimism far removed from the media *coup d'état* at the end of Michael Bogdanov's cycle for the ESC. Bogdanov...is also strikingly anticlerical – an option not taken up here.'[3] The first half of '*Henry VI*' ran from the beginning of Shakespeare's *1 Henry VI*; the second half from the last scene of *1 Henry VI* through to the end of Act 3 of *2 Henry VI*.

Design took a high profile in the production, the set being especially spectacular in '*Henry VI*'. A raked deep stage was used, pierced like a grille from which smoke

---

[1] The play was broadcast on BBC radio on 9 October 1947 (produced by Felix Felton); 31 October 1952 (selected scenes only, produced by Peter Watts); and 7 March 1971 (with *Part 2*, produced by Raymond Raikes).

[2] '*Henry VI*' was first performed on 29 September 1988 and the trilogy on one day on 22 October 1988. The text is published as *The Plantagenets*, 1989.

[3] Michael Ratcliffe, *Observer*, 30 October 1988.

wafted up throughout most of the production, thus enhancing the elaborate lighting effects (by Chris Parry) that were deployed throughout. The costumes were elaborate and, generally, historically accurate, unlike the uniform styles devised for the earlier Stratford productions by Hall and Hands. The first scene was dressed with huge pennons, hanging from the flies and patchworked with armorial bearings; scenes at the French court took place under a forest of hanging strips of brass decorated with the fleur-de-lis and furnished with handles at the bottom so that they could be used as thunder sheets. The dauphin, Alençon, and Orléans 'rode' on spectacularly large gold-bedecked hobbyhorses. A conspicuous political statement was made by having a wooden latticed throne, furnished with a heaven-aspiring back tall enough to tower into the flies, descend to stand upon a prison cage that was thrust up from a central stage trap: power rests upon the curtailment of liberty. That cage was to be used for the death of Mortimer (2.5), and, later, for the death scenes of King Henry and, in *Richard III*, the Duke of Clarence.

Ralph Fiennes as Henry VI gave a splendidly assured performance: in his first scene he was swaddled up to the neck in a white costume with full gold regalia and wore less elaborate but constantly white costumes as the plays proceeded. At first he was a mere spectator at the play of politicians, ignored by his court. But this was no holy fool, victim of 'church-like humours',[1] but a political clear-sighted patriot, honest but made impotent by the savage plotting that besets his court. Joan la Pucelle (Julia Ford) was a plucky public schoolgirl who felled the dauphin with Amazonian karate chops and knocked down Talbot using her shield alone. She conjured her witches on a battlefield, surrounded by English corpses. No spirits appeared, but the bodies raised their heads and stared balefully at her: an effective stage image. Margaret (Penny Downie) appeared in gold, sexy and a (metaphorically) rich prize on the battlefield: later she would be in metallic black, powerful and dangerous. It was a performance which strengthened from sensuality into authority throughout the sequence, and the personality was in no way constrained by the emblematic costuming.

Taken at a fast pace, much to the audience's enjoyment, the production was unashamedly patriotic and heroic. 'Ladders scale the skimpy bulwarks at Orléans and the actors are let loose like trainee marines, using all parts of the theatre, side exits and a turreted gantry.'[2] Central to the conception was David Waller, a stalwart of the company, who played a bluff open-hearted 'growlingly honest'[3] Gloucester. He helped the director expose 'the cant – the words we use and the flags we fly to do our fellow creatures down'.[4] In the first scene the people were visible, lurking nervously behind a curtain. They rushed angrily downstage when news was brought of the loss of France. (In this connection, however, later in the

[1] *2H6* 1.1.247.
[2] Michael Coveney, *Financial Times*, 24 October 1988.
[3] Irving Wardle, *The Times*, 24 October 1988.
[4] See Adrian Noble (talking to Michael Romain), 'Shakespeare on the war-path', *Observer*, 23 October 1988.

16   Julia Ford as Joan la Pucelle in Adrian Noble's 1988 production at Stratford-upon-Avon

play Cade and his followers simply represented popular power without responsibility and were remorselessly dispatched.)

Sources

As I have argued above, the history plays ought really to be redesignated 'political plays'. We can test the validity of this claim by inspecting Shakespeare's use of his historical sources, mainly Edward Hall's *The Union of the Two Noble and Illustre Families of Lancastre and Yorke*, 1548,[1] and Raphael Holinshed's *The Third Volume of Chronicles*, the second edition of 1587. From time to time his verse bears a distinct relationship to their prose; at times Shakespeare combines alternative readings of situation and event (notably in the scenes involving Joan),[2] and at other times he ranges freely backwards and forwards over the years (see the headnotes in the Commentary to Acts 3 and 4 particularly) to create the necessary dramatic structures for his reading of the forms and pressures of the time. For some

[1] Bullough (III, 25) suggests that Shakespeare may conceivably have used Grafton's *A Chronicle at Large* (1569) which used Hall's *Union* almost word for word.
[2] See p. 25 above, n. 4. Hall incorporated the long hostile account of Joan of Arc he found in the Burgundian history of Enguerrand de Monstrelet (Bullough, III, 12).

scholars this has been 'bewildering...Fact and fiction [are blended]... incidents are transposed or altered, until it seems that *1 Henry VI* is not so much a Chronicle play as a fantasia on historical themes.'[1]

It is probably impossible to decide with certainty which passages derive from which chronicler. Philip Brockbank concluded: 'My own prejudices are two: that Shakespeare wrote the plays, and that he read and browsed in more than one chronicle... That Shakespeare used more than one chronicle is demonstrable, but to which he referred and at what points in the preparation of the plays, are questions which can only be imperfectly decided from the evidence.'[2]

Received opinion for a long time was that Hall was the main source.[3] My own findings, which lean heavily on Brockbank's work and which are reported in the headnotes, indicate that more of Hall was transcribed into Holinshed than might have been supposed. I therefore concur with Brockbank when he writes:

There are two reasons for differing from Denny[4] by making Holinshed rather than Hall the basis of the play. In the first place, much of the determining detail owed to Holinshed is trivial,[5] including some slight verbal echoes easily caught up from the page; while that owed to Hall is more obviously significant and memorable. Secondly, the Holinshed reminiscences are more widely scattered. Of the twenty-seven scenes into which modern editions divide, thirteen could derive from either chronicle [1.3 (plus Fabyan), 1.5, 1.6, 2.2, 2.5 (but 2.5.74–92 probably Holinshed), 3.1 (plus Fabyan), 3.2, 3.4, 4.3, 4.4, 4.6, 4.7, 5.5], two are quite independent of both [2.3, 2.4], and five offer evidence too trifling to permit a decision [1.4, 4.2, 5.2, 5.3, 5.4[6]]. Six scenes suggest that Holinshed lay to hand (1.1, 1.2, 2.1, 3.3,[7] 4.1, 5.1), and only one (4.5, the first Talbot scene) shows an indisputable obligation to Hall.[8]

Scholars who have argued for Hall have, unwittingly perhaps, put a construction upon his type of history that may derive from their readings of the plays – or from their own political inclinations. Bullough, for example, writes: 'Hall's aim therefore was to show the evils of dissension in the state, and of wickedness in the individual, to trace the workings of Divine Justice on the sinner himself, on his posterity, and on the unhappy people over whom he ruled.'[9] That may be true of his professed intention as evinced in the introductory pages to his chronicle, but in the course of his work the reader is confronted with a much more modern, secularist, and sceptical kind of history. There are occasional references to God,

[1] Bullough, III, 25.
[2] Brockbank, p. 25.
[3] Wilson, pp. xxxii ff.; Bullough, III, 25; Cairncross and Sanders tend to reprint source material from Hall rather than Holinshed.
[4] C. F. Denny, 'The sources of *1 Henry VI* as an indication of revision', *PQ* (1937), 225–48; Bullough also offers extracts from Hall rather than Holinshed.
[5] For example: 1.1.110–40 (Patay), Boswell-Stone, p. 207; 1.2.64–150 (Joan at Orléans and Touraine), Boswell-Stone, p. 210; 5.1 ('goodly peace' and 'pope'), Boswell-Stone, p. 234.
[6] This contains evidence of debts to Holinshed, see 5.4 headnote in Commentary.
[7] This does contain evidence of debts to Hall: see 3.3.14–15 and 24 nn.
[8] Brockbank, p. 26.
[9] Bullough, III, 11.

to fortune, to classical gods even,[1] but the bulk of the narrative is filled with material explanations of battles and political transactions.

As well as Hall and Holinshed Shakespeare used Robert Fabyan's *The New Chronicles of England and France* (1516) for the retainers' riot in 1.3 and 3.1 (see Appendix 1, p. 199 below), and may have had recourse to Geoffrey of Monmouth's *Historia Regum Britanniae*, Book 8, Chapters 21–3, for the account of how the ailing Uther Pendragon was carried onto the field of battle in a litter, referred to in 3.2.95,[2] and to John Stow's *Chronicles of England* (1580)[3] and Froissart's *Chronicles* (translated by Lord Berners, 1523–5)[4] for specific details.

There is evidence in *1 Henry VI* that Shakespeare quoted from both the Bishops' Bible (see 1.5.9 n.) and the Geneva version (see 2.1.26 n. and 3.3.42 n.).[5] Citations in the Commentary are generally taken from the Geneva text.

---

[1] See, for example, pp. 124, 125, 146.
[2] A translation of the relevant passage is given by Bullough, III, 70–80. Holinshed in his *History of Scotland* tells a similar story of Pendragon's brother, Aurelius Ambrosius (*Chronicles*, 1587 edn, II, 99).
[3] See 2.5 headnote in Commentary.
[4] See 1.2.29–31.
[5] See Noble, pp. 109–13.

NOTE ON THE TEXT

The only authoritative text for this play is that provided by the 1623 First Folio (F) in which the play was printed for the first time; all later editions are derived from that source. The nature and provenance of F – it derives basically from Shakespeare's manuscript – are discussed in the Textual Analysis (pp. 187–95) below. The 'editor' of the Second Folio (F2) made an unusual number of corrections, especially corrections to metre. Some of these have been accepted, although they have no special authority.

The collation in this edition (immediately below each page of text) records all significant departures from F, including variants in lineation, variants in the wording and the placing of stage directions as well as in speech headings. It does not record corrections of misprints or modernisations of spellings except where these may be of some consequence. In the format of the collation, the authority for this edition's reading follows immediately after the quotation from the text. Other readings, if any, follow in chronological order. Readings offered by previous editors are registered only if they must be considered in relationship to recent discussions of the comparatively few textual cruces found in the play, or if they offer a challenging alternative where no certainty is possible. When, as is usually the case, the variant or emendation adopted has been used by a previous editor or suggested by a textual commentator, those authorities are cited in the abbreviated forms *Rowe* and *conj. Theobald* respectively. *Subst.* stands for *substantively*, and indicates that I have not transcribed a later emendation literally – see pp. xiii–xvii above for an explanation of the abbreviations and a full list of the editions and commentaries cited. The form *Eds.* is used for insignificant and obvious editorial practices (minor clarifications and expansions of stage directions or modernisations of proper names, for example, which do not need to be ascribed to one originator), and the form *This edn* is used for innovations of my own. Significant additions to the Folio stage directions are enclosed in square brackets; there is a comparatively large number of these because of the fact that the play derives from an authorial manuscript rather than a playhouse text. In the Commentary an asterisk in the lemma (the key word or phrase printed in bold type) is used to call attention to an emendation in the text; the collation should be consulted for further information.

I have, according to the convention of this edition, modernised and regularised proper names. Sir John Fastolf bears his historical name and not the name Sir John Falstaff which is almost certainly the result of scribal or compositorial intervention. Where past tenses of the verb require an accentuation that they would not receive in modern speech, they are marked with a *grave* accent ('fixèd', 'untunèd'). Unmarked '-ed's can be assumed to have been elided.

I have tried to keep punctuation as light as is consistent with the clarification of sense, often removing line-end commas from F's text, for the reason that a line-ending can itself provide a subtle and flexible pause or break in the sense. The rhythms surpass what Nashe derided as 'the spacious volubility of a drumming decasyllabon'.[1] Previous editors who punctuated heavily gave us texts that impose rhythmic monotony for readers and actors – there is more enjambment in early Shakespeare than might be supposed from some modern editions. Any significant departure from the F punctuation, however, is recorded in the collation. I have not attempted to remove half-lines, nor automatically to expunge metrical irregularity, believing that players can use these for special emphases or effects.

I have followed conventional act and scene divisions. These were determined by eighteenth-century editors – the divisions registered in F are abnormally irregular and inconsistent. The recent Oxford edition, having identified those moments when the stage is momentarily empty, has redefined the scene divisions (see collation). However, this is not going to help readers coming to the text with conventional and familiar act, scene, and line references, and the proliferation of scenic division is untrue to the experience of a theatre audience. 1.4–6, for example, although technically a series of scenes, is really one sequence, and it is not necessary in a playtext to register what are essentially literary conventions. For reasons of theatrical economy, Shakespeare had at least some of the fighting occurring off-stage, thus creating momentary divisions within what are arguably complete scene units. The marked entrances and exits in this and other sequences, therefore, need not be rigorously followed by a modern director.

I have not recorded the location of any scenes, as it seems to me that all scenes in the drama of the English Renaissance 'take place' on the stage, not in 'the Palace of Westminster' or 'Near Bordeaux', and that localisation encourages readers at least to impose expectations appropriate only to naturalist drama.

Headnotes to scenes in the Commentary give references to source material in both Holinshed and Hall – it is very seldom possible to discern which of the chroniclers Shakespeare used. Headnotes also relate the action, where this is possible, to actual places and historical events.

---

[1] Epistle prefixed to Greene's *Menaphon*; see Nashe, I, 311.

The First Part of King Henry VI

LIST OF CHARACTERS

KING HENRY THE SIXTH

DUKE OF BEDFORD, *Regent of France, third son of Henry IV, and uncle to the king*
DUKE OF GLOUCESTER, *Lord Protector, and fourth son of Henry IV*

DUKE OF EXETER, *Thomas Beaufort, great-uncle to the king*
BISHOP OF WINCHESTER, *Henry Beaufort, younger brother to Exeter, later cardinal*
DUKE OF SOMERSET, *Edmund Beaufort, nephew to Exeter*

RICHARD PLANTAGENET, *son of Richard, late Earl of Cambridge; later Regent of France and Duke of York*

EARL OF WARWICK
EARL OF SALISBURY
EARL OF SUFFOLK
LORD TALBOT, *later Earl of Shrewsbury*
JOHN TALBOT, *his son*
EDMUND MORTIMER, *Earl of March*
SIR JOHN FASTOLF
SIR WILLIAM GLANSDALE
SIR THOMAS GARGRAVE
SIR WILLIAM LUCY
WOODVILLE, *Lieutenant of the Tower of London*
MAYOR OF LONDON
VERNON, *of the White Rose or Yorkist faction*
BASSET, *of the Red Rose or Lancastrian faction*
A LAWYER *of the Temple*
A PAPAL LEGATE
GAOLERS, *to Mortimer*

CHARLES, *Dauphin, and later King, of France*
REIGNIER, *Duke of Anjou and titular King of Naples*
DUKE OF ALENÇON
BASTARD OF ORLÉANS
DUKE OF BURGUNDY
GENERAL *of the French army at Bordeaux*
GOVERNOR OF PARIS
MASTER GUNNER, *of Orléans*
A BOY, *son of the Master Gunner*
JOAN LA PUCELLE, *also called Joan of Arc*
SHEPHERD, *father of Joan la Pucelle*
MARGARET, *daughter of Reignier*
COUNTESS OF AUVERGNE
PORTER *of the Countess of Auvergne*
French SERGEANT
French SENTINEL

French SOLDIER
French SCOUT
FIENDS, *appearing to Joan la Pucelle*

Attendant lords, warders of the Tower, English and French heralds, soldiers, courtiers, servants

Notes

F does not supply a list of characters; one was first given by Rowe.

KING HENRY THE SIXTH (1421–71) Son of Henry V. (1387–1422) whom he succeeded when nine months old. The events of the play comprise a dramatic collage of episodes framed by the death of his father and his marriage in 1445 to Margaret of Anjou. However, some of the losses of French territories reported in 1.1 took place well after this date. References in the text to the king's tender years (3.1.71, 3.1.133, 5.1.21) suggest that the role in this part of the sequence may have been taken by a boy player.

DUKE OF BEDFORD (1389–1435) John of Lancaster, third son of Henry IV. Regent of France, he relieved Orléans in 1429 and arranged for the execution of Joan la Pucelle at Rouen in 1431.

DUKE OF GLOUCESTER (1391–1447) Humphrey of Lancaster, youngest son of Henry IV. At his brother Henry V's death he claimed the regency, but had to defer to Bedford and accept the title 'Protector of England' which he held from 1427 to 1429. He was the constant enemy of his uncle, the Bishop of Winchester. After a relationship with the Lady Jaquet, wife of John of Brabant (5.5.97), he married Eleanor Cobham who figures largely in *2H6*. Images of his life can be pursued in S.M. Pratt, 'Shakespeare and Humphrey Duke of Gloucester: a study in myth', *SQ* 16 (1965), 201–16.

DUKE OF EXETER (d. 1427) Thomas Beaufort, eldest son of Henry IV's father John of Gaunt by his mistress Catherine Swynford, who later became his third wife. (John of Gaunt was the fourth son of Edward III.)

BISHOP OF WINCHESTER (d. 1447) Henry Beaufort, the second of Gaunt's illegitimate sons, Chancellor on the accession of Henry V and named guardian of Henry VI. He was made a cardinal in 1426 by Pope Martin V, and led the opposition to Gloucester.

DUKE OF SOMERSET Shakespeare, like the chroniclers, conflated two historical personages. John Beaufort, first Duke of Somerset (1403–44), was 'alive' at the time of 2.4, which alludes to the death of Mortimer in 1425 and draws upon an account of a quarrel in 1435 between John Beaufort and York. In describing this quarrel both Holinshed (p. 185) and Hall (p. 179) wrongly refer to him as Edmund Beaufort. Edmund Beaufort, second Duke of Somerset (1406–55), was in fact John Beaufort's younger brother; he was openly accused of treason by their antagonist Richard Plantagenet, Duke of York in 1452. John Beaufort's death is not recorded in Holinshed or Hall.

RICHARD PLANTAGENET (1411–60) Descended through his mother from the Mortimer line, which derived from Lionel, Duke of Clarence, third son of Edward III. His father, who was descended from Edmund of Langley, fifth son of Edward III and first Duke of York, had been executed in 1415 for conspiring against Henry V. He is restored to his title of Duke of York in 3.1. (For 'Plantagenet' see 2.4.0 SD n.)

EARL OF WARWICK Richard de Beauchamp, Earl of Warwick (1382–1439), who had accompanied Henry V to France, was present at the king's funeral in 1422 (see 1.1, Holinshed, p. 134, Hall, p. 114), and was charged with the education of the infant Henry VI in 1428. He was dead (Holinshed, p. 193; Hall, p. 191) by the time of the truce signed at Tours in 1444 (see 5.5, Holinshed, p. 206; Hall, p. 203). His title was inherited in 1449 by his son-in-law Richard Neville, Earl of Warwick (1428–71), known as the 'Kingmaker'.

EARL OF SALISBURY (1388–1428) Thomas de Montacute or Montague, fourth Earl of

Salisbury, had been one of Henry V's most able leaders and, with Talbot, one of the foremost English soldiers in France after Henry's death. He besieged Orléans in 1428 and died of injuries received from a cannon ball at Tourelles.

EARL OF SUFFOLK (1396–1450) William de la Pole, fourth Earl and later Duke of Suffolk, served with success in France until he was captured by Joan of Arc after she had raised the siege of Orléans. He married the widowed Countess of Salisbury and emerged as an advocate of peace with France in opposition to Humphrey, Duke of Gloucester, who after Bedford's death led the war party. He has a large role in *2H6*.

LORD TALBOT (1388?–1453) first Earl of Shrewsbury and the most brilliant soldier of his day (see 1.4.41–2 n.). He was captured at the battle of Patay and imprisoned for two years until 1431. He took Bordeaux but was defeated and slain at Castillon.

JOHN TALBOT The chroniclers relate the heroic death of Talbot's son John, Lord Lisle, along with that of his bastard son Henry Talbot (Holinshed, p. 236; Hall, pp. 228–9).

EDMUND MORTIMER (1391–1425) fifth Earl of March, who had been recognised as heir-presumptive by Richard II in 1398. He was uncle to Richard Plantagenet. Previous editors have argued that Shakespeare confused him with his uncle, Sir Edmund Mortimer (1376–1409?); see 2.5.74 n. The author did, however, attribute to him some of the misfortunes of his cousin Sir John Mortimer (see 2.5 headnote) who was executed in 1424. Edmund, unlike Sir John, 'was not imprisoned when Henry [IV] succeeded to the throne – as was the dramatic Mortimer [see 2.5.23–5] – but served in France, and bore offices of trust' (Boswell-Stone, p. 219). The identifications do not matter: he serves the play as sole representative of the line.

SIR JOHN FASTOLF (1378?–1459) A Norfolk landowner who distinguished himself at Agincourt and subsequently held high offices in France. However, the Tudor chroniclers and Shakespeare followed a tradition which branded him as a coward (because of his imprudent actions at the battle of Patay) and which derives from the fifteenth-century *Chronique* of Monstrelet. Throughout the Folio text and in all editions of the play before that of Theobald he is called 'Falstaffe', because, no doubt, of scribal or compositorial confusion with the famous character in *1* and *2 Henry IV*. Editors since Wilson have reverted, inexplicably, to 'Falstaff': see George Walton Williams, 'Fastolf or Falstaff', *ELR* 5 (1975), 308–12. For an argument that Fastolf is a figure for Shakespeare's contemporary, Lord Cobham, see Alice-Lyle Scoufos, *Shakespeare's Typological Satire*, 1979, pp. 134–65.

SIR WILLIAM GLANSDALE The name is spelt 'Glasdale' in the chronicles (see Boswell-Stone, p. 210 n.).

SIR THOMAS GARGRAVE Nothing is known of him beyond what is mentioned in the chronicles (Holinshed, p. 161; Hall, p. 145).

SIR WILLIAM LUCY The name of the Sheriff of Warwickshire during the reign of Henry VI; Shakespeare may have used Sir William's name because he was an ancestor of Sir Thomas Lucy (1532–1600), a local magnate, of Charlecote near Stratford-upon-Avon.

WOODVILLE (d. *c.* 1441) Richard Woodville was Lieutenant of Calais and a loyal Lancastrian. However, his son transferred his allegiance to the Yorkist cause and his granddaughter Elizabeth married Edward IV in 1464.

VERNON A Sir John Vernon is mentioned as being with Talbot when he was killed at Castillon (Hall, p. 228, Holinshed, p. 235). Sir Richard Vernon was Speaker of the House of Commons at the Leicester parliament of 1425, although he is not mentioned by Holinshed (p. 146).

BASSET The name for Vernon's antagonist in 3.4 seems to have been taken from Peter Basset who was Chamberlain to Henry V at the time of the king's death (Hall, p. 113) and therefore a Lancastrian.

CHARLES (1403–61) The dauphin (heir apparent), who succeeded his father as Charles

VII in 1422 although he was not crowned at Rheims until 1429.

REIGNIER (1409–80) Duke of Anjou and Lorraine and, as son of Louis II of Naples, the titular King René I of Naples; brother-in-law of Charles VII. His daughter Margaret married Henry VI in 1445. His appearances in 1.2, 2.1 and 3.2 are unhistorical. See 1.1.94 n.

DUKE OF ALENÇON (1409–76) Jean, fifth Duke, companion in arms to Joan of Arc.

BASTARD OF ORLÉANS (1403?–68) Jean, Count Dunois, illegitimate son of Louis, Duke of Orléans, and nephew of King Charles VI.

DUKE OF BURGUNDY (1396–1467) Philip the Good who, by the Treaty of Troyes (1420), became an ally of the English; with Bedford, he was named co-regent of France by Henry V. After 1435, however, he transferred his allegiance to Charles VII.

JOAN LA PUCELLE (1412–31) Jeanne d'Arc (see 2.2.20 n.), born at Domrémy; saviour of the French, for whom she raised the siege of Orléans, won the battle of Patay, and had Charles crowned at Rheims. After being abandoned by those whom she had served as a champion, she fell into the hands of the Burgundians who sold her to the English. She was declared a heretic and burnt alive at Rouen.

MARGARET (1430–82) Daughter of Reignier of Anjou, who married Henry VI by proxy at Nancy in 1445 (see Ralph Griffiths, *The Reign of Henry VI*, 1981, p. 315; compare *2H6* 1.1.5, which places the wedding at Tours). She plays a large part in *2* and *3H6*.

COUNTESS OF AUVERGNE She appears in 2.3, a scene that has no basis in the chronicles; an invented character. (It may be that there is a veiled allusion to Mary Stuart who had, in 1558, married the young 'Prince Dauphin d'Auvergne' (an honorary title of sixteenth-century dauphins) who became François I of France. See Alice-Lyle Scoufos, *Shakespeare's Typological Satire*, 1979, p. 144.)

THE FIRST PART OF HENRY THE SIXTH

1.1 *Dead march. Enter the funeral of King Henry the Fifth, attended on by the* DUKE OF BEDFORD, *Regent of France, the* DUKE OF GLOU-CESTER, *Protector, the* DUKE OF EXETER, [*the* EARL OF] WARWICK, *the* BISHOP OF WINCHESTER, *and the* DUKE OF SOMERSET; [*Heralds, etc.*]

BEDFORD Hung be the heavens with black! Yield, day, to night!
       Comets, importing change of times and states,

Act 1, Scene 1   1.1] *Capell subst.; Actus Primus. Scæna Prima.* F   0 SD.3 GLOUCESTER] *Rowe;* Gloster F   0 SD.4 HERALDS, *etc.*] *Malone; not in* F   1 Yield, day,] *Oxford;* yield day F

Act 1, Scene 1

1.1 F distinguishes 1.1, 2.1, 3.1–4, and 4.1 as in this text but then designates the present 5.1, 2 as 4.2, 3 and the present 5.5 as Act 5 (see Textual Analysis, p. 191 below). Other act and scene divisions derive from Pope and Capell.

Shakespeare condenses scattered events from Henry VI's reign into a forceful dramatic prelude to the play: Henry V's funeral took place on 7 November 1422. After an impressive processional entrance, the ceremony of burial (in Westminster Abbey, according to the sources) is interrupted by news of the collapse of Henry V's empire, conveyed with apocalyptic overtones. Of the towns mentioned in 60–1 and 65, Guyenne was in fact lost in 1451, Rheims in 1429, Paris in 1436, and Gisors and Rouen in 1449 (for Orléans see 157 n.). Charles VII was crowned as a child in Poitiers a few weeks after Henry V's death and crowned again seven years later in Rheims (see 92 below).

Shakespeare would seem to have read Gloucester's encomium of Henry V in Hall (pp. 112–13 – see Appendix 1, p. 196 below). Holinshed's version (pp. 133–4) is shorter and does not contain the phrase 'what shall I say' (see 15 n.). The account of the division between Winchester and Gloucester is in Holinshed, pp. 146–54 (Hall, pp. 130–7). Shakespeare displaces the explanation of the loss of Paris (Holinshed, p. 185; Hall, p. 179; see Appendix 1, p. 197 below) to give it prominence. The account of the battle of Patay (1429) which is narrated at length by the Third Messenger (103 ff.) is in Holinshed, p. 165 (Hall, pp. 149–50). Holinshed (p. 147) and Hall (p. 131) both record Winchester's plan to seize the king (1425?). It is

evident, however, that the author had Holinshed to hand when writing this scene (see 112 n.).

0 SD.1 *Dead march* 'The dead march was played by the drum alone, probably muffled' (Long, p. 6).

0 SD.1 *funeral* Holinshed notes: 'His body embalmed and closed in lead, was laid in a chariot royal, richly apparelled with cloth of gold. Upon his coffin was laid a representation of his person, adorned with robes, diadem, sceptre, and ball, like a king' (p. 134). Engravings from Shakespeare's time indicate that noble mourners at funerals wore hooded cloaks – see T. Lant's drawing of the funeral procession of Sir Philip Sidney, 1587 (illustration 1, p. 6 above); compare 17 below and *2H6* 2.4.0 SD.

0 SD.3–4 *the* EARL...SOMERSET Neither Warwick nor Somerset has a part in the action until 2.4, nor is an exit marked for either. It might be most convenient for them to leave with the coffin at 45.

1–5 The movement of the verse and some of the imagery are strongly reminiscent of Zenocrate's funeral scene in Marlowe's *2 Tamburlaine* 3.2.1–15.

1 **Hung...black** Shakespeare signals the theatricality of the scene with a hyperbolic metaphor that derives from the practice of draping the sides of the stage with black for performances of tragedies (see Hattaway, p. 24). The 'heavens' was a designation for the underside of the 'hut' that was constructed over the stage in certain playhouses.

1 *Yield...night** The apocalyptic apostrophe recalls Isa. 13.10.

2 **importing** portending (*OED* Import *v* 5d), although the apocalyptic tenor of the speech

Brandish your crystal tresses in the sky,
And with them scourge the bad revolting stars
That have consented unto Henry's death: 5
King Henry the Fifth, too famous to live long!
England ne'er lost a king of so much worth.
GLOUCESTER England ne'er had a king until his time:
Virtue he had, deserving to command;
His brandished sword did blind men with his beams,   10
His arms spread wider than a dragon's wings;
His sparkling eyes, replete with wrathful fire,
More dazzled and drove back his enemies
Than midday sun fierce bent against their faces.
What should I say? His deeds exceed all speech: 15
He ne'er lift up his hand but conquerèd.
EXETER We mourn in black; why mourn we not in blood?
Henry is dead, and never shall revive;
Upon a wooden coffin we attend,
And Death's dishonourable victory   20
We with our stately presence glorify
Like captives bound to a triumphant car.
What? Shall we curse the planets of mishap

---

3 crystal] F; crested *conj. Warburton*   6 King Henry] F; Henry *Pope*   10 his] F; its *Pope*

suggests that 'causing' (*OED* Import *v* 4) may be appropriate; compare the comet portending revenge at 3.2.31–2.

3 **Brandish** Flourish; flash (*OED* sv *v* 4).

3 **crystal** clear, bright (*OED* sv *adj* B2).

3 **tresses** 'Comet' derives from a Greek word meaning 'long-haired star'.

4 **revolting** rebelling; the epithet works proleptically to provide a figure for the reign of Henry VI.

5 **have...unto** were accessaries to (*OED* Consent *v* 7).

6 **too...long** Compare the proverb 'Those that God loves do not live long' (Dent G251).

9 **Virtue** Power, merit.

10 **his** its.

10–12 **dragon's...fire** Compare the dragon slain by Redcross in *FQ*, I, xi: 'with his waving wings displayed wide' (stanza 18), 'His blazing eyes...Did burn with wrath, and sparkled living fire' (stanza 14). For the dragon in the Apocalypse, see Rev. 12.3 ff.

12 **sparkling eyes** 'Dragon' derives from a

Greek word meaning 'to see clearly, to stare', and, more remotely, 'to flash'.

12 **replete with** full of.

15 **What...say?** Words fail me (a common phrase in Hall).

16 **lift** lifted (Abbott 341).

16 **his hand** i.e. bearing a sword.

16 **but conquerèd** without conquering.

17 **in blood** by shedding the blood of the rebellious French. Exeter here rebukes Bedford for the fatalism of his opening speech.

18 **revive** live again (*OED* sv *v* 2).

19 **wooden** unfeeling, insensitive.

21 **presence** company.

22 **car** chariot. The image recalls not only the Triumph of Death in Petrarch's *Trionfi* but the entry of Marlowe's Tamburlaine, the scourge of Asia, in his chariot drawn by captive kings in *1 Tamburlaine* 4.3. The line also echoes (or is echoed by) his *Edward II* 1.1.174: 'With captive kings at his triumphant car'.

23 **of mishap** unlucky, evil.

That plotted thus our glory's overthrow?
Or shall we think the subtle-witted French   25
Conjurers and sorcerers, that, afraid of him,
By magic verses have contrived his end?
WINCHESTER He was a king blest of the King of Kings:
Unto the French, the dreadful judgement-day
So dreadful will not be as was his sight.   30
The battles of the Lord of Hosts he fought:
The church's prayers made him so prosperous.
GLOUCESTER The church? Where is it? Had not churchmen
    prayed,
His thread of life had not so soon decayed.
None do you like but an effeminate prince   35
Whom like a schoolboy you may overawe.
WINCHESTER Gloucester, whate'er we like, thou art Protector
And lookest to command the prince and realm.
Thy wife is proud; she holdeth thee in awe
More than God or religious churchmen may.   40
GLOUCESTER Name not religion, for thou lov'st the flesh,

---

24 glory's] *Rowe;* Glories F   32 church's] *Cam.;* Churches F   33] *Pope;* The...it? / Had ...pray'd F
33 not] F; but *conj. Vaughan*   37 Gloucester] *Eds., throughout;* Gloster F

---

25 subtle-witted devious, treacherous.

26 Conjurers Magicians who raise spirits.

27 magic verses Thomas gives examples of rhyming charms from this period (pp. 211–14). Perhaps there is a more specific and jocular allusion to the belief that the Irish could rid themselves of enemies (and rats) by rhyming them to death; compare *AYLI* 3.2.176–7, and Sidney, *An Apology for Poetry*, ed. G. Shepherd, 1973, p. 237 n. 26.

27 contrived plotted (*OED* Contrive v^1 1b).

28 King of Kings From Rev. 19.16, describing the Last Judgement.

29 dreadful judgement-day See Rev. 6.12–17 for a description of the horrors.

30 his sight the sight of him.

31 Winchester compares Henry V to the Christian warrior-king David who 'fighteth the battles of the lord' (1 Sam. 25.28).

31 Lord of Hosts Isa. 13.4.

32 prosperous successful, fortunate.

33–6 'The panegyrics pronounced upon Henry the fifth are nervously elegant; and this rebuke, which Gloucester gives the canting bishop, is sensibly severe' (Bell).

33 prayed Punning on 'preyed' (Cercignani, p. 233).

34 thread of life Spun by Clotho, one of the three Fates (see Tilley T249).

35 effeminate Not necessarily implying that Henry was unmanly, since the word could, without implying reproach, mean 'gentle' or 'tender' (*OED* sv *adj* 1c).

37 Protector Gloucester had been nominated Protector of England by Henry V during the minority of his heir. Bedford was made regent of the realm of France (Holinshed, p. 136; Hall, p. 115). The Council in fact disallowed Gloucester's claim to the title, and parliament awarded it to Bedford, allowing Gloucester the protectorate during the absence of his brother. These complications are not set out by the chroniclers but may explain Winchester's 'whate'er we like'.

38 prince ruler.

39 holdeth...awe exacts reverence from you, i.e. rules you; the ambitious Eleanor plays a prominent part in *2H6*.

41 thou...flesh you devote yourself to (carnal) pleasure.

And ne'er throughout the year to church thou go'st,
Except it be to pray against thy foes.
BEDFORD Cease, cease these jars and rest your minds in peace;
Let's to the altar. Heralds, wait on us.   45
Instead of gold, we'll offer up our arms –
Since arms avail not now that Henry's dead.
Posterity, await for wretched years
When, at their mothers' moistened eyes, babes shall suck,
Our isle be made a nourish of salt tears,   50
And none but women left to wail the dead.
Henry the Fifth, thy ghost I invocate:
Prosper this realm, keep it from civil broils,
Combat with adverse planets in the heavens.
A far more glorious star thy soul will make   55
Than Julius Caesar or bright –

Enter a MESSENGER

MESSENGER My honourable lords, health to you all!
Sad tidings bring I to you out of France,
Of loss, of slaughter, and discomfiture:
Guyenne, Compiègne, Rheims, Rouen, Orléans,   60
Paris, Gisors, Poitiers, are all quite lost.
BEDFORD What say'st thou, man, before dead Henry's corse?

45 Heralds,] *Pope;* Heralds F   45 us.] ·F; us. *Exit Funeral / Cairncross; us. Exeunt Warwick, Somerset, and Heralds with coffin / Oxford*   47 not...dead.] *This edn;* not,...dead, F   48 Posterity,] *Capell;* Posteritie F   49 moistened] F *subst.;* moist F2   50 nourish] F; marish *Pope*   60 Compiègne] *Oxford;* Champaigne F   60 Rheims, Rouen] *Capell;* Rheims F *subst.*   61 Gisors] F (Guysors)   61 Poitiers] F (Poictiers)

45 The line indicates that an altar may have stood on the stage, perhaps 'discovered' in the tiring-house, and that the hearse and heralds moved up towards it at this point to keep vigil throughout the rest of the scene. Alternatively the funeral may here have left the stage, which would make the references at 62 figurative.
46 **arms** weapons.
48 **await for** look out for.
50 **nourish** Variant of 'nourice' (nurse); the metaphor means that instead of milk there will be only tears for babies to drink. However, Pope's conjecture 'marish' (= marsh) could be easily misread as 'nourish', and is attractive.
52 **invocate** call in prayer. The line indicates that Bedford may have turned to pray at the altar on stage (see 45 n. above).
55 **glorious star** Ovid narrates how Caesar's soul became a 'goodly shining star' (*Metamorphoses* XV, 839 and 944–56). Henry's apotheosis

is to exceed that of the Caesars, and the line concludes an introduction in which Henry V is presented as a classical and biblical hero – in contrast with those who survive him.
56 **bright** – Bedford may have been going on to invoke Augustus, whose glory eclipsed that of Caesar himself – see *Metamorphoses* XV, 959 ff. This is the first in a sequence of interruptions to the ceremonial scenes that stud the play – see p. 11 above.
59 **discomfiture** rout, complete defeat in battle (*OED* sv 1).
60–1 See headnote to this scene.
60 *****Compiègne** The town (F's 'Champaigne') where Joan was captured in 1429.
60 *****Rouen** Capell's insertion of this name seems to be justified by 65 below and was probably caused by eyeskip from one initial 'R' to the other.
62 **corse** corpse, body.

Speak softly, or the loss of those great towns
Will make him burst his lead and rise from death.

GLOUCESTER Is Paris lost? Is Rouen yielded up?   65
If Henry were recalled to life again
These news would cause him once more yield the ghost.

EXETER How were they lost? What treachery was used?

MESSENGER No treachery, but want of men and money.
Amongst the soldiers this is mutterèd: 70
That here you maintain several factions
And, whilst a field should be dispatched and fought,
You are disputing of your generals.
One would have ling'ring wars with little cost,
Another would fly swift but wanteth wings,   75
A third thinks, without expense at all,
By guileful fair words peace may be obtained.
Awake, awake, English nobility!
Let not sloth dim your honours, new begot.
Cropped are the flower-de-luces in your arms: 80
Of England's coat one half is cut away.   [*Exit*]

EXETER Were our tears wanting to this funeral,
These tidings would call forth her flowing tides.

BEDFORD Me they concern; regent I am of France.
Give me my steelèd coat, I'll fight for France.   85

---

65 Rouen] *Cam.;* Roan F   76 third] F; third man F2   80–1 arms: / . . .coat] *This edn;* Armes / . . .Coat, F
81 SD] *Wilson; not in* F   83 her] F; their *Theobald*

64 lead The lining of the coffin (see 0 SD.1
n.).
67 yield the ghost Biblical: see Acts 5.10.
69–73 This is the explanation offered by
Holinshed (p. 185) and by Hall (p. 179) for
the loss of Paris years later in 1436. It is notable that
Shakespeare makes this rebuke of aristocratic
factionalism so prominent (see p. 14 above);
compare 1.2.17.
71 several separate, divisive.
71 factions Trisyllabic; see Cercignani, p.
296.
72 field (1) armed force (*OED* sv *sb* 8b), (2)
battle (*OED* sv *sb* 8a).
73 of about (Abbott 174).
75 Compare the proverb 'He would fain fly but
he wants feathers' (Tilley F164).
75 wanteth lacks.
79 begot acquired (*OED* Beget *v* 1); i.e. on the
battlefield under Henry V.

80 flower-de-luces fleurs-de-lis, the heraldic
symbol of the French monarchy. Since Edward
II's marriage in 1308 to Isabella, daughter of
Philip IV, English rulers had laid claim to the
French throne. Henry V had acquired the title
'King of England and heir of France' by the
Treaty of Troyes (1420) which provided for his
marriage to the Princess Katherine (see *H5* 5.2).
The death of her father Charles VI precipitated
the revolt led by the dauphin (Holinshed, p. 137;
Hall, p. 115).
80 arms coat-of-arms; as also 'coat' at 81.
***81, 161** SD F gives an exit only for 2
MESSENGER (a characteristic of authorial copy),
but the formal design of the scene implies that the
other two should leave the stage immediately they
have delivered their lines.
83 her England's.
84 regent ruler in the monarch's absence.

Away with these disgraceful wailing robes!
[*He removes his mourning cloak*]
Wounds will I lend the French, instead of eyes,
To weep their intermissive miseries.

Enter to them ANOTHER MESSENGER

2 MESSENGER Lords, view these letters, full of bad mischance.
 France is revolted from the English quite,   90
 Except some petty towns of no import;
 The Dauphin Charles is crownèd king in Rheims;
 The Bastard of Orléans with him is joined;
 Reignier, Duke of Anjou, doth take his part;
 The Duke of Alençon flieth to his side.   *Exit*   95
EXETER The dauphin crownèd king? All fly to him?
 O whither shall we fly from this reproach?
GLOUCESTER We will not fly but to our enemies' throats.
 Bedford, if thou be slack, I'll fight it out.
BEDFORD Gloucester, why doubt'st thou of my forwardness?   100
 An army have I mustered in my thoughts,
 Wherewith already France is overrun.

Enter [*a* THIRD] MESSENGER

3 MESSENGER My gracious lords, to add to your laments
 Wherewith you now bedew King Henry's hearse,

---

86 SD] *Oxford subst.; not in* F   89 SH 2 MESSENGER] *Rowe subst.; Mess.* F   92 Dauphin] *Eds., throughout;* Dolphin
F   94 Reignier] *Rowe subst., throughout;* Reynold F; René *Oxford*   95 Duke of] F; Duke *conj. Walker*
96 crownèd] *Rowe;* crown'd F   102 SD *Enter a* THIRD] *This edn; Enter another* F   103 SH 3 MESSENGER] *Rowe
subst.; Mes.* F

---

86 wailing robes mourning garments (a
nonce-use).
*86 SD Like Tamburlaine (*1 Tamburlaine*
1.2.41–2), Bedford lays down his garb of peace
to create a theatrical image that signifies his
translation into a warrior.
87 lend give.
88 intermissive miseries 'their miseries,
which have had only a short intermission from
Henry V's death to my coming amongst them'
(Warburton).
91 petty small (*OED* sv *adj* 1).
92 See headnote to scene.
92 *Dauphin F reads 'Dolphin' throughout,

the common English form until *c.* 1670. Compare
the pun at 1.4.106.
93 Bastard of Orléans Described by Hall,
pp. 144 ff.
94 *Reignier F anomalously reads 'Reynold'
throughout the scene. This probably derives from
the name 'Veignold' mentioned by Hall (p. 145)
but not by Holinshed as being present at the siege
of Orléans with the Bastard. It is possible that
Shakespeare originally intended to use Veignold
as a character, but, prompted by the similarities of
name, decided to combine the role with that of
Reignier.
97 reproach disgrace.

I must inform you of a dismal fight   105
Betwixt the stout Lord Talbot and the French.
WINCHESTER What? Wherein Talbot overcame – is't so?
3 MESSENGER O no; wherein Lord Talbot was o'erthrown:
    The circumstance I'll tell you more at large.
    The tenth of August last, this dreadful lord,   110
    Retiring from the siege of Orléans,
    Having full scarce six thousand in his troop,
    By three and twenty thousand of the French
    Was round encompassèd and set upon:
    No leisure had he to enrank his men.   115
    He wanted pikes to set before his archers;
    In stead whereof sharp stakes plucked out of hedges
    They pitchèd in the ground confusèdly
    To keep the horsemen off from breaking in.
    More than three hours the fight continuèd,   120
    Where valiant Talbot, above human thought,
    Enacted wonders with his sword and lance.
    Hundreds he sent to hell, and none durst stand him;
    Here, there, and everywhere, enragèd he slew.
    The French exclaimed the devil was in arms: 125
    All the whole army stood agazed on him.
    His soldiers, spying his undaunted spirit,
    'A Talbot! A Talbot!' crièd out amain
    And rushed into the bowels of the battle.
    Here had the conquest fully been sealed up,   130

---

112 full scarce] F; scarce full *Rowe*   124 slew] F; flew *Rowe²*   126 the] F; their *conj. Capell*

---

105 dismal calamitous, terrible (*OED* sv *adj* 3 and 4); compare *Mac.* 1.2.53.

105 fight This was the battle of Patay, which was in fact fought after the raising of the siege of Orléans (see 1.2).

109 circumstance details (*OED* sv *sb* 9).

109 at large in full.

110–40 The speech recalls the epic descriptions of battle given by the messengers in *The Spanish Tragedy*.

110 tenth of August Historically, 18 June 1429 (Boswell-Stone, p. 207), about six weeks after the siege of Orléans depicted in the two following scenes. Shakespeare may have adjusted the date to achieve a semblance of accuracy or for metrical reasons.

110 dreadful inspiring dread.

111 See 105 n.

112 full in full.

112 full . . . thousand This agrees with Holinshed's 'not past six thousand' (p. 165) who, in a marginal note, corrects Hall's 'five thousand' (p. 149).

116 pikes Either pikemen or the 'stakes bound with iron sharp at both the ends of the length of five or six foot, to be pitched before the Archers' (Grafton, I, 516–17) devised by Henry V at Agincourt.

119 off Inserted for metrical purposes.

124 The line bears some resemblance to *FQ*, III, i, 66.

126 agazed on astounded at.

128 A To (French *à*).

128 amain with all their strength.

130 sealed up completed, confirmed.

If Sir John Fastolf had not played the coward.
He, being in the vaward, placed behind
With purpose to relieve and follow them,
Cowardly fled, not having struck one stroke.
Hence grew the general wrack and massacre: 135
Enclosèd were they with their enemies.
A base Walloon, to win the dauphin's grace,
Thrust Talbot with a spear into the back –
Whom all France, with their chief assembled strength,
Durst not presume to look once in the face.   140

BEDFORD Is Talbot slain? Then I will slay myself
For living idly here, in pomp and ease,
Whilst such a worthy leader, wanting aid,
Unto his dastard foemen is betrayed.

3 MESSENGER O no, he lives, but is took prisoner,   145
And Lord Scales with him, and Lord Hungerford;
Most of the rest slaughtered or took likewise.

BEDFORD His ransom there is none but I shall pay:
I'll hale the dauphin headlong from his throne,
His crown shall be the ransom of my friend;   150
Four of their lords I'll change for one of ours.
Farewell, my masters; to my task will I;
Bonfires in France forthwith I am to make,
To keep our great Saint George's feast withal.

---

131 Fastolf] *Theobald subst., throughout; Falstaffe* F   132 vaward] *Rowe;* Vauward F; vanguard *Oxford*
137 Walloon] F3; Wallon F   139 their chief] F; their F3   141 slain? Then] *Johnson subst.;* slain then? F *subst.*
148 pay:] *This edn;* pay. F

131 ***Fastolf** The compositors of F (or a scribe), familiar with *H4*, set 'Falstaffe' throughout. Shakespeare, however, would have read in Holinshed (p. 165): 'From this battle departed without any stroke striken Sir John Fastolf, the same year for his valiantness elected into the order of the garter' (Hall, p. 150, also gives 'Sir Ihon Fastolffe').

132 **in . . . behind** stationed in the second rank of the vanguard.

135 **wrack** destruction.

137 **Walloon** Inhabitant of what is now south Belgium; Walloons are not mentioned in the chronicles but 'formed an important part of the Spanish forces under Parma in the Netherlands' (Wilson).

138 An act contrary to military codes of honour.

146 **Scales** Thomas, Lord Scales (d. 1460), distinguished himself in the French wars and was put to death by the Yorkists after the battle of Northampton.

146 **Hungerford** Walter, Baron Hungerford (d. 1449), had fought at Agincourt and was an executor of Henry V's will.

148 The French can expect no ransom but the vengeance I shall exact.

151 **change** exchange; i.e. kill.

153–4 **Bonfires . . . feast** St George was patron saint of England and of the Order of the Garter. Bedford boasts that he will celebrate the saint (not necessarily on his day, 23 April) after wreaking havoc in France.

Ten thousand soldiers with me I will take,   155
Whose bloody deeds shall make all Europe quake.

3 MESSENGER So you had need; 'fore Orléans besieged
    The English army is grown weak and faint,
    The Earl of Salisbury craveth supply
    And hardly keeps his men from mutiny,   160
    Since they, so few, watch such a multitude.   *[Exit]*

EXETER Remember, lords, your oaths to Henry sworn:
    Either to quell the dauphin utterly,
    Or bring him in obedience to your yoke.

BEDFORD I do remember it, and here take my leave   165
    To go about my preparation.   *Exit Bedford*

GLOUCESTER I'll to the Tower with all the haste I can,
    To view th'artillery and munition,
    And then I will proclaim young Henry king.

                            Exit Gloucester

EXETER To Eltham will I, where the young king is,   170
    Being ordained his special governor,
    And for his safety there I'll best devise.   *Exit*

WINCHESTER Each hath his place and function to attend;
    I am left out; for me, nothing remains;
    But long I will not be Jack-out-of-office.   175
    The king from Eltham I intend to steal,
    And sit at chiefest stern of public weal.   *Exit*

---

157 'fore Orléans besieged] *Hanmer subst.*; for Orléans is besieged, F *subst.*   161 SD] *Wilson; not in* F
170, 176 Eltham] *Steevens;* Eltam F   176 steal] *Singer, conj. Mason;* send F   177 SD] F; *Exeunt / Cam.*

---

155 Ten thousand Accords with the figure given by Grafton (I, 583).

157 *'fore Orléans besieged F's reading suggests that the English are besieged within the city rather than besieging it. Hanmer's emendation makes the line conform with 60 above. (Salisbury besieged Orléans in 1428–9.)

159 supply reinforcements (*OED* sv *sb* 5).

161 watch keep under surveillance.

162–4 Based on Henry V's dying exhortation (Holinshed, p. 132; Hall, p. 112).

163 quell slay, destroy.

166 preparation Five syllables (Cercignani, p. 296).

167 Tower The Tower of London.

168 munition powder, shot, shells, etc. (*OED* sv *sb* 2).

170–4 In the chroniclers both Exeter and Winchester had 'custody' of the young prince in 1422 (Holinshed, p. 136; Hall, p. 115), but in 1427 Warwick became 'governor of the young king, instead of Thomas Duke of Excester [*sic*], lately departed to God' (Holinshed, p. 160; Hall, p. 143).

173–7 Winchester's direct address to the audience casts him in the role of a stage villain.

175 Jack...office Proverbial (Tilley J23).

176 Eltham The site of a royal manor in Kent on the road to Canterbury.

176 *steal F's 'send' is probably compositorial dittography after 'intend'; 'steal' provides a rhyme to create a final couplet and accords with the accusation that Winchester 'purposed...to have removed [the king] from Eltham...to Windsor ...to put him in governance as him list' (Holinshed, p. 147; Hall, p. 131).

177 at chiefest stern as steersman (Latin *gubernator*, from which 'governor' derives.).

[1.2] *Sound a flourish. Enter* CHARLES [THE DAUPHIN, THE DUKE
OF] ALENÇON, *and* REIGNIER [DUKE OF ANJOU], *marching with
Drum and Soldiers*

CHARLES Mars his true moving, even as in the heavens
    So in the earth, to this day is not known.
    Late did he shine upon the English side;
    Now we are victors: upon us he smiles.
    What towns of any moment but we have?   5
    At pleasure here we lie near Orléans –
    Otherwhiles the famished English, like pale ghosts,
    Faintly besiege us one hour in a month.
ALENÇON They want their porridge and their fat bull-beeves:
    Either they must be dieted like mules   10
    And have their provender tied to their mouths,
    Or piteous they will look, like drownèd mice.

Act 1, Scene 2   1.2] *Capell subst.; not in* F   0 SD REIGNIER] F4 *subst.; Reigneir* F (*throughout scene*)   6 near] F
subst.; in conj. this edn   6 Orléans –] *This edn;* Orleance: F   7 Otherwhiles] F; The whiles *Capell*

Act 1, Scene 2
*1.2 The scene depicts the attack on the
English besiegers of Orléans by the French in
1428–9 (Holinshed, p. 161; Hall, pp. 144–5),
who may be presumed to be encamped outside
the city but within (see 6) the fortifications thrown
up by the Bastard (Holinshed, p. 161) – unless we
emend 'near', a possible case of partial
dittography after 'here' (6), to 'in'. In theatrical
terms this allows the French forces to exit at 21
into the tiring-house, which here signifies the
interior of the city or fortification wall. (It seems
pedantic, however, to begin a new scene here as
Oxford does.) This sally is not mentioned in the
chronicles, but may have been suggested by a
similar unsuccessful attack led by the Bastard
(Holinshed, p. 161; Hall, p. 145).

Shakespeare followed Holinshed's account of
the meeting of Joan and Charles (pp. 163–4),
but see 67 n. below; Hall gives her a 'foul face'
(p. 148), Holinshed says she was 'of favour...
likesome' (p. 163) – compare 82–4 below.

0 SD.1 **flourish** Sounded on trumpets to
signify the presence of authority (Long, p. 10).

0 SD.2 REIGNIER His role is not really established in the play until 5.3 and his name here
suggests that the player who took the part was
used here simply to swell the scene (see 1.1.94
n.).

0 SD.3 **Drum** Drummer. Presumably the lively
march of the French would provide a dramatic
contrast with the dead march of the play's
opening scene.

1–2 Not until Kepler published his *De Motibus
Stellae Martis* in 1609 could the eccentricity of the
orbit of Mars be understood. Similar accounts of
this phenomenon occur in Sandford's translation
of H. C. Agrippa's *De Vanitate* (1569), p. 43, and
in Nashe (III, 30), but there is no need to
postulate them as sources as previous editors
have done.

1 **his** An expansion of the possessive in *-s*
according to a false etymology (Abbott 217).

5 **moment** importance.

6 **near** See headnote to scene.

7 **Otherwhiles** At times.

8 **Faintly** Half-heartedly (*OED* sv *adv* 3b).

9 Compare the proverb(?) 'He looks as big as if
he had eaten bull beef' (Dent B716). *OED*
records 'bull-beef' as a term of abuse.

9 **porridge** Part of the English soldier's customary diet (Nashe, I, 331); made by stewing
vegetables, herbs, or meat, and often thickened
with barley.

10 **dieted** fed.

12 **like...mice** Compare the proverb 'To
look like a drowned mouse' (Tilley M1237).

REIGNIER Let's raise the siege; why live we idly here?
        Talbot is taken, whom we wont to fear;
        Remaineth none but mad-brained Salisbury,   15
        And he may well in fretting spend his gall:
        Nor men nor money hath he to make war.
CHARLES Sound, sound alarum! We will rush on them.
        Now, for the honour of the forlorn French,
        Him I forgive my death that killeth me   20
        When he sees me go back one foot or fly.

                                        Exeunt

Here alarum; they are beaten back by the English with great loss.
Enter CHARLES, ALENÇON, *and* REIGNIER

CHARLES Who ever saw the like? What men have I?
        Dogs! Cowards! Dastards! I would ne'er have fled
        But that they left me 'midst my enemies.
REIGNIER Salisbury is a desperate homicide: 25
        He fighteth as one weary of his life.
        The other lords, like lions wanting food,
        Do rush upon us as their hungry prey.
ALENÇON Froissart, a countryman of ours, records
        England all Olivers and Rolands bred   30
        During the time Edward the Third did reign.

---

13 live] F; lie *conj. Walker (compare* 6)   **21** fly] F; flee *Oxford*   **21** SD.1 *Exeunt*] F; *Exeunt* / 1.3 *Oxford*
28 hungry] F; hungred *conj. Johnson*   **29** Froissart] *Reed; Froysard* F   **30** bred] *Rowe;* breed F

13 raise the siege cause the English forces to withdraw (*OED* Raise *vb*¹ 27).

14 wont were wont.

15 mad-brained hot-headed.

16 spend his gall work out his bitter spirit.

17 Compare 1.1.69–73 n.

18 alarum In the dialogue the word clearly means a call to attack, presumably sounded on a trumpet (compare 3.2.35 SD). At 21 SD.2 it designates sound effects backstage: 'The term... signifies a battle or onslaught and includes clashes of weapons, drumbeats, trumpet blasts, shouts – anything to make a tumult' (Long, p. 131); compare *2H6* 5.2.3; *H5* 3.Chorus.33 SD. The dialogue and stage directions indicate that the fighting is to take place mainly off-stage – the sound effects act as a kind of theatrical shorthand.

19 forlorn As in 'forlorn hope', refers to 'men who perform their duty at the imminent risk of their life' (*OED*, sv *adj* 3b).

21 fly Oxford's contention that F's 'fly' was in fact pronounced 'flee' to create a rhyme here is unlikely. See Cercignani, p. 251.

21 SD See headnote to scene.

25 homicide murderer.

26 weary...life Compare Eccles. 2.17: 'Thus began I to be weary of my life' (Noble).

27–8 like...prey Compare Ps. 17.12 (from the Prayer of David surrounded by enemies): 'Like as a lion that is greedy of prey', and Dent L316.3.

28 their hungry prey prey to their hunger (transferred epithet).

29–31 In Lord Berners's translation (1523–5) of Froissart's *Chroniques* every Englishman in the victory of the French in 1367 is accounted 'worth a Roland or an Oliver' (ed. W. P. Ker, 6 vols., 1901–3, IV, 429); these two knights of Charlemagne, celebrated in *La Chanson de Roland*, were common Renaissance types of chivalric valour. 'Their exploits are rendered so ridiculously...by the old romancers that from thence arose that saying...of giving one a Roland for his Oliver, to signify the matching of one incredible lie with another' (Warburton); *OED* records this usage, however, only from 1612 (see *OED* Roland).

More truly now may this be verified,
For none but Samsons and Goliases
It sendeth forth to skirmish. One to ten!
Lean raw-boned rascals! Who would e'er suppose   35
They had such courage and audacity?

CHARLES Let's leave this town, for they are hare-brained slaves,
And hunger will enforce them to be more eager.
Of old I know them: rather with their teeth
The walls they'll tear down than forsake the siege.   40

REIGNIER I think by some odd gimmers or device
Their arms are set, like clocks, still to strike on;
Else ne'er could they hold out so as they do.
By my consent, we'll even let them alone.

ALENÇON Be it so.   45

Enter the BASTARD OF ORLÉANS

BASTARD Where's the Prince Dauphin? I have news for him.
CHARLES Bastard of Orléans, thrice welcome to us.
BASTARD Methinks your looks are sad, your cheer appalled.
Hath the late overthrow wrought this offence?
Be not dismayed, for succour is at hand: 50
A holy maid hither with me I bring,
Which, by a vision sent to her from heaven,
Ordainèd is to raise this tedious siege
And drive the English forth the bounds of France.
The spirit of deep prophecy she hath,   55
Exceeding the nine sibyls of old Rome:

37] *Pope subst.;* Let's…Towne, / For…Slaues, F   37 hare-brained] *Dyce;* hayre-brayn'd F   38 them to] F;
them *Pope*   41 gimmers] *Alexander; gimmors* F; gimmals F2   47 SH] *Capell; Dolph.* F *(throughout scene)*
48 appalled] *Steevens;* appal'd F

33 **Samsons** Samson is the Old Testament type of strength: see Judges 14 ff.

33 **Goliases** Goliath is the giant of 1 Sam. 17. 'The form *Golias*…occurs also in Chaucer, and seems to have been used in medieval Latin' (*OED*). It is also to be found in the anonymous *Edmund Ironside* at line 1953.

34 **skirmish** do battle – more fiercely than the modern word suggests (Hart).

35 **raw-boned** skeleton-like.

35 **rascals** lean inferior deer; rabble, rogues.

37 **hare-brained** Compare the proverb 'As mad as a (March) hare' (Tilley H148).

38–40 **hunger…down** Compare the proverb 'Hunger breaks stone walls' (Tilley H811).

38 **eager** fierce (*OED* sv *adj* 5).

41 **gimmers** Corruption of 'gimmals', a mechanism used in clocks 'where one piece moves within another, whence it is taken at large for an engine' (Johnson).

44 **consent** counsel.

48 **cheer appalled** countenance pale with fear.

54 **forth** from (Abbott 156).

55 For the use of prophecy by subversive movements and the concern it caused the government, see Thomas, p. 471.

56 **nine sibyls** The sibyls in antiquity were women reputed to possess powers of prophecy. Classical authorities mention four or ten sibyls, not nine. Shakespeare may, however, have taken the figure from Batman's *The Doome Warning all men to the Judgemente* (1581), p. 36; see Harlow.

What's past and what's to come she can descry.
Speak: shall I call her in? Believe my words
For they are certain and unfallible.

CHARLES Go call her in.

[Exit Bastard]

But first, to try her skill,   60

Reignier, stand thou as dauphin in my place;
Question her proudly; let thy looks be stern;
By this means shall we sound what skill she hath.

Enter [BASTARD *and*] JOAN [LA] PUCELLE [*armed*]

REIGNIER [*As Charles*] Fair maid, is't thou wilt do these wondrous
feats?
PUCELLE Reignier, is't thou that thinkest to beguile me?   65
Where is the dauphin? [*To Charles*] Come, come from
behind;
I know thee well, though never seen before.
Be not amazed: there's nothing hid from me.
In private will I talk with thee apart:
Stand back, you lords, and give us leave awhile.   70
REIGNIER [*To Alençon and Bastard*] She takes upon her bravely at first
dash.

[The Lords withdraw]

PUCELLE Dauphin, I am by birth a shepherd's daughter,

---

58 my words] F; her words *conj. Johnson*   60 SD] *Capell; not in* F   63 SD LA PUCELLE] *Dyce, throughout; Puzel* F
(*the usual spelling until 3.2*)   63 SD *armed*] *Oxford; not in* F   64, 66 SD] *Oxford; not in* F   64 wilt] F; will *conj.*
Capell   71 SD.1, 71 SD.2] *This edn; not in* F

---

59 unfallible Obsolete after the seventeenth
century; see Abbott 442.
   60 try test.
   62 proudly vigorously (*OED* sv *adv* 2).
   63 sound investigate, measure.
   63 SD PUCELLE girl, maid (French). This and
the derivative form 'puzzle' were also used in
English to mean 'drab' or 'whore' (see 1.4.106).
   67 through...before Hall writes: 'she knew
and called him her king, whom she never saw
before' (p. 148). These last words are omitted
by Holinshed, but are not sufficient to constitute
proof that Shakespeare had Hall to hand when
writing this scene.
   68 there's...me The words could be construed as a claim to knowledge acquired through
the 'spirits' Joan conjures at 5.3.3–4, an indication to the audience that she is indeed a witch.

Alternatively they could be taken simply as an
indication of her assurance.
   69–71 The lines indicate that Joan and
Charles stand so close together as to create an
equivocal image to the prurient lords.
   71 She plays her part superbly from the first
encounter (compare *Shr.* 4.2.109).
   71 at first dash Dent (D41.1) records a catchphrase; the words are also open to a bawdy
construction.
   72 shepherd's daughter Although Holinshed
notes (p. 163) that Joan's father was 'a sorry
shepherd', this detail, along with the reference to
England's scourge (129), may indicate that Joan
is casting herself as a French Tamburlaine;
Tamburlaine was originally a 'Scythian shepherd'
(see the title page of the 1590 edn).

My wit untrained in any kind of art.
Heaven and our Lady gracious hath it pleased
To shine on my contemptible estate.   75
Lo, whilst I waited on my tender lambs
And to sun's parching heat displayed my cheeks,
God's mother deignèd to appear to me
And, in a vision full of majesty,
Willed me to leave my base vocation   80
And free my country from calamity;
Her aid she promised and assured success.
In complete glory she revealed herself –
And whereas I was black and swart before
With those clear rays which she infused on me,   85
That beauty am I blest with, which you may see.
Ask me what question thou canst possible,
And I will answer unpremeditated;
My courage try by combat, if thou dar'st,
And thou shalt find that I exceed my sex;   90
Resolve on this: thou shalt be fortunate
If thou receive me for thy warlike mate.

CHARLES Thou hast astonished me with thy high terms.
Only this proof I'll of thy valour make:

76 whilst] *Eds.;* whilest F   86 with, which you] F; which you F2; you may *conj. Cam.*   90 my] F; thy *conj. anon in Cam.*

73 **wit** mind.
73 **art** skill.
77 Elizabethan beauties preserved their fair skins from the sun; compare *TGV* 4.4.151–6.
78 For Reformation writers who counted Catholic rites and mysteries as forms of magic, see Thomas, ch. 3.
83 **complete** Stressed on the first syllable (Cercignani, p. 34).
84 **black** black-haired (*OED* sv *adj* 3a); presumably the boy player wore an obvious blonde wig.
84 **swart** dusky, swarthy; Hall writes of 'her foul face' (p. 148), and it is possible that Shakespeare added the detail to create this seeming miracle.
85–6 Compare 'Beauty is a certain living and spiritual grace, *infused* first by an shining *angel-ray* of God, and thence into men's souls, the forms of their bodies, and their voices; a ray which... ravishes by delighting, and by ravishing inflames us with burning love' (Ficino, *Commentarium in Convivium*, v, vi, *Opera Omnia* (Basel, 1551), p. 391). Castiglione describes beauty as 'an influence of the heavenly bountifulness...like the sun' (*Il Cortegiano*, trans. Sir Thomas Hoby, 1928 edn, p. 304).
85 **With** By virtue of.
85 **infused** shed, diffused.
87 For the transposed adjective, see Abbott 419.
88 **unpremeditated** extempore.
89 **try by combat** The episode is not mentioned by Holinshed but adds action to the scene.
91 **Resolve on** Be assured of.
92 **mate** Equivocal, like 111 and 115–16 below.
93 Charles's deprecation of Joan's rhetoric recalls Marlowe (*1 Tamburlaine* 1.1.19–20, 1.2.106–7, etc.).
93 **terms** style.

In single combat thou shalt buckle with me,   95
And if thou vanquishest, thy words are true;
Otherwise I renounce all confidence.

PUCELLE I am prepared. Here is my keen-edged sword
Decked with fine flower-de-luces on each side –
[*Aside*] The which at Touraine, in Saint Katherine's
churchyard,   100
Out of a great deal of old iron I chose forth.

CHARLES Then come, a God's name; I fear no woman.

PUCELLE And while I live I'll ne'er fly from a man.

Here they fight, and Joan [la] Pucelle overcomes

CHARLES Stay, stay thy hands; thou art an Amazon
And fightest with the sword of Deborah.   105

PUCELLE Christ's mother helps me, else I were too weak.

CHARLES Whoe'er helps thee, 'tis thou that must help me.
Impatiently I burn with thy desire;
My heart and hands thou hast at once subdued.
Excellent Pucelle, if thy name be so,   110
Let me thy servant and not sovereign be;
'Tis the French dauphin sueth to thee thus.

PUCELLE I must not yield to any rites of love

---

97 Otherwise I] F; I otherwise *conj. Seymour*   99 fine] F; five *conj. Steevens (after Holinshed)*   99–100 side – / Aside] *This edn*; side, F   100 churchyard] F; church *Pope*   101 great deal of] F; deal *Dyce*   102 come] F; come on *conj. Oxford*   103 fly from a] F; fly no F2   103 SD la] *Rowe*; de F   113 rites] *Pope*; rights F

95 buckle fight, grapple; also 'copulate' (compare 5.3.28 and *Ado* 5.2.18).

97 confidence (1) trust, (2) intimacy (*OED* sv *sb* 6).

99 fine Holinshed (p. 163) reads 'fiue floure delices': 'fiue' could be easily misread by the compositor as 'fine'.

100–1 The tone of these lines, in keeping with Pucelle's sardonic wit, and the unmetrical nature of 100, suggest that they may well have been intended as a prose aside. (They were so treated in the 1983 BBC television version.)

100 churchyard If the conjecture that the word is part of an aside is not accepted, the extrametrical syllable may be explained by noting that the chronicles read 'churche'. F's '-yard' may therefore be a misreading of the final loop of the MS. 'h' or 'he' as the abbreviation 'y^{d}'.

102 a in (*OED* sv *prep*[1] 10).

103 SD *la Pucelle F's '*de*' (here and elsewhere) is probably an error caused by Com-

positor A. 'The sources agree in treating "puzel" as an epithet and not a place name; contrast "*Ione of Aire*" at 5.4.49' (Wells and Taylor, *Textual Companion*, p. 220).

104 Amazon From the race of fabulous female warriors said to have come from Scythia.

105 Deborah See Judges 4–5. Deborah led her people against their oppressors, the Canaanites; Holinshed, p. 175 (2nd edn only), cites a French chronicler, de Tillet, who likens her to 'Debora, Jahell [i.e. Jael], and Judith'.

108 thy desire (1) desire of thee, (2) the desire with which you have infused me.

110 Excellent Exalted, more than noble (*OED* sv *adj* 2).

110 Pucelle See 63 SD n.

111 servant (1) vassal, (2) worshipper – as of the Virgin Mary, (3) lover.

113 *rites F's 'rights' is, according to *OED* (Right *sb*[2]), an erroneous spelling for 'rites'; compare *MND* 4.1.133.

For my profession's sacred from above;
When I have chasèd all thy foes from hence,   115
Then will I think upon a recompense.
CHARLES Mean time look gracious on thy prostrate thrall.
REIGNIER [*To Alençon*] My lord methinks is very long in talk.
ALENÇON Doubtless he shrives this woman to her smock;
Else ne'er could he so long protract his speech.   120
REIGNIER Shall we disturb him, since he keeps no mean?
ALENÇON He may mean more than we poor men do know;
These women are shrewd tempters with their tongues.
REIGNIER [*To Charles*] My lord, where are you? What devise you on?
Shall we give over Orléans, or no?   125
PUCELLE Why no, I say. Distrustful recreants,
Fight till the last gasp; I will be your guard.
CHARLES What she says, I'll confirm: we'll fight it out.
PUCELLE Assigned am I to be the English scourge.
This night the siege assurèdly I'll raise;   130
Expect Saint Martin's summer, halcyons' days,

---

118 SD] *This edn; not in* F   124 SD] *Oxford; not in* F   125 over] *Rowe;* o're F   125 Orléans] F; Orléans, yea *conj. Oxford*   127 I will] *Capell;* Ile F   131 halcyons'] *Riverside;* Halcyons F *subst.;* halcyon F3 *subst.*

---

114 sacred Past participle of 'sacre' = sanctify (*OED* Sacre *v* 3).

117 prostrate Charles may still be on the ground after the fight.

119 shrives...smock hears this woman's most intimate confessions; with an innuendo (Hulme, p. 123); compare *3H6* 3.2.107–8 and *MV* 1.2.131.

121 keeps no mean is behaving so immoderately. Cercignani (p. 154) argues (*pace* Kökeritz) that this is *not* a pun on 'men'.

123 shrewd mischievous.

124 where...on what are your intentions? what do you decide?

125 *give over abandon.

126 Distrustful Untrustworthy (although *OED*, which glosses this word as 'diffident', gives this meaning only from 1618).

126 recreants cowards (*OED* Recreant *sb* 1).

127 the last gasp Proverbial (Dent G G3).

129 scourge Theologians pointed out that scourges of God – sent by God to punish iniquity – were themselves evil and would die when their tasks were complete (see Calvin, *The Institution of Christian Religion*: 'And this is to be holden in mind, that when God performeth by the wicked that thing which he decreed by his secret judgement, they are not to be excused, as though they did obey his commandment, which indeed of their own evil lust they do purposely break' (trans. T. Norton, 1587 edn, I, xviii, pp. 69–70)). Perhaps this is an ironic evocation of Tamburlaine – see 72 n. above. Other references to the notion are at 2.3.14, 4.2.16, 4.7.77; see also p. 16 above.

131 Expect Saint Martin's summer Look for fair weather after the onset of autumn (the feast of St Martin is 11 November), 'that is expect prosperity after misfortune' (Johnson).

131 halcyons' days Proverbial (Tilley D116); 'Now a seven-night before the Mid-winter day, and as much after, the sea is allayed and calm for the sitting and hatching of the birds Halcyons [kingfishers]' (Pliny's *Naturall Historie*, trans. Holland, 1601, II, xlvii). E.A. Armstrong, *Shakespeare's Imagination*, 1963 edn, p. 43 n., suggests that Shakespeare 'visualised either the mythological nest floating on the sea or a kingfisher diving into a stream'.

Since I have enterèd into these wars.
Glory is like a circle in the water,
Which never ceaseth to enlarge itself
Till, by broad spreading, it disperse to nought: 135
With Henry's death the English circle ends,
Dispersèd are the glories it included.
Now am I like that proud insulting ship
Which Caesar and his fortune bare at once.

CHARLES Was Mahomet inspirèd with a dove?   140
Thou with an eagle art inspirèd then.
Helen, the mother of great Constantine,
Nor yet Saint Philip's daughters were like thee.
Bright star of Venus, fall'n down on the earth,
How may I reverently worship thee enough?   145

ALENÇON Leave off delays and let us raise the siege.

REIGNIER Woman, do what thou canst to save our honours;
Drive them from Orléans and be immortalised.

CHARLES Presently we'll try. Come, let's away about it;
No prophet will I trust if she prove false.   150

Exeunt

---

132 enterèd] *Malone;* entred F; entred thus F2   145 reverently] F; reverent *Dyce²*

133–5 Malone gives analogues for the image and traces it back to Book XIII of the *Punica* of Sylvius Italicus. However, it does not seem beyond Shakespeare's power to have invented it.

138 insulting triumphing, boasting (*OED* Insult *v* 1); the word may also refer to its etymology (Latin *insulto*) and mean 'leaping' or 'bounding'.

139 Caesar…fortune Caesar used the phrase to encourage a sea-captain, fearful for the loss of his ship as he carried Caesar to Brundisium (see North's Plutarch, III, 429–30).

140–3 The references in this passage probably derive from Shakespeare's reading of Henry Howard's *Defensative against the poison of supposed prophecies* (1583), sig. C3ᵛ, fo. 4ᵛ, sig. L14ᵛ; see Wilson, pp. xxv–xxvi, and Harlow.

140 The tale was common that Mahomet was inspired by a dove which he used to feed with wheat out of his ear.

141 eagle The attribute of St John the Evangelist because, like the eagle, he looked on 'the sun of glory'; but also a type of Christ

because it was believed that the bird renewed its youth every ten years by plunging into the ocean (compare *FQ*, I, xi, 34, and also Ps. 103.5).

142 Helen Led by a vision, St Helena is reported to have discovered the wood of the true cross at Jerusalem.

143 Saint Philip's daughters 'Now [Philip] had four daughters, virgins, which did prophesy' (Acts 21.9).

144 A complex conceit: Lucifer is the morning star, the planet Venus before sunrise, and the name also appears in translations of Isa. 14.12: 'How art thou fallen from heaven, O Lucifer, of the morning, and cut down to the ground' (Geneva). Lucifer became the name attributed to Satan before his fall. Charles, who lacks the prowess of Mars (compare 1 above), is ensnared by Joan's charms.

144–5 Compare the Ephesians' idolatrous worship of the image of Diana 'which came down from Jupiter' (Acts 19.35).

149 Presently Immediately.

[1.3] *Enter* GLOUCESTER *with his* SERVINGMEN [*in blue coats*]

GLOUCESTER I am come to survey the Tower this day;
     Since Henry's death I fear there is conveyance.
     Where be these warders that they wait not here?
     [*The Servingmen knock at the gates*]
     Open the gates; 'tis Gloucester that calls.
1 WARDER [*Within*] Who's there that knocks so imperiously?   5
1 SERVINGMAN It is the noble Duke of Gloucester.
2 WARDER [*Within*] Whoe'er he be, you may not be let in.
1 SERVINGMAN Villains, answer you so the Lord Protector?
1 WARDER [*Within*] The Lord protect him. So we answer him;
     We do no otherwise than we are willed.   10
GLOUCESTER Who willed you or whose will stands but mine?
     There's none Protector of the realm but I.
     [*To Servingmen*] Break up the gates; I'll be your warrantise.
     Shall I be flouted thus by dunghill grooms?
     Gloucester's Men rush at the Tower gates,
     and WOODVILLE *the Lieutenant speaks within*

Act 1, Scene 3   1.3] *Capell subst.; not in* F   0 SD *in blue coats*] *Capell subst.; not in* F   3 SD] *Capell subst.; not in* F   5, 7, 9 SD] *Malone; not in* F   5 knocks] F; knocketh *Theobald*   6, 8 SH 1 SERVINGMAN] *This edn;* Glost.I.Man. / and / I.Man. F   13 SD] *Oxford; not in* F

Act 1, Scene 3

*1.3 Another scene of dissension among the English nobility; it takes up the quarrel (1424) between Winchester and Gloucester (Holinshed, p. 147; Hall, p. 131) that broke out at 1.1.33; the account of the attempt by the Mayor to prevent bloodshed (70 ff.) derives from Fabyan, p. 596. The author seems to have forgotten that Winchester was not yet made cardinal: see 19, 36, 42, 55. However, Shakespeare may well have been in addition consulting the *second* bill of complaint made by Gloucester to the king against Winchester in 1441 (Holinshed, pp. 199 ff.; Hall, pp. 197 ff.) after Winchester had been made cardinal. He might also have been led astray by his perusal of Fabyan who notes, *immediately* after his account of the 'Parliament of Bats' (see above): 'This fifth year [1427]...upon the day of the annunciation of our Lady, the Bishop of Winchester with[in] the church of our Lady of Calais was created cardinal' (p. 597). Oxford's emendations which serve to correct these references (see collation and Wells and Taylor, *Textual Companion*, p. 218) are not justified.

0 SD SERVINGMEN For Tudor legislation that

attempted to control over-large retinues, see Williams, pp. 1–2.

0 SD *in blue coats* The customary garb of servingmen (*Shakespeare's England*, II, 112–13).

1 The line indicates that Winchester, with a look, took in the tiring-house façade which served as 'the Tower'.

1 survey inspect.

1 Tower The Tower of London, as at 1.1.167.

2 conveyance dishonest dealing (*OED* sv 11b).

3 warders entrance guards.

4 *Gloucester Trisyllabic here as sometimes elsewhere (Cercignani, p. 275), although F reads '*Gloster*'.

7 he i.e. your master.

8 answer...Protector Compare John 18.22 where an officer 'smote Jesus with his rod, saying, "Answerest thou the high priest so?"'.

10 willed commanded.

13 Break up Tear open.

13 warrantise surety, permission.

14 flouted mocked, insulted.

14 SD.2 within i.e. from within the tiring-house, the door to which served as the gate of the Tower.

WOODVILLE [*Within*] What noise is this? What traitors have we here?   15
GLOUCESTER Lieutenant, is it you whose voice I hear?
    Open the gates; here's Gloucester that would enter.
WOODVILLE [*Within*] Have patience, noble duke; I may not open;
    The Cardinal of Winchester forbids:
    From him I have express commandment   20
    That thou nor none of thine shall be let in.
GLOUCESTER Faint-hearted Woodville, prizest him 'fore me?
    Arrogant Winchester, that haughty prelate
    Whom Henry, our late sovereign, ne'er could brook?
    Thou art no friend to God or to the king.   25
    Open the gates, or I'll shut thee out shortly.
SERVINGMEN Open the gates unto the Lord Protector
    Or we'll burst them open if that you come not quickly.

    Enter to the Protector at the Tower gates
    WINCHESTER *and his Men in tawny coats*

WINCHESTER How now, ambitious Humphrey, what means this?
GLOUCESTER Peeled priest, dost thou command me to be shut out?   30
WINCHESTER I do, thou most usurping proditor
    And not 'Protector' of the king or realm.
GLOUCESTER Stand back, thou manifest conspirator,
    Thou that contrived'st to murder our dead lord,
    Thou that giv'st whores indulgences to sin: 35

15, 18 SD] *Alexander; not in* F   19 The Cardinal] F; My lord *Oxford*   28 Or we'll] F *subst.; Or Pope*   29 Humphrey] *Theobald; Vmpheir* F; umpire F2; vizier *Oxford*   30 me to] F; me *Pope*

19 **Cardinal of Winchester** Beaufort did not receive his red hat until 1427 (Holinshed, p. 146). See headnote and 5.1.28-9 n.
20 ***commandment** Four syllables (Cercignani, p. 293; F reads 'commandement').
22 **prizest** do you respect.
24 **brook** endure.
26 **shut thee out** deprive you of office.
27-8 These lines should perhaps be printed as prose.
28 SD.2 *tawny coats* The uniform of apparitors or summoners, attendants on bishops (*Shakespeare's England*, II, 113).
29 ***Humphrey** F's '*Vmpheir*' is anomalous, and Oxford's emendation 'vizier' is attractive, as is F2's reading 'umpire', a word used at 2.5.29.
30 **Peeled** (1) tonsured; (2) bald as the result of venereal disease.
31 **proditor** traitor.

34 In Hall (p. 131) Gloucester accuses Winchester of procuring a man to 'have slain [Henry V when Prince of Wales] in his bed'.
35 **giv'st...sin** Bishops of Winchester in Shakespeare's time were notorious for owning land on which Southwark bawdy houses were built near the Bankside playhouses (see John Stow, *The Survey of London* (1598), ed. Kingsford, 2 vols., 1908, II, 54–5). Colman, p. 49, hears 'an echo of the Martin Marprelate controversy. "Martin's" opening salvo, fired at the Bishops of London *and Winchester* in October 1588, had been aimed "To the right puissant and terrible priests, my clergy masters of the Confocation-house..."'
35 **indulgences** Papal documents which could be bought and which granted absolution from punishment; the gibe is at the bishop's revenue from the brothels.

I'll canvas thee in thy broad cardinal's hat,
If thou proceed in this thy insolence.
WINCHESTER Nay, stand thou back; I will not budge a foot.
This be Damascus, be thou cursèd Cain
To slay thy brother Abel, if thou wilt.   40
GLOUCESTER I will not slay thee, but I'll drive thee back;
Thy scarlet robes, as a child's bearing-cloth,
I'll use to carry thee out of this place.
WINCHESTER Do what thou dar'st, I beard thee to thy face.
GLOUCESTER What? Am I dared and bearded to my face?   45
Draw, men, for all this privileged place –
                    [*All draw their swords*]
Blue coats to tawny coats. – Priest, beware your beard,
I mean to tug it and to cuff you soundly.
Under my feet I'll stamp thy cardinal's hat;
In spite of pope or dignities of church,   50
Here by the cheeks I'll drag thee up and down.
WINCHESTER Gloucester, thou wilt answer this before the pope.
GLOUCESTER Winchester goose, I cry, 'A rope! A rope!'
Now beat them hence; why do you let them stay?
Thee I'll chase hence, thou wolf in sheep's array.   55

36] F; *not in Oxford*   42 scarlet] F; *purple Oxford*   46 SD] *Oxford; not in* F   47 tawny coats] F; *tawny Pope*   49 I'll] F2; I F   49 cardinal's hat] F; *bishop's mitre Oxford*

36 canvas (1) entangle in a net (hawking term, see *OED* Canvas *v* 1), (2) punish by tossing in a canvas sheet or blanket (*OED* Canvass *v* 1), (3) investigate thoroughly (*OED* Canvass *v*, 4).
36 cardinal's hat The sign of one of the Southwark brothels noted in Stow.
38 I...foot Compare the proverb 'He will not budge an inch (foot)' (Tilley I52).
39 Damascus Near where Cain was reputed to have slain Abel (compare Mandeville, *Travels*, ed. A. W. Pollard, 1900, p. 81).
40 brother Winchester was actually half-brother to Gloucester's father Henry IV.
42 scarlet robes Of a cardinal.
42 bearing-cloth For carrying a child to baptism; compare *WT* 3.3.115 and see Hulme, p. 321.
44 beard defy.
46 Drawing a weapon in a royal dwelling was an offence; compare *Tit.* 2.1.46.
46 privileged enjoying immunity (from violence).
48 tug it Tugging a beard was a calculated insult.
49 *I'll F's 'I' would indicate that the hat was trampled on stage – possible but unlikely in view of the previous line.
50 dignities dignitaries (*OED* Dignity 3b).
51 by the cheeks This may imply that the original player of Winchester was fat (see 1.1.41).
53 Winchester goose A swelling in the groin caused by venereal disease; also, one so infected, or a prostitute. Proverbial (Tilley G366).
53 A rope (1) A hangman's halter, (2) the sound of a parrot's cry (Dent R172.1), hence a term of abuse, (3) Winchester's penis which brought him the clap – see Anne Lancashire, 'Lyly and Shakespeare on the ropes', *JEGP* 68 (1969), 237–44.
55 wolf...array A proverbial figure of hypocrisy (Tilley W614); see Matt. 7.15.

Out, tawny coats! Out, scarlet hypocrite!

*Here Gloucester's Men beat out the Cardinal's Men, and enter
in the hurly-burly the* MAYOR OF LONDON *and his* OFFICERS

MAYOR Fie, lords, that you, being supreme magistrates,
Thus contumeliously should break the peace!
GLOUCESTER Peace, mayor! Thou know'st little of my wrongs.
Here's Beaufort, that regards nor God nor king,   60
Hath here distrained the Tower to his use.
WINCHESTER Here's Gloucester, a foe to citizens,
One that still motions war and never peace,
O'ercharging your free purses with large fines;
That seeks to overthrow religion,   65
Because he is Protector of the realm;
And would have armour here out of the Tower,
To crown himself king and suppress the prince.
GLOUCESTER I will not answer thee with words, but blows.
Here they skirmish again
MAYOR Nought rests for me in this tumultuous strife   70
But to make open proclamation.
Come, officer, as loud as e'er thou canst, cry.
[Hands the Officer a paper]
[OFFICER] All manner of men, assembled here in arms this day,
against God's peace and the king's, we charge and command
you, in his highness' name, to repair to your several dwelling   75
places, and not to wear, handle, or use any sword, weapon, or
dagger henceforward, upon pain of death.
[The fighting ceases]
GLOUCESTER Cardinal, I'll be no breaker of the law;

---

56 scarlet] F; cloakèd *Oxford*   62 Gloucester] *Cam.*; *Gloster* F; *Gloster* too F2   72 canst, cry:] F; canst? / *Cry.* /
Cairncross   72 SD] *This edn; not in* F   73 SH OFFICER] *Hanmer; not in* F   77 SD] *This edn; not in* F   78
Cardinal] F; Bishop *Oxford*

56 scarlet hypocrite The cardinal's red robes
provide Gloucester with a figure of the scarlet
woman of Rev. 17.3–4, a symbol of 'the new
Rome which is the papistry, whose cruelty and
blood-shedding is declared by scarlet' (Geneva
gloss).
56 SD.2 hurly-burly tumult, commotion (the
word had a more dignified connotation then than
now).
57 supreme Accented on the first syllable
(Cercignani, p. 34).
57 magistrates rulers.
58 contumeliously by insulting each other.
59 mayor Could be disyllabic (Cercignani,

p. 357).
61 distrained seized (*OED* Distrain *v* 10b).
63 still motions continually advocates.
64 Freely overburdening your purses with
heavy taxes.
67 armour...Tower The Tower was
London's chief arsenal.
68 suppress deprive of office (*OED* sv *v* 1c).
68 prince ruler (i.e. Henry VI).
70 rests remains.
72 cry The compositor of F may have caught a
SD 'cry' into the text (see collation). Compare
2.1.37 SD.
75 several various.

But we shall meet and break our minds at large.
WINCHESTER Gloucester, we'll meet to thy cost, be sure;   80
Thy heart-blood I will have for this day's work.
MAYOR I'll call for clubs if you will not away.
[*Aside*] This cardinal's more haughty than the devil.
GLOUCESTER Mayor, farewell. Thou dost but what thou mayst.
WINCHESTER Abominable Gloucester, guard thy head,   85
For I intend to have it ere long.
Exeunt[, severally, Gloucester and Winchester with their Servingmen]
MAYOR See the coast cleared and then we will depart. –
[*Aside*] Good God, these nobles should such stomachs
bear!
I myself fight not once in forty year.

Exeunt

[1.4] *Enter the* MASTER GUNNER *of Orléans and his* BOY

GUNNER Sirrah, thou know'st how Orléans is besieged

80 we'll] F; we will *conj. Walker in Cam.*   80 thy] F; thy dear F2   83 SD] *This edn; not in* F   83 cardinal's] F;
bishop is *Oxford*   86 it ere long] F; it e're be long F3; it, ere't be long *Capell*   86 SD] *Dyce; not in* F   88
SD] *This edn; not in* F   88 Good] F; OFFICER Good *conj. Warburton subst.*   **Act 1, Scene 4**   1.4] *Capell subst.;
not in* F   1 SH GUNNER] *This edn; M.Gunner* F

79 **break** reveal (compare *H5* 5.2.245);
perhaps punning on 'breaking heads'.
79 **at large** at length.
81 **heart-blood** life.
82 **call for clubs** summon the help of
London's apprentices to put down this disorder.
'Prentices and clubs' was the traditional rallying
cry (*Shakespeare's England*, 11, 168–9).
85 **Abominable** Unnatural.
87 **coast cleared** Compare the proverb 'The
coast is clear' (Tilley c469).
88 **stomachs** tempers. The stomach was regarded as the seat of anger.
89 **year** A common Elizabethan plural.

Act 1, Scene 4
*1.4 The first part of the scene was probably
set on the main stage, from where the Gunner
could gesture towards the 'piece of ordnance' (15
and n.) situated within the tiring-house or, more
probably, outside the playhouse (see illustration
3, p. 10 above). (On the other hand, there could
have been a property gun on stage, the noise
being produced by 'chambers' outside the play-

house.) The tiring-house balcony or the roof of a
portico represented 'yonder tower' (11) on which
Salisbury, Talbot and the other English nobles
appeared. Alternatively, if the tiring-house façade
was concave, the shot could have been imagined
to have passed from one side of its balcony to the
other.
Although both the Gunner and his Boy have
left the stage at 21, I have followed tradition and
not begun a new scene there because I did not
want to divide further 1.4–1.6 which in fact
constitute one continuous theatrical sequence.
Salisbury was mortally wounded in 1428, i.e.
about four months before Joan met Charles in
March 1429 (see 1.2). The details are given in
Holinshed, pp. 161–2 (Hall, p. 145); Talbot was
not in fact exchanged for Santrailles until 1433
(Boswell-Stone, p. 214) but, according to Holinshed (p. 174) and Hall (p. 164), 'without delay'
after the battle of Patay. The attributes of Talbot
(41–2) are taken from Hall's encomium after the
narrative of his death in 1453 (p. 230).
1 **Sirrah** Used to address inferiors.

And how the English have the suburbs won.

BOY Father, I know, and oft have shot at them,
  Howe'er unfortunate I missed my aim.

GUNNER But now thou shalt not. Be thou ruled by me: 5
  Chief master gunner am I of this town;
  Something I must do to procure me grace.
  The prince's espials have informèd me
  How the English, in the suburbs close entrenched,
  Went, through a secret grate of iron bars   10
  In yonder tower, to overpeer the city,
  And thence discover how with most advantage
  They may vex us with shot or with assault.
  To intercept this inconvenience,
  A piece of ordnance 'gainst it I have placed   15
  And even these three days watched if I could see them.
  Now do thou watch, for I can stay no longer.
  If thou spy'st any, run and bring me word,
  And thou shalt find me at the governor's.   *Exit*

BOY Father, I warrant you, take you no care;   20
  I'll never trouble you if I may spy them.   *Exit*

4 unfortunate] *Eds.*; vnfortunate, F   8 prince's espials] F *subst.*; Princes 'spials *Pope*; Prince' espials *Cairncross*   10 Went] F; Wont *Steevens, conj. Tyrwhitt*   13 They may vex us] F; Vex us they may *conj. Cairncross;* They may us vex *conj. Oxford*   16–17] *Cairncross, conj. Vaughan;* And...dayes haue I watcht, / If...watch, / For...longer. F   21 SD.1 *Exit*] F; *Exit* / 1.6 *Oxford*

2 **English...won** In fact Holinshed (p. 161) records how the Bastard 'destroyed the suburbs' but the English took 'the bulwark of the bridge, with a great tower standing at the end of the same'.

4 ***Howe'er unfortunate** Although unfortunately.

7 **grace** honour.

8 **espials** spies.

10 **Went** Were accustomed (see *OED* Go v 32b).

11 **overpeer** look down on.

13 **vex** harass.

14 **inconvenience** harm.

15 The line could be taken to indicate that no gun is seen by the audience. In fact the scene could be performed equally well with or without this property.

15 **piece of ordnance** mounted gun or a cannon. If this was to be seen by the audience 68 SD would indicate that it was a non-practical property gun.

15 **'gainst** opposite, aimed at.

16 ***watched** F's 'have I watched' seems to have been caught from the line before.

19 And you will have brought me advancement (see 7).

20 **take you no care** have no worries.

21 SD.1 **on the turrets** See illustration 3, p. 10 above. If these castle-like structures did not exist, the words perhaps constitute an authorial description of the function to which Shakespeare wanted the tiring-house balcony (or a private box – see headnote) to be put (compare the 'turret' of 3.2.30 and '*on the walls*' of 3.2.40 SD). If the performance was designed for an early playhouse without a stage canopy (which in this scene would have created a sight-line problem for spectators below it), it is conceivable that '*the turrets*' indicated that the playhouse hut was to be used: see G. Wickham, '"Heavens", machinery, and pillars in the Theatre and other early playhouses', in H. Berry (ed.), *The First Public Playhouse: The Theatre in Shoreditch, 1576–1598,* 1979.

Enter SALISBURY *and* TALBOT *on the turrets, with*
[SIR WILLIAM GLANSDALE, SIR THOMAS GARGRAVE *and*] *others*

SALISBURY Talbot, my life, my joy, again returned!
How wert thou handled, being prisoner,
Or by what means gots thou to be released?
Discourse, I prithee, on this turret's top.   25
TALBOT The Earl of Bedford had a prisoner,
Called the brave Lord Ponton de Santrailles;
For him was I exchanged and ransomèd.
But with a baser man-of-arms by far
Once in contempt they would have bartered me;   30
Which I disdaining, scorned, and cravèd death
Rather than I would be so pilled-esteemed;
In fine, redeemed I was as I desired.
But O, the treacherous Fastolf wounds my heart,
Whom with my bare fists I would execute   35
If I now had him brought into my power.
SALISBURY Yet tell'st thou not how thou wert entertained.
TALBOT With scoffs and scorns and contumelious taunts;
In open market-place produced they me
To be a public spectacle to all.   40
'Here', said they, 'is the terror of the French,
The scarecrow that affrights our children so.'
Then broke I from the officers that led me
And with my nails digged stones out of the ground
To hurl at the beholders of my shame.   45
My grisly countenance made others fly;

---

21 SD.2 SIR WILLIAM...*and*] *Capell; not in* F   21 SD.3 GLANSDALE] F; Glasdale *Oxford*   26 Earl] F; Duke
Theobald   27 Santrailles] *Capell; Santrayle* F   28 ransomèd] *Pope;* ransom'd F   32 pilled-] *Capell;*
pil'd F; vilde- *Pope*

24 **gots thou** did you manage; the form is
more euphonic than 'got'st' (Abbott 340).
26 **Earl** F's reading. In fact Bedford had been
created duke in 1415. Shakespeare probably
made this mistake after reading of the Earl of
Arundel's capture of 'the valiant captain called
Pouton de Santrailles' at Beauvais in 1431
(Holinshed, p. 174; Hall, p. 164).
29 **baser** of lower rank.
29 **man-of-arms** soldier.
· 32 ***pilled-esteemed** esteemed as a beggar
(obsolete form of the past participle of 'peel' (=
rob) (*OED* Pilled *ppl adj* 4)). Compare *OED*'s

citations of 'pilled-pated', 'pilled-skinned'. (Many
editors follow Pope and emend to 'vile-esteemed',
citing Sonnet 121.)
33 **In fine** In short.
33 **redeemed** ransomed.
34 **Fastolf** See 1.1.131 n.
37 **entertained** treated.
41–2 Talbot's prowess became a folk legend:
'the French women to affray their children,
would tell them that the Talbot cometh' (E.K.'s
gloss to June in Spenser's *The Shepheardes
Calender* (1579), fol. 25; compare 2.3.16).
42 **scarecrow** bogy (*OED* sv *sb* 2b).
46 **grisly** grim.

None durst come near for fear of sudden death.
In iron walls they deemed me not secure:
So great fear of my name 'mongst them were spread
That they supposed I could rend bars of steel   50
And spurn in pieces posts of adamant.
Wherefore a guard of chosen shot I had
That walked about me every minute-while;
And if I did but stir out of my bed,
Ready they were to shoot me to the heart.   55

Enter the BOY *with a linstock*

SALISBURY I grieve to hear what torments you endured;
          But we will be revenged sufficiently.
          Now it is supper-time in Orléans.
          Here, through this grate, I count each one,
          And view the Frenchmen how they fortify.   60
          Let us look in, the sight will much delight thee. –
          Sir Thomas Gargrave and Sir William Glansdale,
          Let me have your express opinions
          Where is best place to make our batt'ry next?
GARGRAVE I think at the North Gate, for there stands lords.   65

---

49 were] F; *was Rowe*   55 SD *linstock*] F; *linstock, and exit / Cairncross*   65 stands] F; *stand* F2   65 lords] F;
Lou *Oxford*

---

49 **were** For the subjunctive in dependent
clauses in association with 'know', 'think', etc.,
see Abbott 301.
51 **spurn in** kick to (*OED* Spurn v^1 5b).
51 **posts of adamant** Virgil speaks of
adamante columnae (*Aeneid* VI, 552); adamant is a
legendary mineral of the greatest durability.
52 **chosen shot** picked musketeers (*OED* Shot
sb^1 21a).
53 **every minute-while** at intervals of a
minute (see *OED* While *sb* 6c; Abbott 430).
55 SD The Boy's entrance here creates a suspense that lasts until he shoots – unless we de-
duce that 18 indicates that some stage directions
are missing and that he simply passes over the
stage here: Walter Hodges suggests (privately):
'His linstock is either already alight, or...he
lights it; or...he could blow on it, or by swinging
it around bring it alive, and then with significant
gestures and a smoking or blazing linstock, he
goes out again to do what we know he will do.'
The instruction '*they shoot*' (68 SD) is for the
stage-keepers (see headnote). Alternatively, if the
gun was on stage, he could have remained on

stage or returned (with the Gunner – to make
sense of '*They shoot*' at 68 SD) immediately before
the ordnance is fired at 68. (This does not accord
with the chroniclers, who have the son firing the
gun (Holinshed, pp. 161–2; Hall, p. 145).)
55 SD **linstock** A stick with one end cleft to
hold burning lint or the gunner's match.
59 **grate** There were possibly windows at the
sides of the stage balcony (Chambers, III, 58–9
n., 93 n.). If the characters appeared at one of
these, the players would point towards the
audience as they listed the details of the town's
defences. Alternatively, use may have been made
of an upper private box, some of which seem to
have been screened by what Sir John Davies
called a 'grate' (Epigram 3, '*In Rufum*', *Epi-
grammes* (1593?)).
63 **express** definite.
64 **make our batt'ry** direct our fire.
65 **stands** For the use of a singular verb with a
plural subject see Abbott 333.
65 **lords** F's reading is weak, but so is Oxford's
'[the bastile of saint] Lou' (from Holinshed).

GLANSDALE And I here, at the bulwark of the bridge.
TALBOT For aught I see, this city must be famished
　　　Or with light skirmishes enfeeblèd.
　　　　Here they shoot, and Salisbury [and Gargrave] fall down
　　　　　　　　　　　　　　　　　　[Exit Boy]
SALISBURY O Lord, have mercy on us, wretched sinners!
GARGRAVE O Lord, have mercy on me, woeful man!　　　　70
TALBOT What chance is this that suddenly hath crossed us?
　　　Speak, Salisbury – at least if thou canst, speak!
　　　How far'st thou, mirror of all martial men?
　　　One of thy eyes and thy cheek's side struck off?
　　　Accursèd tower, accursèd fatal hand　　　　　75
　　　That hath contrived this woeful tragedy!
　　　In thirteen battles Salisbury o'ercame;
　　　Henry the Fifth he first trained to the wars.
　　　Whilst any trump did sound or drum struck up
　　　His sword did ne'er leave striking in the field.　　　80
　　　Yet liv'st thou, Salisbury? Though thy speech doth fail,
　　　One eye thou hast to look to heaven for grace:
　　　The sun with one eye vieweth all the world.
　　　Heaven, be thou gracious to none alive
　　　If Salisbury wants mercy at thy hands! –　　　　85
　　　Sir Thomas Gargrave, hast thou any life?
　　　Speak unto Talbot, nay look up to him. –
　　　Bear hence his body; I will help to bury it.
　　　　　[Exeunt some with the body of Gargrave]

---

68 SD.1 *shoot*] *Rowe; shot* F   68 SD.1 *fall*] *Capell; falls* F   68 SD.2 *Exit Boy*] *This edn; not in* F   86–8] *Conj. H.*
Brooks in Cairncross; 88 precedes 86–7 in F   88 SD] *Cairncross; not in* F

66 bulwark fortification (*OED sv sb* 1).
67 famished starved out (*OED* Famish *v* 2).
68 SD.1 Here they shoot See 55 SD n. For
'*Here*' in SDs (compare 96 SD and 102 SD below),
see Textual Analysis, p. 191.
68 SD.1 fall down Hodges suggests privately
that 'Salisbury, Gargrave *et al.* come out onto the
open part of the upper stage, staggering and
falling about', smeared with 'blood' or 'with a
clout of red-painted cloth held to the face'. The
staging recalls the death scene of Antony (*Ant.*
4.15).
68 SD.2 *Exit Boy* This is necessary if it has
been decided to keep the Boy on stage from 55.
69–70 This recalls the opening petition of
the Litany.

71 chance mischance (*OED sv sb* 2).
71 crossed thwarted.
73 mirror pattern, exemplar.
76 contrived plotted.
77 Salisbury Trisyllabic.
82–3 Polyphemus brings the same comforting
conceit to Galatea: 'This one round eye of mine
is like a mighty target. Why? / Views not the sun
all things from heaven? Yet but one only eye /
Hath he' (*Metamorphoses* XIII, 1001–3).
*88 Placed before 86 in F. What follows indicates that the body cannot be that of Salisbury.
Oxford explain 'by the assumption that this misplaced line was an ambiguous marginal addition,
which Compositor A inserted in the wrong place'
(Wells and Taylor, *Textual Companion*, p. 221).

Salisbury, cheer thy spirit with this comfort,
Thou shalt not die whiles –   90
He beckons with his hand and smiles on me
As who should say, 'When I am dead and gone,
Remember to avenge me on the French.'
Plantagenet, I will; and, like thee, Nero,
Play on the lute, beholding the towns burn.   95
Wretched shall France be only in my name.
Here an alarum and it thunders and lightens
What stir is this? What tumult's in the heavens?
Whence cometh this alarum and the noise?

Enter a MESSENGER

MESSENGER My lord, my lord, the French have gathered head:
The dauphin, with one Joan la Pucelle joined,   100
A holy prophetess new risen up,
Is come with a great power to raise the siege.
Here Salisbury lifteth himself up and groans
TALBOT Hear, hear, how dying Salisbury doth groan;
It irks his heart he cannot be revenged.
Frenchmen, I'll be a Salisbury to you.   105
Puzel or pucelle, dolphin or dog-fish,
Your hearts I'll stamp out with my horse's heels
And make a quagmire of your mingled brains. –

---

94 like thee, Nero] *Malone;* like thee F; Nero-like will F2 *subst.;* Nero-like *Pope*   98 the] F; this *Pope*   100
la] *Cam., throughout; de* F   106 pucelle] *Theobald; Pussel* F

92 As who As one who.
92 dead and gone Proverbial (Dent DD9).
94 Plantagenet Salisbury's family name was Montacute, but he was descended from the house of Anjou by the marriage of the first Lord Montacute to Alice, great-granddaughter of Edward I.
94 *like thee, Nero F omits 'Nero', but the emendation is obviously warranted as Talbot imagines the towns in France burning in revenge. The story of Nero commanding the city of Rome to be set on fire and playing on the harp as he watched it burn is retold in Grafton, I, 61.
96 only in at the mere sound of (Abbott 161).
96 SD *thunders and lightens Drums could be used for thunder (or a cannonball rolled in an iron trough) and fireworks for lightning (see Jonson, *Every Man in his Humour* (1601), Prologue; Hattaway, pp. 31–2).

99 gathered head rallied their forces together.
102 SD *groans Prefiguring the havoc wrought by Joan on the English.
106 Puzel Obsolete form of 'pucelle', here meaning 'harlot' (*OED* Pucelle 2); see 1.2.63 SD n. Oxford cites another meaning from Cotgrave: 'the river pilchard; or a young or little shadfish'.
106 *pucelle The word could mean both 'maid' (*OED* sv 1) and 'slut' (*OED* sv 2) in the period.
106 dolphin . . . dog-fish Punning on the current pronunciation of 'dauphin' (see 1.1.92 n.); 'dogfish' was used as a term of abuse (*OED* sv 2); the dolphin and dogfish ranked high and low in the hierarchies of bestiaries (for the dogfish see Webster, *The Duchess of Malfi* 3.5.125 ff.).
107–8 The grisly image is reminiscent of the rant of Tamburlaine; compare 4.7.77–80.

Convey we Salisbury into his tent,
And then try what these dastard Frenchmen dare.   110

Alarum. Exeunt

[**1.5**] *Here an alarum again, and* TALBOT *pursueth the* DAUPHIN, *and driveth him; then enter* JOAN LA PUCELLE *driving Englishmen before her* [*and exit after them*]. *Then enter* TALBOT

TALBOT Where is my strength, my valour, and my force?
Our English troops retire, I cannot stay them;
A woman clad in armour chaseth men.

Enter PUCELLE [*with Soldiers*]

Here, here she comes — I'll have a bout with thee;
Devil or devil's dam, I'll conjure thee: 5
Blood will I draw on thee — thou art a witch —
And straightway give thy soul to him thou serv'st.
PUCELLE Come, come; 'tis only I that must disgrace thee.

Here they fight

TALBOT Heavens, can you suffer hell so to prevail?
My breast I'll burst with straining of my courage   10

---

109 we] *Cairncross, conj. Vaughan;* me F   **110** then] *Conj. Walker in Cam.;* then wee'le F   **110** what these] F; what *Pope*   **Act 1, Scene 5   1.5**] *Capell subst.; not in* F   **0** SD.2 LA PUCELLE] *Theobald; de Puzel,* F   **0** SD.2 *and exit after them*] *Dyce; not in* F   **3** men] *This edn, conj. Vaughan;* them F   **3** SD *with Soldiers*] *This edn; not in* F   **6** thee — ...witch —] *Dyce;* thee,...witch F   **6** art a] F; arrant *conj. Cairncross*

***109–10** F's 'me' for 'we' is probably the result of an m/w misreading. The hypermetric 'then wee'le' is probably, as Cairncross conjectures, 'due to consequent emendation of the sense'.

Act 1, Scene 5
***1.5** Joan's attack on the English forces at Orléans took place in April and May of 1429 (Holinshed, pp. 164–5; Hall, pp. 148–9). Shakespeare invented the encounter between Joan and Talbot (see 12 SD n. below).

0, 3, 8, 12, 14 SD The stage directions in this scene indicate that the preliminary bouts of skirmishing should move back and forth across the stage until Joan breaks away from Talbot at 13 to exit at 18 through a central opening which represents a city gate. Alternatively 14 SD, instead of being a vague descriptive (authorial?) direction, may indicate that Joan leaves the main stage to reappear aloft and deliver 15–18 from

there.

2 stay stop.

3 ***men** F's 'them' was probably caught from the preceding line.

4 bout Sexual innuendo as in 3.2.56–8 (compare *Rom.* 2.1.17 ff. and *H5* 5.2.292) based on a possible punning jingle with French *con* in 'conjure' (5) which means 'send back to hell' (compare *Rom.* 2.1.26).

5 Devil...dam See Tilley D225.

6–7 For 'scratching', the belief that a witch lost her power if blood was drawn from her, see Thomas, pp. 633–4, 649.

7 him (1) the devil, (2) the dauphin.

8 disgrace eclipse, surpass (*OED* sb *v* 2).

9 hell...prevail Compare Matt. 16.18: 'upon this rock will I build my church; and the gates of hell shall not prevail against it' (Bishops' Bible) — Geneva reads 'shall not overcome it'.

10 courage vigour, wrath (*OED* sv *sb* 3a, b).

And from my shoulders crack my arms asunder
But I will chastise this high-minded strumpet.

They fight again

PUCELLE Talbot, farewell, thy hour is not yet come;
I must go victual Orléans forthwith.

A short alarum, then [she pauses before entering] the town with Soldiers

O'ertake me if thou canst: I scorn thy strength.   15
Go, go, cheer up thy hunger-starvèd men;
Help Salisbury to make his testament.
This day is ours, as many more shall be.   *Exit*

TALBOT My thoughts are whirlèd like a potter's wheel;
I know not where I am nor what I do.   20
A witch by fear, not force, like Hannibal,
Drives back our troops and conquers as she lists:
So bees with smoke and doves with noisome stench
Are from their hives and houses driven away.
They called us, for our fierceness, English dogs;   25
Now like to whelps we crying run away.

A short alarum

[*Shouts*] Hark, countrymen: either renew the fight,
Or tear the lions out of England's coat.
Renounce your soil, give sheep in lions' stead:
Sheep run not half so treacherous from the wolf,   30
Or horse or oxen from the leopard,

---

14 SD *she…entering*] *This edn; not in* F   16 hunger-] *Rowe;* hungry- F   21 Hannibal,] F; Hannibal *Oxford*
27 SD] *This edn; not in* F   29 soil] F; style *conj. Dyce;* shield *conj. Vaughan*

12 **high-minded** arrogant.

12 SD The ensuing dialogue gives no evidence to a modern director as to whether or not Joan defeats Talbot (with the help of magic?) or whether she withdraws from the duel to protect her own skin. 'In the 1975 production at the Oregon Shakespearean Festival, Joan made several magical signs in the air with her sword before the combat; Talbot then fought at half speed, moving as if wading in molasses' (Alan C. Dessen, *Elizabethan Stage Conventions and Modern Interpreters*, 1984, p. 113).

13 **thy…come** Compare John 7.30: 'Then they sought to take him, but no man laid hands on him, because his hour was not yet come.'

15 **O'ertake** Strike (*OED* Overtake *v* 2).

16 ***hunger-starvèd*** Compare *3H6* 1.4.5; 'starvèd' here means 'killed' or 'withered' (*OED* Starve *v* 6a, b), so Rowe's emendation of a pre-

sumed compositorial sophistication (F's 'hungry') is justified.

21 **by fear…Hannibal** The tale is told in Livy, XXII, 6–7, and North's Plutarch, V, 97, of how Hannibal commanded his men to tie lit torches to the horns of two thousand oxen and thus deceived the Romans into thinking they were outnumbered.

23 **noisome** noxious.

28 Three lions passant were quartered with the fleur-de-lis in the English coat-of-arms.

29 **soil** country.

29 **give** display in your armorial bearings (*OED* sv *v* 24).

30 **Sheep…treacherous** Sheep are not half as treacherous and untrustworthy when they run.

31 **leopard** The metre suggests that here, exceptionally, the word was trisyllabic (compare Cercignani, pp. 69, 312).

As you fly from your oft-subduèd slaves.

Alarum. Here [enter Soldiers to] another skirmish

It will not be: retire into your trenches;
You all consented unto Salisbury's death
For none would strike a stroke in his revenge.   35
Pucelle is entered into Orléans
In spite of us or aught that we could do.

                                        [Exeunt Soldiers]

O, would I were to die with Salisbury!
The shame hereof will make me hide my head.

                                    Exit. Alarum. Retreat

[1.6] *Flourish. Enter on the walls* PUCELLE; [CHARLES THE]
DAUPHIN, REIGNIER, ALENÇON, *and Soldiers [with colours, below]*

PUCELLE Advance our waving colours on the walls;
Rescued is Orléans from the English.
Thus Joan la Pucelle hath performed her word.
CHARLES Divinest creature, Astraea's daughter,
How shall I honour thee for this success?   5
Thy promises are like Adonis' gardens
That one day bloomed and fruitful were the next. –

---

32 SD *enter...to*] *This edn; not in* F   37 SD] *Oxford; not in* F   **Act 1, Scene 6**   1.6] *Capell subst.; not in* F
0 SD.1 *Flourish*] *As Collier; after / retreat, / (1.5.39 SD)* F   0 SD.2 *with colours, below*] *This edn; not in* F
2 English.] F; English wolves F2   6 gardens] *Hanmer;* Garden F

33 It...be It is hopeless (Dent B112.2).

33 retire...trenches The line suggests a
possible exit over the side of the stage into the
yard at 39.

34 consented unto acquiesced in (*OED*
Consent *v* 6).

35 his revenge revenge for him.

39 Proverbial (Dent HH18).

39 SD *Retreat* Sounded by drums and
trumpets.

Act 1, Scene 6
*1.6 The action continues from the previous
scene. It would seem that Joan makes only a brief
appearance alone aloft – Charles does not address
her directly after 7, and the balcony could be
clear for the next scene.

1 Advance Raise aloft.

3 performed her word Biblical (1 Kings
8.20).

4 Astraea's daughter Astraea, goddess of
justice and daughter of Jupiter, lived on earth
during the golden age until the wickedness of the
iron age caused her to take her place again among
the stars (*Metamorphoses* 1, 169–70).

6 Adonis' gardens In Plato (*Phaedrus* 276b), a
forcing bed and symbol of transience, but in
Spenser (*FQ*, III, vi, 29–50), as in Pliny (*Nat.
Hist.* XIX, 4), the gardens are a place of
generation and fertility. (The allusion was the
subject of a major scholarly debate among
eighteenth-century commentators; this may be
pursued in Johnson's note.)

France, triumph in thy glorious prophetess!
Recovered is the town of Orléans;
More blessed hap did ne'er befall our state.   10

[*Exit Pucelle*]

REIGNIER Why ring not bells aloud throughout the town?
Dauphin, command the citizens make bonfires
And feast and banquet in the open streets
To celebrate the joy that God hath given us.

ALENÇON All French will be replete with mirth and joy·   15
When they shall hear how we have played the men.

CHARLES 'Tis Joan, not we, by whom the day is won;
For which I will divide my crown with her,
And all the priests and friars in my realm
Shall in procession sing her endless praise.   20
A statelier pyramis to her I'll rear
Than Rhodope's of Memphis ever was.
In memory of her, when she is dead,
Her ashes, in an urn more precious
Than the rich-jewelled coffer of Darius,   25
Transported shall be at high festivals
Before the kings and queens of France.
No longer on Saint Denis will we cry,
But Joan la Pucelle shall be France's saint.

11] *Conj. Steevens;* Why ring not out the Bells alowd, / Throughout...Towne? F   **22** of] *Dyce, conj. Capell;* or F
25 rich-jewelled coffer] F *subst.;* rich jewel-coffer *conj. Steevens*   **27** France.] F; France up-borne *conj. Capell*

10 hap event (*OED* sv *sb*¹ 2).

*11 As the compositor seems to have anticipated the '-out the' from the end of the line and printed 'not out the', I have printed Steevens's conjecture.

16 played the men acted the parts of warriors (Dent PP13).

18–29 'I think he means to call her strumpet all the while he is making his loud praise of her' (Johnson).

21 pyramis The old form of 'pyramid' which could also designate an obelisk or pinnacle (*OED* Pyramid *sb* 3).

22 Rhodope An infamous strumpet who, by marriage, became Queen of Memphis and was supposed to have built the third pyramid.

22 *of F's 'or', which suggests another prince of Memphis, is unlikely.

24 ashes An ominous anticipation of Joan's end.

25 rich-jewelled...Darius After taking Gaza, Alexander found a rich coffer among Darius's jewels and in it kept the works of Homer, which he valued highly. The story is told in North's Plutarch (IV, 305, 308 – see Harlow); the detail of the coffer being carried in procession is found in Nashe, I, 359. F's reading makes the coffer jewelled; North, Nashe, and Puttenham (*Arte of English Poesie* (1589), p. 12) refer to a jewel-coffer, i.e. something intended to contain jewels.

28 on...cry will we call upon Saint Denis. Saint Denis, the first Bishop of Paris, was the patron saint of France.

29 France's saint Joan was beatified only in 1909 and canonised in 1920.

Come in, and let us banquet royally   30
After this golden day of victory.

Flourish. Exeunt

2.1 *Enter [aloft] a [French]* SERGEANT OF A BAND *with two*
SENTINELS

SERGEANT Sirs, take your places and be vigilant;
    If any noise or soldier you perceive
    Near to the walls, by some apparent sign
    Let us have knowledge at the court of guard.
1 SENTINEL Sergeant, you shall.

[Exit Sergeant]
            Thus are poor servitors,   5
    When others sleep upon their quiet beds,
    Constrained to watch in darkness, rain, and cold.

Enter TALBOT, BEDFORD, *and* BURGUNDY [*and Soldiers*],
    with scaling-ladders, their drums beating a dead march

Act 2, Scene 1   2.1] *Capell subst.; Actus Secundus. Scena Prima.* F   0 SD *aloft*] *This edn; to the Gate Capell; not in*
F   0 SD *French*] *Capell; not in* F   5 SH 1 SENTINEL] *Capell subst.; Sent.* F   7 SD] *As* F; *before* 0 SD *conj. this edn;
transferred to 2.2.6, Cairncross; transferred to 2.2.0, Riverside*   7 SD *and Soldiers*] *Capell subst.; not in* F

30–1 The general invitation serves to clear the
stage with an impressive exit.

Act 2, Scene 1
    2.1 Talbot's recapture of Orléans is invented,
although Shakespeare did adapt some details
(11–12 and 37, 38 SDs) from chronicle accounts
of the recapture of Le Mans in 1428 (Holinshed,
p. 160; Hall, p. 143). Perhaps Shakespeare
wished to set 'a partial (and fictitious) recovery in
France' (Bullough, III, 27) against the emergent
rivalry between York and Lancaster. The
dauphin's recourse to witchcraft (16–18) is
deplored by the chroniclers (Holinshed, p. 171;
Hall, p. 151). Burgundy and Reignier (see 1.1.94
n.) are introduced, unhistorically, to prepare for
their parts later in the play.
    Shakespeare begins the scene with a theatrical
montage, 'cutting' from the French defenders on
the stage balcony to the English attackers who
enter silently at 7.
    0 SD *aloft* The scene could be equally well
played on a stage with no area aloft if the English
were to enter the playhouse yard (see 7 SD) and

climb up onto the stage; see Nevill Coghill, *The
Triple Bond*, ed. Joseph G. Price, 1975, p. 236.
    0 SD SERGEANT OF A BAND Leader of a
troop; a higher rank than a modern sergeant
(*OED* Sergeant *sb* 9).
    3 apparent clear, obvious.
    4 court of guard guard-house (see *OED*
Corps de garde 2).
    5 servitors soldiers (*OED* sv 3).
    7 SD.2 scaling-ladders Also employed at the
battle of Harfleur in *H5* 3.1. Evidence that they
were used on stage in siege scenes comes from
Jasper Mayne's encomium of Ben Jonson who
'laid'st no sieges to the music-room' (see Hattaway, p. 29).
    7 SD.2 dead march Not necessarily a funeral
march, but any march played on muffled drums
(see *OED* Dead *adj* 14, and compare J. S.
Manifold, *The Music in English Drama from
Shakespeare to Purcell*, 1956, p. 30). Perhaps, however, the body of Salisbury was here carried
across the stage in a funeral procession from
which Talbot and the others break off to seize the
'opportunity' (13) of a surprise attack. Other

TALBOT Lord regent, and redoubted Burgundy,
By whose approach the regions of Artois,
Wallon, and Picardy are friends to us, 10
This happy night the Frenchmen are secure,
Having all day caroused and banqueted;
Embrace we then this opportunity,
As fitting best to quittance their deceit
Contrived by art and baleful sorcery. 15
BEDFORD Coward of France, how much he wrongs his fame,
Despairing of his own arm's fortitude,
To join with witches and the help of hell!
BURGUNDY Traitors have never other company.
But what's that Pucelle whom they term so pure? 20
TALBOT A maid, they say.
BEDFORD A maid? And be so martial?
BURGUNDY Pray God she prove not masculine ere long,
If underneath the standard of the French
She carry armour as she hath begun.
TALBOT Well, let them practise and converse with spirits. 25
God is our fortress, in whose conquering name
Let us resolve to scale their flinty bulwarks.
BEDFORD Ascend, brave Talbot, we will follow thee.

22 long,] *Eds.;* long: F 24 begun.] F; begun – *Oxford*

editors, following Wilson, needlessly conjectured that that SD was a 'prompter's note' (Wilson, p. 138, n. 7), and had been caught from 2.2 – on the grounds that a 'dead march' was employed only at funerals. (See Textual Analysis, pp. 189 below. The problem is further discussed by Long, pp. 20–2; Greg, *Folio*, p. 189.) The device serves as a theatrical quotation of the play's opening funeral sequence, but is prefixed to a scene in which the English are victorious.

8 **redoubted** distinguished.

9–10 Burgundy's defection made the forces of these Netherlands regions the allies of the English.

9 **approach** arrival.

10 **Wallon** Wallonia, the south-eastern area of modern Belgium.

11 **This happy night** By good fortune tonight.

11 **secure** free from care (the Latinate meaning).

14 **quittance** repay.

15 **Contrived** Plotted.

15 **art** magical power; short for 'art magic' (*ars magica*).

16 **Coward** The dauphin.

16 **wrongs his fame** harms his reputation.

17 **fortitude** strength (*OED* sv 1).

20 **Pucelle** For F's 'Puzell' see 1.2.63 SD n.

22 **prove not masculine** (1) does not turn out to be male, (2) is revealed to be a woman (by becoming pregnant).

23 **standard...French** (1) French colours, (2) the dauphin's penis (see Partridge, p. 191).

24 **carry armour** (1) wear armour, (2) bear the weight of the dauphin (in copulation).

25 **practise** (1) conspire (*OED* sv v 9), (2) have (sexual) intercourse (*OED* sv v 10; compare *Per.* 4.2.125).

25 **converse** (1) talk, (2) be sexually intimate (*OED* sv v 2b).

26 **God...fortress** David's words in 2 Sam. 22.2 run thus: 'The Lord is my rock and my fortress.' (The Bishops' Bible here reads 'castle' (Noble).)

28–34 The three leaders use three ladders to climb to the balcony over the stage, Talbot in the centre, the other two on either side (see 2.1.7 SD n.). Oxford, however, conjectures that Bedford and Burgundy 'make their attack' from offstage.

TALBOT Not all together; better far, I guess,
    That we do make our entrance several ways,   30
    That if it chance that one of us do fail,
    The other yet may rise against their force.
BEDFORD Agreed. I'll to yond corner.
BURGUNDY   And I to this.
TALBOT And here will Talbot mount, or make his grave.
    Now, Salisbury, for thee and for the right   35
    Of English Henry, shall this night appear
    How much in duty I am bound to both.
[*The English, having scaled the walls,*] *cry, 'Saint George!', 'A Talbot!'*
SENTINELS Arm, arm! The enemy doth make assault! [*Alarum*]

The French [Sentinels] leap o'er the walls in their shirts
[*and exeunt. The English exeunt aloft*]. *Enter several ways [below]*
BASTARD, ALENÇON, REIGNIER, *half ready and half unready*

ALENÇON How now, my lords? What, all unready so?
BASTARD Unready? Ay, and glad we 'scaped so well.   40
REIGNIER 'Twas time, I trow, to wake and leave our beds,
    Hearing alarums at our chamber doors.
ALENÇON Of all exploits since first I followed arms,
    Ne'er heard I of a warlike enterprise
    More venturous or desperate than this.   45
BASTARD I think this Talbot be a fiend of hell.
REIGNIER If not of hell, the heavens sure favour him.
ALENÇON Here cometh Charles; I marvel how he sped.

Enter CHARLES *and* JOAN [LA PUCELLE]

29 all together] *Rowe;* altogether F   **31** fail] F; fall *Cairncross*   **33** this.] F; this. *Exeunt severally Bedford and Burgundy, with some soldiers. / Oxford*   **37** SD] *Theobald subst.; Cry. S. George. A Talbot.* F (*after 38*)   **38** SH SEN-TINELS] *Eds.; Sent.* F   **38** SD.1 *Alarum*] *Oxford; not in* F   **38** SD.2 *Sentinels*] *This edn; not in* F   **38** SD.3 *and exeunt...aloft*] *This edn; not in* F   **38** SD.3 *below*] *This edn; not in* F

29 *all together i.e. by the same ladder.
30 several separate.
32 rise...force scale their defences despite their resistance.
35-7 Unlike Tamburlaine, 'even when Talbot seems bent on a most private course of honor... he nevertheless conceives of it as consistent with his patriotic duty' (James C. Bulman, *The Heroic Idiom of Shakespearian Tragedy*, 1985, p. 31).
35 right just claim.
36 shall it shall (Abbott 404).
***37** SD, **38** SD See headnote. My SDs suggest that the English, having scaled the walls, take up positions upstage of the French who, despite their protestations (5-7), have fallen asleep. The scaling-ladders still in position obviate the need for players actually to leap the eight or nine feet to the stage below.
38 SD.3 *below* The sequence that follows could conceivably have been played aloft, but the main stage would be less crowded and make the flight of the French at 77 more dramatic (and comic).
38 SD.4 ready dressed.
45 venturous daring.
48 marvel...sped wonder how he fared.

BASTARD [*Aside*] Tut, holy Joan was his defensive guard.

CHARLES Is this thy cunning, thou deceitful dame?   50
        Didst thou at first, to flatter us withal,
        Make us partakers of a little gain,
        That now our loss might be ten times so much?

PUCELLE Wherefore is Charles impatient with his friend?
        At all times will you have have my power alike?   55
        Sleeping or waking, must I still prevail,
        Or will you blame and lay the fault on me? –
        Improvident soldiers, had your watch been good,
        This sudden mischief never could have fall'n.

CHARLES Duke of Alençon, this was your default,   60
        That, being captain of the watch tonight,
        Did look no better to that weighty charge.

ALENÇON Had all your quarters been as safely kept
        As that whereof I had the government,
        We had not been thus shamefully surprised.   65

BASTARD Mine was secure.

REIGNIER   And so was mine, my lord.

CHARLES And for myself, most part of all this night,
        Within her quarter and mine own precinct
        I was employed in passing to and fro
        About relieving of the sentinels.   70
        Then how or which way should they first break in?

PUCELLE Question, my lords, no further of the case,
        How or which way. 'Tis sure they found some place
        But weakly guarded where the breach was made.
        And now there rests no other shift but this: 75
        To gather our soldiers, scattered and dispersed,

49 SD] *This edn; not in* F

49 **holy** A sexual quibble (Partridge, p. 121).
49 **defensive** protecting.
50 **cunning** witchcraft.
51 **flatter** encourage (with false hopes).
54 **impatient** irritable, angry (*OED sv adj* 1).
54 **friend** companion, mistress (compare French *amie*).
56 **still prevail** (1) always overcome, (2) always seduce (as at 5.4.78).
58 **Improvident** Negligent, unwary (*OED sv adj* 2).
59 **mischief** calamity.

59 **fall'n** happened.
60 **default** failure, fault (*OED sv sb* 4).
61 **tonight** last night.
62 **charge** duty.
63 If all the military sectors of the town had been as securely guarded.
68 **quarter** (1) sector, (2) chamber.
68 **precinct** area of command.
70 **About** Concerned with.
74 **But** Only.
75 **rests** remains.
75 **shift** stratagem.

And lay new platforms to endamage them.
          [*They move towards one door*]

Alarum. Enter an [ENGLISH] SOLDIER *crying, 'A Talbot! A Talbot!'*
[*The French*] *fly* [*across the stage*] *leaving their clothes behind* [*and exeunt*]

SOLDIER I'll be so bold to take what they have left.
          The cry of 'Talbot' serves me for a sword,
          For I have loaden me with many spoils,   80
          Using no other weapon but his name.   *Exit*

[2.2] *Enter* TALBOT, BEDFORD, BURGUNDY, [*a* CAPTAIN, *and others*]

BEDFORD The day begins to break and night is fled,
          Whose pitchy mantle over-veiled the earth.
          Here sound retreat and cease our hot pursuit.
                    Retreat [*sounded*]
TALBOT Bring forth the body of old Salisbury
          And here advance it in the market-place,   5
          The middle cincture of this cursèd town.

          [*Dead march. Enter with the body of* SALISBURY]

77 SD.1] *This edn; Exeunt* F; *not in Capell*   77 SD.2–3] *This edn; Alarum . . . a Souldier . . . Talbot: they . . . behind.* F
77 SD.3] *and exeunt*] *Oxford; not in* F   **Act 2, Scene 2**   2.2] *Capell subst.; not in* F   o SD *a . . . others*] *Capell; not in* F   3 SD *sounded*] *Capell; not in* F   6 cincture] *This edn; centure* F; *centre* F2   6 SD] *Cairncross; not in* F

77 **lay new platforms** make fresh plans.
77 SD.2 *A Talbot* See 1.1.128 n.
77 SD.3 Editors since Capell have suppressed F's '*Exeunt*'. However, it is reasonable to restore it (without so creating another scene) on the grounds that Shakespeare may have been following the chroniclers closely. They noted that 'some of them, being not out of their beds, got up in their shirts, and leapt over the walls. Other ran naked out of the gates' (Holinshed, p. 160; Hall, p. 143). The non-illusionistic conventions of the Elizabethan stage made it possible for the tiring-house entrances to signify the exterior of the gates of Orléans at the beginning of the scene and the interior of them here (Hattaway, p. 26). Joan and the French, therefore, probably made towards one door, were surprised by the entrance of the soldier, and fled across the stage to exit from another, so following their troops 'out of the city'.
78 **bold** forward.

Act 2, Scene 2
*2.2 The sequence continues. Salisbury was extolled by Hall (p. 144) and Holinshed (p. 162).
2 **pitchy** black; compare *FQ*, I, v, 20: 'grisly Night . . . in a foul black pitchy mantle clad', and Dent MM7.
5 **advance** bring forth; or perhaps 'raise aloft on a bier' (*OED* Advance *v* 9).
6 ***cincture*** enclosure (*OED* sv *sb* 2 – which cites the earliest example of this rare usage from 1627). Spenser uses the phrase 'middle centre' at *FQ*, v, v, 5, which would support the traditional emendation to 'centre'.

Now have I paid my vow unto his soul:
For every drop of blood was drawn from him
There hath at least five Frenchmen died tonight;
And that hereafter ages may behold   10
What ruin happened in revenge of him,
Within their chiefest temple I'll erect
A tomb, wherein his corpse shall be interred;
Upon the which, that every one may read,
Shall be engraved the sack of Orléans,   15
The treacherous manner of his mournful death,
And what a terror he had been to France.

                                        [*Exit funeral*]

But, lords, in all our bloody massacre
I muse we met not with the dauphin's grace,
His new-come champion, virtuous Joan of Arc,   20
Nor any of his false confederates.

BEDFORD 'Tis thought, Lord Talbot, when the fight began,
Roused on the sudden from their droswy beds,
They did amongst the troops of armèd men
Leap o'er the walls for refuge in the field.   25

BURGUNDY Myself, as far as I could well discern
For smoke and dusky vapours of the night,
Am sure I scared the dauphin and his trull,
When arm in arm they both came swiftly running,
Like to a pair of loving turtle-doves   30
That could not live asunder day or night.
After that things are set in order here,
We'll follow them with all the power we have.

                    Enter a MESSENGER

17 SD] *Cairncross; not in* F   20 Arc] *Rowe;* Acre F

7 **my vow** See 1.4.94, 105–10.
8 **was** For the omitted 'that', see Abbott 244.
9 **hath** For the singular construction, see Abbott 335.
10 **hereafter** future.
10–17 Salisbury's body was, according to the chroniclers (Holinshed, p. 162; Hall, p. 145), conveyed back to England for burial at Bissam.
16 **mournful** deplorable (*OED* sv *adj* 3).
19 **muse** wonder.
19 **the dauphin's grace** (1) his grace the dauphin, (2) the dauphin's pet goddess or trull.
20 **champion** One who fights on behalf of another.

20 **virtuous** Ironic; the word allows Talbot to attribute to Joan both unwomanly valour and unchastity.
20 *****Arc** F reads *Acre*, probably an i/c misreading of the *Aire* found at 5.4.49. Holinshed (p. 163) reads 'Are'; the word does not occur in Hall or Grafton.
21 **confederates** accomplices, plotters (*OED* Confederate *sb* 2).
27 **For** Despite.
28 **trull** strumpet.
30 **turtle-doves** Proverbial for constancy (Tilley T624).
33 **power** forces (*OED* sv *sb*[1] 9).

MESSENGER All hail, my lords! Which of this princely train
    Call ye the warlike Talbot, for his acts   35
    So much applauded through the realm of France?
TALBOT Here is the Talbot. Who would speak with him?
MESSENGER The virtuous lady, Countess of Auvergne,
    With modesty admiring thy renown,
    By me entreats, great lord, thou wouldst vouchsafe   40
    To visit her poor castle where she lies,
    That she may boast she hath beheld the man
    Whose glory fills the world with loud report.
BURGUNDY Is it even so? Nay, then I see our wars
    Will turn into a peaceful comic sport,   45
    When ladies crave to be encountered with.
    You may not, my lord, despise her gentle suit.
TALBOT Ne'er trust me then; for when a world of men
    Could not prevail with all their oratory,
    Yet hath a woman's kindness overruled –   50
    [*To Messenger*] And therefore tell her I return great thanks,
    And in submission will attend on her –
    Will not your honours bear me company?
BEDFORD No, truly, 'tis more than manners will;
    And I have heard it said unbidden guests   55
    Are often welcomest when they are gone.
TALBOT Well then, alone, since there's no remedy,
    I mean to prove this lady's courtesy.
    Come hither, captain. *Whispers* You perceive my mind?
CAPTAIN I do, my lord, and mean accordingly.   60

                                    Exeunt

---

38 Auvergne] *Rowe;* Ouergne F   51 SD] *This edn; not in* F   54 'tis] F; *it is Malone*   59 SD] *As Johnson; after the line in* F

34–60 The episode has no basis in the chronicles; see 2.3 headnote.

34 All hail Often used in Shakespeare, as here, to introduce an episode of treachery (see E. A. Armstrong, *Shakespeare's Imagination*, 1946). This is an allusion to Judas, although he does not speak these words in Matt. 26.29. In the York and Chester mystery plays, however, he does.

34–6 Which...France? The question contrasts with Pucelle's immediate recognition of Charles in 1.2.

35–6 acts...applauded The metaphor insultingly reduces Talbot from hero to player.

37 would wishes to.

41 lies dwells.

43 report (1) acclaim, (2) din of cannon.

45 comic raising mirth or delight.

46 encountered with (1) met, (2) made love to (Partridge, p. 99).

47 gentle courteous.

48 Ne'er...then Proverbial(?) (Dent T558.1).

48 world great number.

49 oratory eloquence (*OED* sv *sb*² 2).

50 overruled prevailed (*OED* Overrule *v* 3).

52 in submission deferentially (*OED* Submission 2).

54 manners will etiquette demands.

55–6 unbidden...gone Proverbial (Tilley G475 and W259).

58 prove try, test.

59 perceive my mind grasp my plan.

60 mean intend to act (*OED* sv *v*¹ 1f).

[2.3] *Enter [the]* COUNTESS [OF AUVERGNE *and her* PORTER]

COUNTESS Porter, remember what I gave in charge,
    And when you have done so, bring the keys to me.
PORTER Madam, I will. *Exit*
COUNTESS The plot is laid; if all things fall out right,
    I shall as famous be by this exploit   5
    As Scythian Tomyris by Cyrus' death.
    Great is the rumour of this dreadful knight,
    And his achievements of no less account;
    Fain would mine eyes be witness with mine ears
    To give their censure of these rare reports.   10

Enter MESSENGER *and* TALBOT

MESSENGER Madam, according as your ladyship desired,
    By message craved, so is Lord Talbot come.
COUNTESS And he is welcome. What! Is this the man?
MESSENGER Madam, it is.
COUNTESS   Is this the scourge of France?
    Is this the Talbot, so much feared abroad   15
    That with his name the mothers still their babes?
    I see report is fabulous and false:

Act 2, Scene 3   2.3] *Capell subst.; not in* F   0 SD *and her* PORTER] *Pope; not in* F   11] F; According…desir'd
Cairncross; Madam…ladyship *Pope*   15 abroad] *Johnson;* abroad? F

Act 2, Scene 3

*2.3 The episode was invented by Shakespeare, although Wilson (pp. xix–xx) suggests that Shakespeare may have known that certain English gentlemen were in the habit of visiting local castles and nunneries during the siege of Rouen in 1591. Such visits are recorded in Sir Thomas Coningsby's *Journal of the Siege of Rouen* (partially reprinted in Bullough, III, 80–6).

1 **gave in charge** commanded.

6 **Scythian…death** Scythia was a name given to various regions in south-eastern Europe between the Carpathian mountains and the river Don. Tomyris was, according to Herodotus (I, ccv ff.), Queen of the Massagetae (an Asian tribe from east of the Caspian), although Thomas Cooper's *Thesaurus* (1565), following Justin or Orosius, calls her 'Queen of Scythia' (see under 'Cyrus'). She slew Cyrus, King of Persia, in 529 BC after he had put her captured son to death. In revenge she had his head thrown into a wineskin of human blood. Eustache Deschamps included her in his list of the Nine Female Worthies (see J. Huizinga, *The Waning of the Middle Ages*, 1955, p. 72; compare *FQ*, II, x, 56, *3H6* 1.4.114, and Jonson's *Masque of Queens*).

7–10 Shakespeare recalls the phraseology of the biblical account (1 Kings 10.6–7, 2 Chron. 9.5–6) of the compliments paid by the Queen of Sheba to King Solomon.

7 **rumour** fame, report.

7 **dreadful** causing dread, fearful.

10 **censure** judgement, opinion (*OED* sv sb 3).

14 **scourge** See 1.2.129 n.

15 **abroad** everywhere.

16 See 1.4.41–2 n.

16 **still** quieten.

17 **report…false** Compare the proverb 'Fame (Report) is a liar' (Tilley F44).

17 **fabulous** fictitious.

I thought I should have seen some Hercules,
A second Hector, for his grim aspect
And large proportion of his strong-knit limbs.   20
Alas, this is a child, a silly dwarf!
It cannot be this weak and writhled shrimp
Should strike such terror to his enemies.

TALBOT Madam, I have been bold to trouble you;
But since your ladyship is not at leisure   25
I'll sort some other time to visit you. [*Going*]

COUNTESS What means he now? Go ask him whither he goes.

MESSENGER Stay, my Lord Talbot, for my lady craves
To know the cause of your abrupt departure.

TALBOT Marry, for that she's in a wrong belief,   30
I go to certify her Talbot's here.

Enter PORTER *with keys*

COUNTESS If thou be he, then art thou prisoner.

TALBOT Prisoner! To whom?

COUNTESS   To me, bloodthirsty lord,
And for that cause I trained thee to my house.
Long time thy shadow hath been thrall to me,   35
For in my gallery thy picture hangs;
But now the substance shall endure the like,
And I will chain these legs and arms of thine,
That hast by tyranny these many years

---

21 silly] F; seely *Oxford*   26 SD] *Capell; not in* F   27] *Pope (omitting* him); What...now? / Goe...goes? F

19 **for...aspect** because of his stern countenance.
19 **aspect** Accented on the second syllable (Cercignani, p. 37).
20 **proportion** size (*OED* sv *sb* 5).
21 **silly** feeble, frail.
22 **writhled** wrinkled. On the basis of this, Cairncross conjectures that the same actor played Talbot and later Richard of Gloucester (*Richard III*). It is not necessary, however, to take the countess literally. Talbot's 'person', according to Hall, was 'fearful, and terrible to his adversaries present' (p. 230), although André Thévet, *Pourtraits et vies des hommes illustres*, 2 vols. (1584), notes that Talbot was 'd'assez moyenne stature' (I, f. 282ʳ).
26 **sort** arrange.

30 **Marry** A mild oath; originally an invocation of the Virgin Mary.
30 **for...belief** because she labours under a misapprehension.
31 Talbot claims his going will prove her inability to imprison him.
31 **certify** inform.
33 **bloodthirsty** Like Cyrus – see 6 n.
34 **trained** lured (as of a falcon).
35 **shadow** image, portrait; used here, as the countess implies, for maleficent magic (see Thomas, pp. 612–14). Shakespeare often makes play with the antonyms of shadow and substance (37) – see *R2* 4.1.297–9, *TGV* 4.4.115–20.
35 **thrall** slave.
37 **the like** i.e. being hanged.
39 **tyranny** violence.

Wasted our country, slain our citizens,   40
And sent our sons and husbands captivate.
TALBOT Ha, ha, ha!
COUNTESS Laughest thou, wretch? Thy mirth shall turn to moan.
TALBOT I laugh to see your ladyship so fond
To think that you have aught but Talbot's shadow   45
Whereon to practise your severity.
COUNTESS Why, art not thou the man?
TALBOT   I am indeed.
COUNTESS Then have I substance too.
TALBOT No, no, I am but shadow of myself:
You are deceived, my substance is not here;   50
For what you see is but the smallest part
And least proportion of humanity:
I tell you, madam, were the whole frame here,
It is of such a spacious lofty pitch
Your roof were not sufficient to contain't.   55
COUNTESS This is a riddling merchant for the nonce:
He will be here, and yet he is not here;
How can these contrarieties agree?
TALBOT That will I show you presently.
Winds his horn; drums strike up; a peal of ordnance

Enter Soldiers

How say you, madam? Are you now persuaded   60
That Talbot is but shadow of himself?
These are his substance, sinews, arms, and strength,
With which he yoketh your rebellious necks,
Razeth your cities, and subverts your towns,
And in a moment makes them desolate.   65
COUNTESS Victorious Talbot, pardon my abuse;

43] *Pope;* Laughest...Wretch? / Thy...moane. F   **59** That] F; That, madam *conj. Steevens*

41 captivate into captivity.
44 fond foolish.
52 least...humanity smallest part of the substantial body (of my forces).
53 the whole frame (1) my own body, (2) the composition of my army.
54 pitch elevation.
56 riddling merchant purveyor of riddles (as used in spells and divinations); for this contemptuous use of 'merchant' compare *Rom.* 2.4.145.
56 for the nonce as occasion requires.

58 contrarieties discrepancies, contradictions (*OED* Contrariety 2b).
59 presently immediately.
59 SD.1 Winds Sounds; 'typical Robin Hood' (Cairncross).
59 SD.1 a peal of ordnance Cannon were commonly used in the public playhouses for sound effects (Hattaway, pp. 31–2); possibly the stage doors were 'blown in'.
64 subverts destroys.
66 abuse imposture, deceit.

I find thou art no less than fame hath bruited,
And more than may be gathered by thy shape.
Let my presumption not provoke thy wrath,
For I am sorry that with reverence   70
I did not entertain thee as thou art.

TALBOT Be not dismayed, fair lady, nor misconster
The mind of Talbot as you did mistake
The outward composition of his body.
What you have done hath not offended me,   75
Nor other satisfaction do I crave
But only, with your patience, that we may
Taste of your wine and see what cates you have,
For soldiers' stomachs always serve them well.

COUNTESS With all my heart, and think me honourèd   80
To feast so great a warrior in my house.

Exeunt

[2.4] *Enter* RICHARD PLANTAGENET, WARWICK, SOMERSET, POLE
[EARL OF SUFFOLK, VERNON *and a* LAWYER]

PLANTAGENET Great lords and gentlemen, what means this silence?
Dare no man answer in a case of truth?

Act 2, Scene 4   2.4] *Capell subst.; not in* F   0 SD.1 POLE] *Eds.; Poole, and others* F   0 SD.2 EARL OF
SUFFOLK] *Riverside; not in* F   0 SD.2 VERNON] *Capell; not in* F   0 SD.2 *and a* LAWYER] *Eds., conj. Vaughan; not in*
F   1 SH PLANTAGENET] *Rowe, throughout; Yorke* F   1] *Pope; Great...Gentlemen, / What...silence?* F

67 fame hath bruited rumour has noised
abroad.
68 by from.
71 entertain receive (*OED* sv *v* 12).
71 as thou art great man that you are.
72 misconster misconstrue.
73 mistake (1) wrongly apprehend, (2) mis-
understand.
74 composition constitution.
77 patience permission.
78 cates delicacies.
79 stomachs (1) (sexual) appetites, (2)
courage.

Act 2, Scene 4
2.4 The scene is fictitious. Shakespeare
imagines the Wars of the Roses to have broken
out among young noblemen studying law in the
Temple. Plantagenet's quarrel with John Beaufort, Earl of Somerset, and his brother Edmund

(seemingly the character in this scene – see 76 n.)
had extended over many years (see 2.5.45–50,
111–14, which sets the quarrel with John on
'January 19, 1425, the historic date of Mortimer's
death' (Boswell-Stone, p. 218)). The enmity
between Richard Plantagenet and Edmund
Beaufort is described in Holinshed, p. 185, and
Hall, p. 179.

0 SD PLANTAGENET The badge (a broom
plant, *planta genista*) adopted as a symbol of
humility by Geoffrey of Anjou, father of Henry II
and founder of the dynasty that ruled England
until the succession of the Tudors in 1485.

2 case of truth A legal matter to be resolved
by appeal to the facts of the case, as opposed to
a case of conscience (*OED* Case *sb*¹ 7) in which
ethical considerations arise. The details of the
case are undefined, perhaps in deference to the
censorship, but obviously concern a claim by
Plantagenet to the crown.

SUFFOLK Within the Temple hall we were too loud;
     The garden here is more convenient.

PLANTAGENET Then say at once if I maintained the truth –   5
     Or else was wrangling Somerset in th'error?

SUFFOLK Faith, I have been a truant in the law
     And never yet could frame my will to it,
     And therefore frame the law unto my will.

SOMERSET Judge you, my Lord of Warwick, then between us.   10

WARWICK Between two hawks, which flies the higher pitch,
     Between two dogs, which hath the deeper mouth,
     Between two blades, which bears the better temper,
     Between two horses, which doth bear him best,
     Between two girls, which hath the merriest eye,   15
     I have perhaps some shallow spirit of judgement;
     But in these nice sharp quillets of the law,
     Good faith, I am no wiser than a daw.

PLANTAGENET Tut, tut, here is a mannerly forbearance:
     The truth appears so naked on my side   20
     That any purblind eye may find it out.

SOMERSET And on my side it is so well apparelled,
     So clear, so shining, and so evident,
     That it will glimmer through a blind man's eye.

PLANTAGENET Since you are tongue-tied and so loath to speak,   25
     In dumb significants proclaim your thoughts:
     Let him that is a true-born gentleman

---

6 error] F; right *conj. Johnson*   13 bears] F; shows *conj. this edn;* hath *conj. anon in Cam.*

---

3 Temple hall Hall of the (Inner or Middle) Temple in Fleet Street, one of the London 'houses of court' or legal societies which admit lawyers to practise at the bar; so called because the buildings had originally belonged to the Knights Templars.

3 were should have been.

4 garden The scene demands a rose brier; see 30 n.

4 convenient suitable, appropriate (*OED* sv *adj* 4).

6 Unless Johnson's conjecture of 'right' for 'error' is accepted, the line should be delivered in a jocular manner.

6 else if that is not believed (*OED* Else *adv* 4c).

6 wrangling (1) quarrelsome, (2) disputing (an academic point).

7 truant idler.

9 frame adapt.

11 pitch The highest point of a flight.

12 deeper mouth more resonant bark.

13 bears The compositor may well have caught this word from the line below. I conjecture 'shows' as a likely reading.

14 bear him carry himself.

17 nice fine.

17 quillets subtleties.

18 daw jackdaw; proverbial for its stupidity (Tilley D50).

20 The...naked Proverbial (Tilley T589).

21 purblind short-sighted (*OED* sv *adj* 2b).

22 apparelled ordered, set out; answers 'naked' at 20.

24 glimmer...eye Compare the proverb 'A blind man might see that' (Dent M82).

25 tongue-tied Tilley T416.

26 dumb significants silent gestures, dumb show.

27 true-born The first use recorded in *OED*.

And stands upon the honour of his birth,
If he suppose that I have pleaded truth,
From off this brier pluck a white rose with me.   30
SOMERSET Let him that is no coward nor no flatterer,
But dare maintain the party of the truth,
Pluck a red rose from off this thorn with me.
WARWICK I love no colours; and without all colour
Of base insinuating flattery   35
I pluck this white rose with Plantagenet.
SUFFOLK I pluck this red rose with young Somerset,
And say withal I think he held the right.
VERNON Stay, lords and gentlemen, and pluck no more
Till you conclude that he upon whose side   40
The fewest roses are cropped from the tree
Shall yield the other in the right opinion.
SOMERSET Good Master Vernon, it is well objected:
If I have fewest, I subscribe in silence.
PLANTAGENET And I.   45
VERNON Then for the truth and plainness of the case,
I pluck this pale and maiden blossom here,
Giving my verdict on the white rose side.
SOMERSET Prick not your finger as you pluck it off,
Lest, bleeding, you do paint the white rose red   50

41] F; The fewest roses from the tree are cropp'd *Cairncross*

28 **stands upon** insists upon.

29 **suppose** is of the opinion, concludes (*OED* sv *v* 1).

29 **pleaded truth** put the case for truth according to legal procedures.

30 The plucking of the rose, like Eve's plucking of the apple in Eden, precipitates a kind of fall; compare *FQ*, I, xi, 46.

30 **brier** Trees, presumably artificial, were common properties on the Elizabethan stage (Hattaway, pp. 31, 37).

30 **white rose** This had been the badge of Roger, Earl of March, father of the Edmund Mortimer who was Richard's uncle.

32 **party** side (in an argument) (*OED* sv *sb* 5).

33 **red rose** 'Camden says the red rose was the accepted badge of Edmund Plantagenet, who was the second son of Henry III, and of the first Duke of Lancaster, surnamed Crouchback' (Brewer, 'rose').

34 **colours** (1) hues, (2) military ensigns, (3) 'probable but really false pleas in law' (*OED* Colour *sb* 12c).

34 **colour** semblance (*OED* sv *sb* 11).

35 **insinuating** ingratiating.

38 **held the right** (1) took the correct line, (2) plucked the right rose.

40–4 The passage is studded with technical legal terms.

40 **conclude** come to a legal decision (*OED* sv *v* 13).

42 **yield** concede in law (*OED* sv *v* 17).

42 **opinion** professional judgement (*OED* sv *sb* 4).

43 **well objected** 'Properly thrown in our way, justly proposed' (Johnson).

44 **subscribe** concur (literally by adding a signature).

47 **maiden** (1) flawless, (2) uncropped (although *OED* records this use only from 1649).

48 **verdict** opinion (*OED* sv *sb* 3).

And fall on my side so against your will.

VERNON If I, my lord, for my opinion bleed,
Opinion shall be surgeon to my hurt
And keep me on the side where still I am.

SOMERSET Well, well, come on: who else?   55

LAWYER Unless my study and my books be false,
The argument you held was wrong in law;
In sign whereof I pluck a white rose too.

PLANTAGENET Now, Somerset, where is your argument?

SOMERSET Here in my scabbard, meditating that   60
Shall dye your white rose in a bloody red.

PLANTAGENET Meantime your cheeks do counterfeit our roses,
For pale they look with fear, as witnessing
The truth on our side.

SOMERSET   No, Plantagenet,
'Tis not for fear, but anger – that thy cheeks   65
Blush for pure shame to counterfeit our roses,
And yet thy tongue will not confess thy error.

PLANTAGENET Hath not thy rose a canker, Somerset?

SOMERSET Hath not thy rose a thorn, Plantagenet?

PLANTAGENET Ay, sharp and piercing, to maintain his truth,   70
Whiles thy consuming canker eats his falsehood.

SOMERSET .Well, I'll find friends to wear my bleeding roses,
That shall maintain what I have said is true,
Where false Plantagenet dare not be seen.

PLANTAGENET Now, by this maiden blossom in my hand,   75
I scorn thee and thy fashion, peevish boy.

---

57 law] *This edn, conj. anon in Cam.;* you F   76 fashion] F; passion *Pope;* faction *Theobald*

51 fall on 'desert to...Prob[ably] a jesting perversion of "fall off" = revolt' (Wilson).

52 for...bleed suffer for my judgement or allegiance.

53 Opinion My reputation (*OED* sv *sb* 6), punning on 42.

54 still always.

55 well, well 'Well, well is a word of malice' (Dent w369).

57 *wrong in law 'as opposed to wrong in fact' (Cairncross); F's 'in you' was probably due to the earlier 'you' in the line.

60 meditating that reflecting upon what; for this transitive use of the verb see *OED* Meditate *v* 1, 2.

62 counterfeit imitate.

68 canker Larva that feeds on rosebuds.

69 Hath...thorn Compare the proverb 'No rose without a thorn' (Tilley R182).

70, 71 his its.

76 fashion ways, demeanour (*OED* sv *sb* 5, 6) or possibly Plantagenet gestures scornfully to the red rose placed behind Somerset's ear (for that fashion see *John* 1.1.142).

76 peevish foolish.

76 boy A term of abuse; however, 'John Beaufort, then Earl of Somerset, was older than Richard [Plantagenet], who calls him "Boy"... the former being at that time nearly twenty-one, while the latter was about thirteen. The subsequent action, however, shows that "Somerset" is John's brother, Edmund Beaufort, whom Richard, in 1452, openly accused of treason [Holinshed, p. 230; Hall, p. 226; *2H6* 5.2]' (Boswell-Stone, p. 218).

SUFFOLK Turn not thy scorns this way, Plantagenet.

PLANTAGENET Proud Pole, I will, and scorn both him and thee.

SUFFOLK I'll turn my part thereof into thy throat.

SOMERSET Away, away, good William de la Pole!   80
We grace the yeoman by conversing with him.

WARWICK Now, by God's will, thou wrong'st him, Somerset.
His grandfather was Lionel, Duke of Clarence,
Third son to the third Edward, King of England:
Spring crestless yeomen from so deep a root?   85

PLANTAGENET He bears him on the place's privilege,
Or durst not for his craven heart say thus.

SOMERSET By him that made me, I'll maintain my words
On any plot of ground in Christendom.
Was not thy father, Richard, Earl of Cambridge,   90
For treason executed in our late king's days?
And, by his treason, stand'st not thou attainted,
Corrupted, and exempt from ancient gentry?
His trespass yet lives guilty in thy blood,
And till thou be restored thou art a yeoman.   95

PLANTAGENET My father was attachèd, not attainted,
Condemned to die for treason, but no traitor;
And that I'll prove on better men than Somerset,

91 executed] F; headed *Pope*

77 **scorns** taunts.

78 **Pole** The family name of the Dukes of Suffolk.

79 **turn** fling back.

81 **grace** (1) treat courteously, (2) ennoble (by according him the ducal title of 'your grace').

81 **yeoman** Under the rank of gentleman; a freeholder of land to the value of forty shillings. The titles of Plantagenet's father and his heirs were forfeited to the crown when Henry V executed him for treason.

83 **grandfather** ancestor (*OED* sv *sb* 3). Clarence was his great-great-grandfather on his mother's side.

85 **crestless** (1) not having the right to a heraldic crest, (2) lacking the top of his family tree (punning on 'root'), (3) cowardly (like a 'crest-fallen' cock).

86 He behaves thus only because of the sanctuary the Temple affords him.

86 **privilege** sanctuary; the protection from arrest granted to certain places (*OED* Privilege *sb* 7); see 1.3.46 and Williams, pp. 227–8. The Temple had been founded as a religious house.

87 **craven** Said of a cock that is 'not game' (*OED* sv *adj* 2b), a response to 'crest-fallen' at 85; compare *Shr.* 2.1.225–7.

90 **Richard** Both father and son bore this name.

91 **late king's days** The reign of Henry V (see *H5* 2.2.66–181).

92 **attainted** condemned (*OED* Attaint *v* 6); Shakespeare evokes the false etymology that links the word to 'tainted', infected in the blood.

93 **Corrupted** Legally deprived of all rights of rank and title (by 'corruption of blood' – see *OED* Corruption 2b).

93 **exempt** excluded.

93 **gentry** rank of gentleman.

95 **restored** given back your titles and lands (see 81 n,).

96 Plantagenet implies that his father was illegally executed in that he was merely divested of title and not indicted by a bill of attainder; see Williams, p. 378.

96 **attachèd** arrested.

98 **prove** By challenging to a duel.

Were growing time once ripened to my will.
For your partaker Pole and you yourself,   100
I'll note you in my book of memory
To scourge you for this apprehension:
Look to it well, and say you are well warned.

SOMERSET Ah, thou shalt find us ready for thee still;
And know us by these colours for thy foes,   105
For these my friends in spite of thee shall wear.

PLANTAGENET And, by my soul, this pale and angry rose,
As cognisance of my blood-drinking hate,
Will I for ever, and my faction, wear
Until it wither with me to my grave,   110
Or flourish to the height of my degree.

SUFFOLK Go forward, and be choked with thy ambition!
And so farewell, until I meet thee next.   *Exit*

SOMERSET Have with thee, Pole. Farewell, ambitious Richard.

                                                        Exit

PLANTAGENET How I am braved and must perforce endure it!   115

WARWICK This blot that they object against your house
Shall be wiped out in the next parliament,
Called for the truce of Winchester and Gloucester;
And if thou be not then created York,
I will not live to be accounted Warwick.   120
Meantime, in signal of my love to thee,
Against proud Somerset and William Pole
Will I upon thy party wear this rose.
And here I prophesy: this brawl today,
Grown to this faction in the Temple garden,   125

---

102 this apprehension] F; misapprehension *conj. Vaughan;* this reprehension *Theobald*   117 wiped] F2; whipt F

99 If ever I have the opportunity.

100 **partaker** part-taker, ally.

101 **note** (1) list, (2) brand, stigmatise (*OED* Note *v*² 7b, c).

102 **apprehension** (mis)conception, opinion.

104 **still** always.

108 **cognisance** token.

108 **blood-drinking** Alluding to the belief that the burning of choler could be quelled only with blood; compare *John* 3.1.341–2 and *3H6* 2.1.79–80.

111 **flourish** (1) shoot forth (*OED* sv *v* 1), (2) prosper (*OED* sv *v* 2).

111 **degree** rank.

114 **Have with thee** I'll go along with you (Dent HH10).

115 **braved** scorned.

116 **object** bring forward.

117 *****wiped out** Extends the 'blot' metaphor, but F's 'Whipt [whipped] out' is just possible, meaning 'quickly disposed of' (for the usage, compare *WT* 4.3.89, 92).

121 **in signal** as a token.

123 **party** side.

124 **brawl** quarrel.

125 **faction** factious quarrel (*OED* sv *sb* 4b).

Shall send, between the red rose and the white,
A thousand souls to death and deadly night.
PLANTAGENET Good Master Vernon, I am bound to you,
That you on my behalf would pluck a flower.
VERNON In your behalf still will I wear the same.   130
LAWYER And so will I.
PLANTAGENET   Thanks, gentle sir.
Come, let us four to dinner. I dare say
This quarrel will drink blood another day.

Exeunt

[2.5] *Enter* MORTIMER, *brought in a chair, and* GAOLERS

MORTIMER Kind keepers of my weak decaying age,
Let dying Mortimer here rest himself.
Even like a man new halèd from the rack,
So fare my limbs with long imprisonment;
And these grey locks, the pursuivants of death,   5

127 A] F; Ten *Collier MS.*   131] F2; And...I. / Thankes gentle. F; And...*gentlemen conj. anon in Cam.*; And...
gentles *Oxford*   Act 2, Scene 5   2.5] *Capell subst.; not in* F   3 rack] *Pope;* Wrack F

127 **deadly** deathly.
*131 F2's regularisation is the simplest of those proposed (see collation).
132 **four to dinner** Alludes to the custom of dining in 'messes' of four; compare *LLL* 4.3.203.

Act 2, Scene 5
*2.5 Shakespeare invented the episode of Plantagenet's visit to the imprisoned Mortimer. Holinshed writes (p. 144; Hall, p. 128) that in 1425 'Edmund Mortimer, the last Earl of March of that name (which long time had been restrained from his liberty, and finally waxed lame) deceased without issue, whose inheritance descended to the lord Richard Plantagenet, son and heir to Richard Earl of Cambridge, beheaded...at the town of Southampton.' Shakespeare follows the chroniclers who attribute to the historical Edmund Mortimer – who was declared heir presumptive to Richard II in 1398, who remained free during Henry V's reign (compare 23–5) and who, under Henry VI, was 'honourably exiled as Lord-Lieutenant of Ireland from 1423 to 1425 when he died' (Bullough, III, 28 n.) – the misfortunes of his cousin Sir John

Mortimer who lay in irons in the Tower until he was beheaded in 1424 (Holinshed, p. 144; Hall, p. 128; Boswell-Stone, pp. 219–20 n.). Compare *2H6* 2.2.41–2, where Shakespeare assumes that Mortimer's captivity under Glendower lasted until his death. The fusion of the two characters suits Shakespeare's desire to portray Mortimer as one of the decaying heroes from the reign of Henry V. 74–92 derive from York's oration to the parliament of 1460 (Holinshed, pp. 262–3; Hall, pp. 245–8). Sanders also notes 'extra material found in Stowe's *Chronicles of England*, 1580, concerning the agreements drawn up between Henry and the Duke of York'.
1 **keepers** (1) goalers, (2) nurses (*OED* Keeper 1e).
3 ***rack** *OED* claims that F's 'Wrack' is an erroneous form of 'rack' (an instrument of torture); Shakespeare may, however, have meant 'shipwreck' ('wrack').
5 **grey...death** Compare the proverb 'Grey hairs are death's blossoms' (Tilley H31).
5 **pursuivants** royal messengers (with power to serve summonses and execute arrest warrants).

Nestor-like agèd in an age of care,
Argue the end of Edmund Mortimer.
These eyes, like lamps whose wasting oil is spent,
Wax dim, as drawing to their exigent;
Weak shoulders, overborne with burdening grief,   10
And pitchless arms, like to a withered vine
That droops his sapless branches to the ground.
Yet are these feet, whose strengthless stay is numb
(Unable to support this lump of clay),
Swift-wingèd with desire to get a grave –   15
As witting I no other comfort have.
But tell me, keeper, will my nephew come?

1 KEEPER Richard Plantagenet, my lord, will come:
We sent unto the Temple, unto his chamber,
And answer was returned that he will come.   20

MORTIMER Enough; my soul shall then be satisfied.
Poor gentleman! His wrong doth equal mine.
Since Henry Monmouth first began to reign,
Before whose glory I was great in arms,
This loathsome sequestration have I had;   25
And even since then hath Richard been obscured,
Deprived of honour and inheritance.
But now the arbitrator of despairs,
Just Death, kind umpire of men's miseries,

6–7] *As* F; *7 precedes 6 in Oxford*   6 an age] F; *a cage Collier MS.*   11 like to] F; *are like conj. Cairncross*   18, 33
SH 1 KEEPER] *Capell; Keeper.* F   19 unto his] F; *his* F2; *to his Rowe*

6–7 Oxford's reversal of these lines is attractive as 'Mortimer is more plausibly compared to
Nestor than are his "Locks" or "death"' (Wells
and Taylor, *Textual Companion*, p. 222).
6 Nestor The oldest of the Greek leaders at
Troy and a type of old age.
7 Argue Evince.
8–9 Compare 1 Sam. 3.2: 'Eli...his eyes
began to wax dim that he could not see. And yea
the light of God went out...' The gloss in the
Geneva Bible explains the last phrase as 'the
lamps which burnt in the night'.
8 like...spent Compare the proverb 'There
is no oil left in the lamp' (Tilley O29).
9 exigent end, extremity.
10–12 The lack of a principal verb in this
sentence suggests that a line has been lost.
11 pithless without marrow, weak.

13 stay is numb support is paralysed.
15 Swift-wingèd Like Mercury.
16 As witting As if they knew.
17 nephew Richard's mother Anne was sister
to Edmund Mortimer, fifth Earl of March.
21 my...satisfied Compare Isa. 53.10–11:
'Yet the Lord would break him, and make him
subject to infirmities...He shall see the travail of
his soul and shall be satisfied.' The prophet
Mortimer quotes Isaiah again at 103.
22 His wrong The wrong he has suffered.
23 Henry Monmouth Henry V.
25 sequestration (1) imprisonment, (2) loss of
property.
29 umpire In law, one called in when arbitrators
(see 28) cannot agree (*OED* sv *sb* 2); 'he that
terminates or concludes misery. The expression
is harsh and forced' (Johnson).

With sweet enlargement doth dismiss me hence.   30
I would his troubles likewise were expired,
That so he might recover what was lost.

Enter RICHARD [PLANTAGENET]

1 KEEPER My lord, your loving nephew now is come.
MORTIMER Richard Plantagenet, my friend, is he come?
PLANTAGENET Ay, noble uncle, thus ignobly used;   35
    Your nephew, late-despisèd Richard, comes.
MORTIMER Direct mine arms I may embrace his neck
    And in his bosom spend my latter gasp.
    O, tell me when my lips do touch his cheeks,
    That I may kindly give one fainting kiss.   40
             [Embraces him]
    And now declare, sweet stem from York's great stock,
    Why didst thou say of late thou wert despised?
PLANTAGENET First, lean thine agèd back against mine arm,
    And in that ease I'll tell thee my disease.
    This day, in argument upon a case,   45
    Some words there grew 'twixt Somerset and me:
    Among which terms he used his lavish tongue
    And did upbraid me with my father's death,
    Which obloquy set bars before my tongue,
    Else with the like I had requited him.   50
    Therefore, good uncle, for my father's sake,
    In honour of a true Plantagenet,
    And for alliance' sake, declare the cause
    My father, Earl of Cambridge, lost his head.
MORTIMER That cause, fair nephew, that imprisoned me   55
    And hath detained me all my flow'ring youth
    Within a loathsome dungeon, there to pine,

34 is he] F; is *Cairncross*   35 SH PLANTAGENET] *Rowe, throughout; Rich.* F   36 late-despisèd] *Capell;* late despised F   40 SD] *This edn; not in* F

30 enlargement release.
31 his Richard's.
31 expired ended (like my life).
35 ignobly contrary to your noble rank.
36 *late-despisèd lately treated with contempt.
38 latter final (*OED* sv *adj* 3).
40 kindly (1) lovingly, (2) to a kinsman.
41 sweet...stock Plantagenet was the nephew of Aumerle in *R2*, who appears later as York in *H5*.

44 disease 'uneasiness, discontent' (Johnson).
45 case See 2.4.2 n.
46 words high words, altercations (*OED* Word *sb* 5).
47 lavish tongue unrestrained or licentious language.
49 obloquy reproach, disgrace.
53 alliance' kinship's (*OED* sv *sb* 1).
53 declare explain (*OED* sv *v* 1).

Was cursèd instrument of his decease.
PLANTAGENET Discover more at large what cause that was,
 For I am ignorant and cannot guess.   60
MORTIMER I will, if that my fading breath permit
 And death approach not ere my tale be done.
 Henry the Fourth, grandfather to this king,
 Deposed his nephew Richard, Edward's son,
 The first-begotten and the lawful heir   65
 Of Edward king, the third of that descent;
 During whose reign the Percys of the north,
 Finding his usurpation most unjust,
 Endeavoured my advancement to the throne.
 The reason moved these warlike lords to this   70
 Was for that (young Richard thus removed,
 Leaving no heir begotten of his body)
 I was the next by birth and parentage:
 For by my mother I derivèd am
 From Lionel, Duke of Clarence, third son   75
 To King Edward the Third; whereas the king
 From John of Gaunt doth bring his pedigree,
 Being but fourth of that heroic line.
 But mark: as in this haughty great attempt
 They labourèd to plant the rightful heir,   80
 I lost my liberty, and they their lives.

---

71 young] F; *young King* F2 75 third] F; *the third* F2 76 To...Third] F; *Unto the third King Edward conj.*
Cairncross 76 the king] *Oxford; he* F; *Bolingbroke Pope*

59 **Discover...large** Reveal more fully.

64 **nephew** Richard II was Henry's cousin; the words were frequently interchanged.

64 **Edward's** The Black Prince's (eldest son of Edward III).

67 **whose** Henry IV's.

67 **Percys** The Earl of Northumberland and Hotspur his son.

69 **advancement** elevation (*OED* sv 1).

70–1 **reason...that** For the omitted and then inserted 'that' see Abbott 285 ('for that' = because).

71 **young** Richard was in fact 33 when he was murdered. It does not seem necessary to adopt F2's 'young King' to correct the metre here.

74 **mother** female forebear (*OED* sv *sb* 1e); compare 2.4.83 n. Mortimer's grandmother

Philippa was daughter of the Duke of Clarence. Previous editors, taking 'mother' in the modern sense, argued that Shakespeare here confused Edmund, fifth Earl of March (1391–1425), with his uncle, Sir Edmund Mortimer (1376–?1409).

74 **derivèd** descended.

75 **Lionel...Clarence** 1338–68, third son of Edward III.

76–8 **whereas...line** Henry IV (Bullingbrook) was son of John of Gaunt, fourth son of Edward III.

76 ***the king** This emendation (of F's 'he') is necessary to make the passage both metrical and comprehensible. Perhaps the MS. read 'the k.' of which, if the 'k' were obscure, 'he' is a possible misreading.

79 **haughty** high, noble (*OED* sv *adj* 3).

Long after this, when Henry the Fifth
(Succeeding his father Bullingbrook) did reign,
Thy father, Earl of Cambridge then, derived
From famous Edmund Langley, Duke of York,   85
Marrying my sister, that thy mother was,
Again, in pity of my hard distress,
Levied an army, weening to redeem
And have installed me in the diadem.
But, as the rest, so fell that noble earl   90
And was beheaded. Thus the Mortimers,
In whom the title rested, were suppressed.
PLANTAGENET Of which, my lord, your honour is the last.
MORTIMER True; and thou seest that I no issue have,
And that my fainting words do warrant death.   95
Thou art my heir; the rest I wish thee gather;
But yet be wary in thy studious care.
PLANTAGENET Thy grave admonishments prevail with me.
But yet methinks my father's execution
Was nothing less than bloody tyranny.   100
MORTIMER With silence, nephew, be thou politic;
Strong-fixèd is the house of Lancaster,
And like a mountain, not to be removed.
But now thy uncle is removing hence,
As princes do their courts when they are cloyed   105
With long continuance in a settled place.
PLANTAGENET O uncle, would some part of my young years

---

82 Henry] F; Henry named *conj. Seymour in Cam.*   84 Cambridge then,] *Cairncross;* Cambridge, then F   102
Strong-fixed] *Theobald subst.;* Strong fixed F

82 Henry Here trisyllabic (?) (Cercignani, p. 358).

84–5 Plantagenet's father, Richard, Earl of Cambridge (died 1415), son of Edward III's fifth son, married Anne Mortimer.

88–91 The Earl of Cambridge's treason is exposed in *H5* 2.2.

88 Levied an army This is not mentioned in *H5* 2.2, but Holinshed (not Hall) notes that Cambridge and Gray 'had conspired together with a power of men to them associate' (p. 71).

88 weening intending.

88 redeem reclaim (the diadem, 89).

89 diadem crown, sovereignty (*OED* sv *sb* 2).

95 warrant signify, promise (*OED* sv *v* 4e).

96 gather (1) infer, (2) regain (his inheritance).

97 studious diligent.

98 grave (1) solemn, (2) delivered on the point of death (compare *Rom.* 3.1.98).

98 admonishments warnings.

100 tyranny outrage, villainy (*OED* sv *sb* 3b).

101 politic prudent.

103 Compare Ps. 125.1: 'as mount Zion, which can not be removed'; and Isa. 54.10; see also Dent M1214.1.

104 removing departing (= dying).

Might but redeem the passage of your age.

MORTIMER Thou dost then wrong me, as that slaughterer doth
Which giveth many wounds when one will kill.   110
Mourn not, except thou sorrow for my good;
Only give order for my funeral.
And so farewell; and fair be all thy hopes,
And prosperous be thy life in peace and war. *Dies*

PLANTAGENET And peace, no war, befall thy parting soul!   115
In prison hast thou spent a pilgrimage,
And like a hermit overpassed thy days.
Well, I will lock his counsel in my breast,
And what I do imagine, let that rest.
Keepers, convey him hence; and I myself   120
Will see his burial better than his life.
       Exeunt [Gaolers, bearing out the body of Mortimer]
Here dies the dusky torch of Mortimer,
Choked with ambition of the meaner sort.
And for those wrongs, those bitter injuries,
Which Somerset hath offered to my house,   125
I doubt not but with honour to redress.
And therefore haste I to the parliament,
Either to be restorèd to my blood,
Or make mine ill th'advantage of my good.   *Exit*

---

108 passage] F; passing *Cairncross*   113 be all] F; befall *Theobald*   121 SD] *Capell subst.; Exit.* F   122 dies] F;
lies *conj. Warburton*   129 mine ill] *Cairncross;* my will F; my ill *Theobald*

108 redeem be exchanged for, buy back (*OED* sv *v* 7b).

111 except unless.

112 give order make arrangements for (*OED* Order *sb* 22).

116 pilgrimage Gen. 47.9 is only the first of a number of occurrences of this metaphor in the Bible; compare Dent L249.

117 overpassed spent (literally 'travelled over' – as on the pilgrimage of 116).

119 imagine A play on the phrase 'to imagine (= plot) the death of' (*OED* Imagine *v* 3), a capital offence of treason (see Williams, p. 275).

121 better than his life more fitting than the manner in which he spent his days.

122 dusky dim (perhaps referring also to the near blindness of Mortimer).

123 the meaner sort people of less noble birth (referring to the Lancastrians); the usual meaning is 'people of ignoble birth'.

124 injuries (1) affronts, (2) wounds.

126 redress cure (*OED* sv *v*¹ 10b).

128 blood inherited rank (*OED* sv *sb* 13).

129 *mine ill F's 'my will' is probably due to a misreading of the last two letters of 'mine' as 'w'. If the emendation is not accepted, the line would mean 'or make my ambition a way to serve my advantage' rather than 'or turn the wrongs offered me to my advantage'.

3.1 *Flourish. Enter* KING [HENRY], EXETER, GLOUCESTER, WIN-
CHESTER, WARWICK, SOMERSET, SUFFOLK, RICHARD PLANTA-
GENET [*and others*]. *Gloucester offers to put up a bill; Winchester snatches
it, tears it*

WINCHESTER Com'st thou with deep premeditated lines,
     With written pamphlets studiously devised?
     Humphrey of Gloucester, if thou canst accuse
     Or aught intend'st to lay unto my charge,
     Do it without invention, suddenly;   5
     As I with sudden and extemporal speech
     Purpose to answer what thou canst object.
GLOUCESTER Presumptuous priest, this place commands my
        patience,
     Or thou shouldst find thou hast dishonoured me.
     Think not, although in writing I preferred   10
     The manner of thy vile outrageous crimes,
     That therefore I have forged, or am not able
     Verbatim to rehearse the method of my pen.
     No, prelate: such is thy audacious wickedness,
     Thy lewd, pestiferous, and dissentious pranks,   15
     As very infants prattle of thy pride.
     Thou art a most pernicious usurer,

Act 3, Scene 1   3.1] *Capell subst.; Actus Tertius. Scena Prima.* F   0 SD.3 *and others*] *Malone; not in* F   1 deep
premeditated] F; deep-premeditated *Dyce*

Act 3, Scene 1
   3.1 The quarrel between Gloucester and Winchester is continued from 1.3. The details are
drawn from Holinshed, p. 147 (Hall, p. 131).
The invective against Winchester (14–18) may
have been derived from the chroniclers' character
sketch which appears after they have told of his
death (Holinshed, p. 212; Hall, p. 240). The
details of the uprising (76–85) derive from
Fabyan, p. 596. Details of the reconciliation
appear in Holinshed, p. 154 (Hall, p. 138).
   0 SD *offers...bill* attempts to present a list of
accusations.
   1 lines written statements (*OED* Line *sb*² 23a).
   5 invention prolonged search for subject
matter.
   5 suddenly without premeditation.
   7 object lay to my charge (*OED* sv *v* 5).
   8 this place i.e. the parliament (which was
held at Leicester; Holinshed, p. 146; Hall, p.
130).

   10 preferred put forward.
   12 forged fabricated lies.
   13 Verbatim Verbally (?) (*OED* sv *adv* 3).
   13 rehearse...pen repeat the gist of what I
have written. ('Method' = a summary (*OED* sv *sb*
6c)).
   15 lewd wicked.
   15 pestiferous deadly.
   15 pranks malicious acts (*OED* Prank *sb*² a).
   16 As very That even; for this use of 'as' see
Abbott 109.
   17 pernicious wicked (*OED* sv *adj*¹ b).
   17 usurer Winchester's wealth derived, according to the chroniclers, from the Bull Legatine
that he had purchased in Rome (Holinshed, p. 156;
Hall, p. 139), and also from his revenues from the
Southwark brothels (see 1.3.35 n.). Gloucester
may be using the trope of 'the two usuries' (*MM*
3.2.6), money-lending and copulation, which
bred interest and issue respectively.

Froward by nature, enemy to peace,
Lascivious, wanton, more than well beseems
A man of thy profession and degree.   20
And for thy treachery, what's more manifest,
In that thou laid'st a trap to take my life
As well at London Bridge as at the Tower?
Beside, I fear me, if thy thoughts were sifted,
The king, thy sovereign, is not quite exempt   25
From envious malice of thy swelling heart.

WINCHESTER Gloucester, I do defy thee. – Lords, vouchsafe
To give me hearing what I shall reply.
If I were covetous, ambitious, or perverse,
As he will have me, how am I so poor?   30
Or how haps it I seek not to advance
Or raise myself, but keep my wonted calling?
And for dissension, who preferreth peace
More than I do? – except I be provoked.
No, my good lords, it is not that offends,   35
It is not that that hath incensed the duke:
It is because no one should sway but he,
No one but he should be about the king,
And that engenders thunder in his breast
And makes him roar these accusations forth.   40
But he shall know I am as good –

GLOUCESTER   As good!
Thou bastard of my grandfather!

WINCHESTER Ay, lordly sir; for what are you, I pray,
But one imperious in another's throne?

GLOUCESTER Am I not Protector, saucy priest?   45

WINCHESTER And am not I a prelate of the church?

GLOUCESTER Yes, as an outlaw in a castle keeps,

---

29 If I were] F; If *Cairncross*   31 it] F; that *conj. Cairncross*   41 good –] F2; good. F

18 **Froward** Perverse, evilly disposed.
20 **thy profession** The qualities of a good bishop are set out in 1 Tim. 3.2–7.
25–6 **exempt...heart** Noble (p. 111) compares the line from the catechism 'to bear no malice nor hatred in my heart' (Book of Common Prayer).
26 **envious** evil, spiteful (*OED* sv *adj* 2).
26 **swelling** proud (*OED* sv *ppl adj* 7a).
28 **me** For the redundant object see Abbott 414.

35 **that** For the omitted 'which' see Abbott 244.
37 **sway** rule.
42 **bastard...grandfather** Winchester was an illegitimate son of John of Gaunt by his mistress Catherine Swynford, who later became his third wife.
44 **imperious** ruling (*OED* sv *adj* 2).
45 **saucy** insolent.
47 **keeps** lives (for his defence).

And useth it to patronage his theft.

WINCHESTER Unreverent Gloucester!

GLOUCESTER   Thou art reverend
Touching thy spiritual function, not thy life.   50

WINCHESTER Rome shall remedy this.

WARWICK   Roam thither then.
[*To Gloucester*] My lord, it were your duty to forbear.

SOMERSET Ay, see the bishop be not overborne.
[*To Winchester*] Methinks my lord should be religious,
And know the office that belongs to such.   55

WARWICK Methinks his lordship should be humbler:
It fitteth not a prelate so to plead.

SOMERSET Yes, when his holy state is touched so near.

WARWICK State holy or unhallowed, what of that?
Is not his grace Protector to the king?   60

PLANTAGENET [*Aside*] Plantagenet, I see, must hold his tongue,
Lest it be said, 'Speak, sirrah, when you should;
Must your bold verdict entertalk with lords?'
Else would I have a fling at Winchester.

KING HENRY Uncles of Gloucester and of Winchester,   65
The special watchmen of our English weal,

---

49 reverend] F3; reuerent F   51–2 WARWICK...forbear.] F; *Glou....then. / War....forbear. Hanmer and most eds.*   52 SD] *This edn; not in* F; *To Win. / Hanmer*   52–3] F; *Som....forbear. / War....over-borne Theobald*   53 see] F; *so Sisson* (*New Readings*)   54 SD] *This edn; not in* F   61 SD] *Hanmer; not in* F

48 **patronage** uphold, defend.

49 ***reverend** F's 'reverent' was not distinguished from 'reverend' in the period.

50 **Touching** With regard to.

51–5 F's reading can stand, without any need to redistribute speakers (see collation), if we assume that Warwick interrupts the altercation by putting Winchester down and then trying to calm Gloucester – even though he takes his side in the quarrel. Sisson, however, emends 'see' at 53 to 'so', and argues that 'Somerset...replies to Warwick, "You say it is his duty to forbear, but the danger is that he will be overborne, and so driven to appeal to Rome"' (*New Readings*, II, 70).

51 **Rome...Roam** The evidence for both these words being pronounced to rhyme with 'room' is reviewed by Cercignani, p. 185.

53 **Yes,** see that the man does not suppress his 'spiritual function' (50).

54 **religious** 'A person given up to a religious ...life, esp. in the Church of Rome' (*OED sv sb* 1)

55 **office** duty (Latin *officium*).

56 **humbler** Trisyllabic (Wilson).

57 **plead** wrangle (*OED sv v* 1b).

58 **holy...near** ecclesiastical office is affected so closely.

60 **his grace** the Duke of Gloucester.

63 **verdict** opinion (*OED sv sb* 3).

63 **entertalk** It is difficult to decide whether F offers one or two words here. Hart glosses as 'engage in conversation' and cites *Metamorphoses* II, 201: 'While Phoebus and his reckless son were entertalking this'. (Compare F's 'enterchanging' at *Rom.* 1.1.113.) The word, however, does not appear in *OED*. The context indicates that the meaning is 'interrupt'.

64 **fling at** verbal encounter with.

65 These are Henry's first words in the trilogy.

66 **watchmen** The word could designate angels (*OED sv sb* 3b); see Dan. 4.10 gloss (Geneva version).

66 **weal** well-being, state.

I would prevail, if prayers might prevail,
To join your hearts in love and amity.
O, what a scandal is it to our crown,
That two such noble peers as ye should jar!   70
Believe me, lords, my tender years can tell
Civil dissension is a viperous worm
That gnaws the bowels of the commonwealth.
A noise within: 'Down with the tawny-coats!'
What tumult's this?

WARWICK   An uproar, I dare warrant,
Begun through malice of the bishop's men.   75
A noise again: 'Stones! Stones!'

Enter MAYOR [OF LONDON, *attended*]

MAYOR O, my good lords, and virtuous Henry,
Pity the city of London, pity us!
The bishop and the Duke of Gloucester's men,
Forbidden late to carry any weapon,
Have filled their pockets full of pebble-stones   80
And, banding themselves in contrary parts,
Do pelt so fast at one another's pate
That many have their giddy brains knocked out.
Our windows are broke down in every street,
And we for fear compelled to shut our shops.   85

Enter [SERVINGMEN] *in skirmish with bloody pates*

KING HENRY We charge you, on allegiance to ourself,
To hold your slaught'ring hands and keep the peace.

---

74 What] *Capell; King.* What F   75 SD.2 OF LONDON, *attended*] *Capell; not in* F   82 pate] F; pates *Pope*   85 SD
SERVINGMEN] *Capell subst.; not in* F

67 prayers Not necessarily to God. The word can mean simply 'entreaties' (*OED* 4).

68 love and amity Such a phrase from the Book of Common Prayer comes naturally to Henry's lips.

70 jar be at odds.

71 my tender years Historically Henry was only five at the time of the quarrel and it was Bedford who 'rebuked' the lords (Holinshed, p. 146; Hall, p. 130).

72–3 Emrys Jones, *The Origins of Shakespeare*, 1977, p. 124, detects a reference to Lydgate's *The Serpent of Division* which was reprinted in 1590.

72 viperous worm malignant serpent.

73 gnaws...commonwealth The allusion is

to the myth that the female viper was killed by her young eating their way out at birth (see Pliny, *Nat. Hist.* x, 62, and compare *Per.* 1.1.64–5) rather than to Aesop's fable of the snake in the bosom.

74 uproar insurrection of the populace (*OED* sv *sb* 1).

78 bishop i.e. bishop's.

79 late recently.

81 contrary parts opposing gangs; 'contrary' is accented on the second syllable (Cercignani, p. 41).

83 giddy mad with anger (*OED* sv *adj* 1b).

84 windows shutters (a probable meaning; see *Shakespeare's England*, I, 14).

Pray, Uncle Gloucester, mitigate this strife.

1 SERVINGMAN Nay, if we be forbidden stones, we'll fall to it with
    our teeth.   90

2 SERVINGMAN Do what you dare, we are as resolute.

Skirmish again

GLOUCESTER You of my household, leave this peevish broil
    And set this unaccustomed fight aside.

3 SERVINGMAN My lord, we know your grace to be a man
    Just and upright and, for your royal birth,   95
    Inferior to none but to his majesty;
    And ere that we will suffer such a prince,
    So kind a father of the commonweal,
    To be disgracèd by an inkhorn mate,
    We and our wives and children all will fight   100
    And have our bodies slaughtered by thy foes.

1 SERVINGMAN Ay, and the very parings of our nails
    Shall pitch a field when we are dead.

Begin [the skirmish] again

GLOUCESTER   Stay, stay, I say!
    And if you love me, as you say you do,
    Let me persuade you to forbear a while.   105

KING HENRY O, how this discord doth afflict my soul.
    Can you, my Lord of Winchester, behold
    My sighs and tears, and will not once relent?
    Who should be pitiful, if you be not?
    Or who should study to prefer a peace   110
    If holy churchmen take delight in broils?

WARWICK Yield, my lord protector; yield, Winchester;
    Except you mean with obstinate repulse
    To stay your sovereign and destroy the realm.
    You see what mischief – and what murder too –   115
    Hath been enacted through your enmity;

---

101 have] F; leave *conj. Walker*

---

88 **mitigate** appease (*OED* sv *v* 1).

92 **peevish** senseless, perverse.

93 **unaccustomed** (1) strange, (2) contrary to order.

99 **disgracèd** Punning on the ducal title that occurs at 60 above.

99 **inkhorn mate** pedantic churl.

102 **parings...nails** Proverbially the last possession of a miser (Tilley P52).

103 **pitch a field** fortify a battlefield (as with stakes).

103 **Stay** Cease.

110 **prefer** promote (*OED* sv *v* 2).

113 **Except** Unless.

113 **repulse** refusal (*OED* sv *sb* 2).

115 **mischief** harm, evil (*OED* sv *sb* 2).

116 **enacted** recorded as in a chronicle for posterity (?) (*OED* Enact *v* 1).

Then be at peace, except ye thirst for blood.

WINCHESTER He shall submit, or I will never yield.

GLOUCESTER Compassion on the king commands me stoop,
Or I would see his heart out, ere the priest   120
Should ever get that privilege of me.

WARWICK Behold, my Lord of Winchester, the duke
Hath banished moody discontented fury,
As by his smoothèd brows it doth appear:
Why look you still so stern and tragical?   125

GLOUCESTER Here, Winchester, I offer thee my hand.

[Winchester turns away]

KING HENRY Fie, Uncle Beaufort! I have heard you preach
That malice was a great and grievous sin;
And will not you maintain the thing you teach,
But prove a chief offender in the same?   130

WARWICK Sweet king! The bishop hath a kindly gird.
For shame, my Lord of Winchester, relent!
What, shall a child instruct you what to do?

WINCHESTER Well, Duke of Gloucester, I will yield to thee;
Love for thy love and hand for hand I give.   135

GLOUCESTER *[Aside]* Ay, but I fear me, with a hollow heart. –
See here, my friends and loving countrymen,
This token serveth for a flag of truce
Betwixt ourselves and all our followers:
So help me God, as I dissemble not.   140

WINCHESTER So help me God! *[Aside]* As I intend it not.

KING HENRY O loving uncle, kind Duke of Gloucester,
How joyful am I made by this contract. –
Away, my masters, trouble us no more,
But join in friendship as your lords have done.   145

1 SERVINGMAN Content; I'll to the surgeon's.

2 SERVINGMAN   And so will I.

---

126 SD] *This edn; not in* F   136 SD] *Collier; not in* F   141 SD] *Pope (after* SH); *not in* F   142 uncle,] F; uncle,
most *conj. Steevens*   142 kind] F; gentle *Pope; and kind Collier*[2]   146] *Cam.;* 1. *Seru.*....Surgeons. / 2. *Seru.*....I F

120 **his** i.e. Winchester's.
121 **privilege of** advantage over (*OED* Privilege *sb* 2d).
123 **moody** arrogant, haughty (*OED* sv *adj* 2).
129 Compare Rom. 2.2.1: 'Thou therefore, which teachest another, teachest thou not thyself?'
131 **kindly gird** appropriate reprimand.
133 **a child** This may be evidence that the king's role was taken by a boy.

136 **hollow** insincere, false.
138 **This token** The handshake.
*141 SD The aside may be unnecessary if Winchester means that he does not intend to dissemble.
143 **contract** Stressed on the second syllable (Cercignani, p. 38).
144 **masters** An ironic and jocular form of address to the servingmen.

3 SERVINGMAN And I will see what physic the tavern affords.

Exeunt [Servingmen, Mayor and the rest]

WARWICK Accept this scroll, most gracious sovereign,
    Which in the right of Richard Plantagenet
    We do exhibit to your majesty.   150

GLOUCESTER Well urged, my Lord of Warwick; for, sweet prince,
    And if your grace mark every circumstance,
    You have great reason to do Richard right,
    Especially for those occasions
    At Eltham Place I told your majesty.   155

KING HENRY And those occasions, uncle, were of force. –
    Therefore, my loving lords, our pleasure is
    That Richard be restorèd to his blood.

WARWICK Let Richard be restorèd to his blood:
    So shall his father's wrongs be recompensed.   160

WINCHESTER As will the rest, so willeth Winchester.

KING HENRY If Richard will be true, not that alone
    But all the whole inheritance I give
    That doth belong unto the house of York,
    From whence you spring by lineal descent.   165

PLANTAGENET Thy humble servant vows obedience
    And humble service till the point of death.

KING HENRY Stoop then, and set your knee against my foot;

[Plantagenet kneels]

    And in reguerdon of that duty done,
    I girt thee with the valiant sword of York: 170
    Rise, Richard, like a true Plantagenet,
    And rise created princely Duke of York.

YORK And so thrive Richard as thy foes may fall!

---

147 SD] *Capell subst.; Exeunt* F   **162** that] F2; *that all* F   **167** humble] F; *faithful Pope*   **168** SD] *This edn; not in*
F   **173** SH YORK] *Eds.; Rich.* F

147 physic remedy.
148 scroll document (*OED* sv *sb* 2).
149 in the right in support of the claim.
150 exhibit submit for consideration; a legal
term (*OED* sv *v* 5a).
152 And if If (Abbott 103).
154 occasions reasons, details (of which);
pronounced with four syllables (Cercignani,
p. 308).
156 of force compelling.
158 restorèd...blood See 2.5.128 n.

162 true loyal.
162 *alone F's 'all alone' is either dittography
or anticipation of 'all' in the next line.
166 humble Pope's conjecture 'faithful' is
attractive as F's reading is probably an anticipation of 'humble' in the next line.
168 Stoop Kneel (*OED* sv *v*¹ 1).
169 reguerdon reward.
170 girt Old form of 'gird'.
172 princely of the royal blood.

And as my duty springs, [*Rising*] so perish they
That grudge one thought against your majesty!   175
ALL Welcome, high prince, the mighty Duke of York!
SOMERSET [*Aside*] Perish, base prince, ignoble Duke of York!
GLOUCESTER Now will it best avail your majesty
    To cross the seas and to be crowned in France.
    The presence of a king engenders love   180
    Amongst his subjects and his loyal friends,
    As it disanimates his enemies.
KING HENRY When Gloucester says the word, King Henry goes;
    For friendly counsel cuts off many foes.
GLOUCESTER Your ships already are in readiness.   185

          Sennet. Flourish. Exeunt [all but Exeter]

EXETER Ay, we may march in England, or in France,
    Not seeing what is likely to ensue.
    This late dissension grown betwixt the peers
    Burns under feignèd ashes of forged love,
    And will at last break out into a flame;   190
    As festered members rot but by degree
    Till bones and flesh and sinews fall away,
    So will this base and envious discord breed.
    And now I fear that fatal prophecy
    Which in the time of Henry named the Fifth   195
    Was in the mouth of every sucking babe:
    That Henry born at Monmouth should win all,

---

174 SD] *Capell; not in* F   177 SD] *Rowe; not in* F   185 SD *all but Exeter*] *Capell; Exeunt. Manet Exeter* F

174 springs grows (*OED* Spring *v*¹ 8).

175 grudge one thought entertain a single hostile thought.

177 ignoble low-born (*OED* sv *adj* 1).

179 Henry did not go to France until 1430, four years after the events dramatised here.

182 disanimates disheartens.

185 SD *Sennet* A processional march usually performed by a group of trumpets, sometimes by hautboys or cornets; the term calls 'attention to the presence of authority or the dignity of government' (Long, p. 10).

186–200 Compare Exeter's second prophecy at 4.1.182 ff.

189 Compare Horace, *Odes* II, 1, 'To Pollio Writing a History of the Civil Wars', 7–8: 'incedis per ignes / suppositos cineri doloso' (you are walking, as it were, over fires hidden beneath treacherous ashes) – see Baldwin, II, 534 – and compare the proverb 'Fire that's closest kept

burns most of all' (Tilley F265).

189 forged counterfeit.

191 members parts of the body.

191 by degree in stages.

193 'So will the malignity of this discord propagate itself and advance' (Johnson).

194 fatal prophecy What follows is based on the chroniclers' account of a premonition of Henry V. 'But when he heard reported the place of his nativity; were it that he was warned by some prophecy, or had some foreknowledge, or else judged himself of his son's fortune, he said unto the Lord Fitz Hugh his trusty chamberlain these words: "My lord, I Henry born at Monmouth, shall long reign and all lose"' (Holinshed, p. 129; Hall, p. 108).

196 Compare Ps. 8.2: 'Out of the mouth of babes and sucklings'; see also Matt. 21.16.

197 Henry...Monmouth Henry V.

And Henry born at Windsor should lose all:
Which is so plain that Exeter doth wish
His days may finish ere that hapless time.   *Exit*   200

3.2 *Enter* [LA] PUCELLE *disguised, with four* SOLDIERS *with sacks upon their backs*

PUCELLE These are the city gates, the gates of Rouen,
Through which our policy must make a breach.
Take heed, be wary how you place your words,
Talk like the vulgar sort of market-men
That come to gather money for their corn.   5
If we have entrance, as I hope we shall,
And that we find the slothful watch but weak,
I'll by a sign give notice to our friends,
That Charles the Dauphin may encounter them.
1 SOLDIER Our sacks shall be a mean to sack the city,   10
And we be lords and rulers over Rouen;
Therefore we'll knock.
                            Knock
WATCH [*Within*] *Qui là?*

198 should lose] F2; loose F   **Act 3, Scene 2**   3.2] *Capell subst.; Scæna Secunda.* F   **0** SD PUCELLE] *Rowe;*
Pucell F (*throughout the rest of the play, except* Ione *at* 5.2.0 SD)   **10** SH 1 SOLDIER] *Capell; Souldier.* F   **13**
SD] *Capell; not in* F   **13** *Qui là?*] *Sisson; Che la.* F; *Qui est là? / Malone*

198 **Henry...Windsor** Henry VI.
198 *should lose F2's emendation of F's
'loose' has been widely accepted on metrical and
rhetorical grounds.
199–200 In the chronicles Exeter dies after
the reconciliation of Gloucester and Winchester
(Holinshed, p. 155; Hall, p. 138); in Shakespeare
he survives until the end of the play.
200 **hapless** unfortunate, wretched.

Act 3, Scene 2
3.2 The fictitious loss and recovery of Rouen in
one day is based on the chroniclers' account of
the capture from the French of the Castle of
Cornill in 1441 by Sir Francis Arragonois
(Holinshed, p. 198; Hall, p. 197) with further
details from Fabyan's account of this incident (p.
615). Details from the account of the capture of
Le Mans (the burning cresset (25 SD)) in 1428
are also used (Holinshed, p. 159; Hall, p. 142).
Bedford's death (110–14) took place in 1435
(Holinshed, p. 184; Hall, p. 178). The anecdote

about Pendragon (95 ff.) probably comes from
Geoffrey of Monmouth. The scene seems
designed to contrast Pucelle with Talbot.
0 SD **four** This is the figure given by Fabyan
(p. 615); Hall and Holinshed say six.
1 **city gates** Conveniently signified by the
tiring-house entrance (Hattaway, p. 25).
2 **policy** stratagem.
3 **place** arrange (*OED* sv v 1b).
4–5 Fabyan notes that the men were 'speaking
French' and were come 'to sell' their 'fruits'
(p. 615).
4 **vulgar** ordinary.
4 **market-men** people come to market.
5 **corn** grain.
7 **that** if.
9 **encounter** assail.
13 **Qui là?* Who [goes] there? The omission
of *va* may be an attempt to create a pidgin French.
F's *Che* for *Qui* is paralleled in Nashe's 'Cheuela'
(1, 359).

PUCELLE *Paysans, la pauvre gent de France:*
      Poor market folks that come to sell their corn.   15
WATCH [*Opening the gate*] Enter; go in. The market bell is rung.
PUCELLE Now, Rouen, I'll shake thy bulwarks to the ground.

                                                                  Exeunt

      Enter CHARLES, BASTARD, ALENÇON[, REIGNIER *and Forces*]

CHARLES Saint Denis bless this happy stratagem
      And once again we'll sleep secure in Rouen.
BASTARD Here entered Pucelle and her practisants;   20
      Now she is there, how will she specify
      Here is the best and safest passage in?
REIGNIER By thrusting out a torch from yonder tower,
      Which, once discerned, shows that her meaning is:
      No way to that, for weakness, which she entered.   25

      Enter [LA] PUCELLE *on the top, thrusting out a torch burning*

PUCELLE Behold, this is the happy wedding-torch
      That joineth Rouen unto her countrymen,
      But burning fatal to the Talbonites.
BASTARD See, noble Charles, the beacon of our friend;
      The burning torch in yonder turret stands.   30
CHARLES Now shine it like a comet of revenge,
      A prophet to the fall of all our foes!
REIGNIER Defer no time; delays have dangerous ends;
      Enter and cry, 'The dauphin!' presently,

14] *Sanders; Peasuns la pouure gens de Fraunce*, F   16 SD] *This edn; not in* F   17 SD.1 *Exeunt*] F; *Exeunt / 3.3 Oxford*
17 SD.2 REIGNIER *and Forces*] *Cam.; not in* F   21 specify] *Rowe;* specifie? F   22 Here] F; *Where Rowe*   23
SH] F *subst.;* ALENÇON *Capell*   28 Talbonites] F; Talbotites *Theobald;* Talbotines *Hanmer*

14 Peasants, the poor tribe of France. *Gent* (feminine) derives from Latin *gens* and means 'race' or 'tribe'.

16 market bell 'The ringing of the bell, which announced the opening of business, was intended to give all buyers and sellers an equal chance, and to prevent wholesale buyers cornering the market' (*Shakespeare's England*, I, 316).

18 Saint Denis See 1.6.28 n.

19 secure free from care (*OED* sv *adj* 1).

20 practisants 'confederates in stratagem' (Johnson).

22 Here This, the F reading (compare Rowe's 'Where'), is substantiated by 24–5.

25 No...weakness No gate is as weakly guarded as that.

25 SD *top* Compare *Temp.* 3.3.17. Probably the hut, shown in the de Witt drawing of the Swan, from which the trumpet was sounded to announce the play. Both the 'tower' of 23 and the 'turret' of 30 could be so designated. The word may be a figurative description from the nautical 'top-castle', a platform placed high on a mast.

28 Talbonites Followers of Talbot (formed from a Latinised version of his name).

31 shine it may it shine.

31 comet See 1.1.2 n.

32 prophet portent (*OED* sv *sb* 5b).

33 Defer Waste (*OED* sv *v*¹ 4).

33 delays...ends Compare the proverb 'Delay breeds danger' (Tilley D195).

34 presently immediately.

And then do execution on the watch.   35

                                             Alarum. [*Exeunt*]

An alarum. [*Enter*] TALBOT *in an excursion*

TALBOT France, thou shalt rue this treason with thy tears,
          If Talbot but survive thy treachery.
        ' Pucelle, that witch, that damnèd sorceress,
          Hath wrought this hellish mischief unawares,
          That hardly we escaped the pride of France.   *Exit*   40

An alarum; excursions. BEDFORD *brought in sick in a chair.*
Enter TALBOT *and* BURGUNDY *without; within,* [LA] PUCELLE,
CHARLES, BASTARD, [ALENÇON,] *and* REIGNIER *on the walls*

PUCELLE Good morrow, gallants; want ye corn for bread?
          I think the Duke of Burgundy will fast
          Before he'll buy again at such a rate.
          'Twas full of darnel: do you like the taste?
BURGUNDY Scoff on, vile fiend and shameless courtesan!   45
          I trust ere long to choke thee with thine own,
          And make thee curse the harvest of that corn.
CHARLES Your grace may starve, perhaps, before that time.
BEDFORD O let no words, but deeds, revenge this treason.
PUCELLE What will you do, good greybeard? Break a lance   50
          And run a-tilt at Death within a chair?

---

35 SD.1 *Exeunt*] Capell *subst.; not in* F; *Exeunt* / 3.4 Oxford   40 pride] F; *prize* Theobald 40 SD.1 *Exit*] F *subst.; Exit* /
3.5 Oxford   40 SD.3 BURGUNDY] Rowe; *Burgonie* F (*throughout scene*)   40 SD.4 ALENÇON] Hanmer; *not in* F   41
Good] F3; *God* F   50–1] Pope *subst.;* What...gray-beard? / Break...Death, / Within a Chayre. F

35 **do...watch** kill the guards.
35 SD.1–2 **Alarum...alarum* See 1.2.18 n.
and, for the two 'alarums', see Textual Analysis,
p. 190 below. 'Exeunts' commonly have to be
inserted in sequences like this: see J. S. Cunning-
ham (ed.), *Tamburlaine the Great*, 1981, pp. 86–7.
35 SD.2 **excursion** sortie; individual soldiers
would pass across the stage to simulate a battle
(see A. Harbage, *A Theatre for Shakespeare*, 1955,
p. 52).
39 **mischief** calamity, harm.
39 **unawares** unperceived (*OED* sv *adv* 3b).
40 **hardly** with difficulty.
40 **pride** 'haughty power' (Warburton).
40 SD.3 *without; within* The formula suggests that Shakespeare intended Joan and the rest
to appear at a tiring-house window or possibly a
box or 'room' that could also have been occupied

by spectators at other performances.
41–4 The lines imply that the French may
have disdainfully pelted the English below with
corn from the sacks they had carried in.
44 **darnel** A weed of the *lolium* family, used
figuratively in the manner of the 'tares' in the
parables of the sower in Matt. 13. The 'choke' of
46 continues the reference ('...the thorns
sprung up, and choked them' – Matt. 13.7).
According to Gerard's *Herbal*, darnel affects the
eyes, and it may therefore have been used by Joan
to dim the vision of the guards.
48 **starve** die (*OED* sv *v* 1).
49 **words...deeds** Proverbial (Tilley w820).
50 **greybeard** In a contemptuous sense; the
Duke of Bedford was in fact only 36 at this time.
51 **run a-tilt** make a lance charge.
51 **within** in (*OED* sv *prep* 1).

TALBOT Foul fiend of France and hag of all despite,
Encompassed with thy lustful paramours,
Becomes it thee to taunt his valiant age
And twit with cowardice a man half dead? 55
Damsel, I'll have a bout with you again,
Or else let Talbot perish with this shame.

PUCELLE Are ye so hot, sir? – Yet, Pucelle, hold thy peace;
If Talbot do but thunder, rain will follow.
They [the English] whisper together in council
God speed the parliament! Who shall be the speaker? 60

TALBOT Dare ye come forth and meet us in the field?

PUCELLE Belike your lordship takes us then for fools,
To try if that our own be ours or no.

TALBOT I speak not to that railing Hecate,
But unto thee, Alençon, and the rest. 65
Will ye, like soldiers, come and fight it out?

ALENÇON Seigneur, no.

TALBOT Seigneur, hang! Base muleteers of France,
Like peasant footboys do they keep the walls
And dare not take up arms like gentlemen. 70

PUCELLE Away, captains; let's get us from the walls,
For Talbot means no goodness by his looks.
Goodbye, my lord; we came but to tell you
That we are here.

Exeunt from the walls

TALBOT And there will we be too, ere it be long, 75
Or else reproach be Talbot's greatest fame.

---

59 SD *the English*] *Capell; not in* F   67, 68 Seigneur] *This edn;* Seignior F   68 muleteers] *Rowe;* Muleters F
71 Away, captains] F; Captains, away *Rowe*   73 Goodbye] F *subst.* (God b'uy); God be wi' you *Rowe*

52 **hag** witch (*OED* sv sb¹ 2).

52 **of all despite** all-malignant (Wilson).

56 **bout** See 1.5.4 n.

58 **hot** (1) angry, (2) ardent, lustful.

59 Compare the proverb 'After thunder comes rain' (Tilley T275).

60 **speaker** (1) spokesman, (2) president of the council.

64 **Hecate** Here trisyllabic; as Cynthia she was goddess of the moon, as Proserpina goddess of Hades and hence became patron of witches.

67 **Seigneur, no** A catchphrase, perhaps derived from 'Signior Nobody'. It is found in Jonson's *The Case is Altered* (1597) 5.7.18, Armin's *Two Maids of Moreclacke* (1608) (ed. Grosart, 1880, p. 111), *The Noble Soldier* (1626)

(Bullen's *Old Plays*, 1882–5, I, 325), etc. (Hart gives further examples.)

67, 68 *Seigneur Lord. F's 'Seignior' was the customary spelling of both *seigneur* (French) and *signior* (Italian).

68 **Base muleteers** Mule-drivers of low birth; 'muleteers' was accented on the first syllable (Cercignani, p. 40).

69 **footboys** Boy servants on foot accompanying mounted knights.

69 **keep** rest within.

73 *Goodbye F's 'God b'uy' may indicate a false etymology – 'redeem' rather than the more common abbreviation of 'be with you' ('Goodbye'); compare *Ham.* 2.1.66.

Vow, Burgundy, by honour of thy house,
Pricked on by public wrongs sustained in France,
Either to get the town again or die.
And I, as sure as English Henry lives,   80
And as his father here was conqueror,
As sure as in this late-betrayèd town
Great Cœur-de-lion's heart was burièd,
So sure I swear to get the town or die.
BURGUNDY My vows are equal partners with thy vows.   85
TALBOT But, ere we go, regard this dying prince,
The valiant Duke of Bedford. – Come, my lord,
We will bestow you in some better place,
Fitter for sickness and for crazy age.
BEDFORD Lord Talbot, do not so dishonour me;   90
Here will I sit, before the walls of Rouen,
And will be partner of your weal or woe.
BURGUNDY Courageous Bedford, let us now persuade you –
BEDFORD Not to be gone from hence; for once I read
That stout Pendragon, in his litter sick,   95
Came to the field and vanquishèd his foes.
Methinks I should revive the soldiers' hearts
Because I ever found them as myself.
TALBOT Undaunted spirit in a dying breast;
Then be it so: heavens keep old Bedford safe!   100
And now no more ado, brave Burgundy,
But gather we our forces out of hand
And set upon our boasting enemy.
                    Exit [with Burgundy and Forces into the town]

---

82 late-betrayèd] *Cam.;* late betrayed F   83 Cœur-de-lion's] *Eds.; Cordelions* F   93 you –] *This edn;* you. F
103 SD.1 *with...Forces] Capell; not in* F   103 SD.1 *into the town] Dyce; not in* F

---

78 Pricked on Goaded.
81 Rouen was besieged by Henry V and starved into submission in January 1419.
82 *late recently.
83 Richard I 'willed his heart to be conveyed unto Rouen and there buried, in testimony of the love which he had ever borne unto that city' (Holinshed, II, 270). Richard earned the nickname during his imprisonment by Leopold, Archduke of Austria, by slaying a lion and tearing the heart out of its body (Fabyan, p. 304).
84 get capture (*OED* sv *v* 4).
86 regard (1) observe, (2) look after.

89 crazy frail, sickly (*OED* sv *adj* 2).
95–6 Geoffrey of Monmouth (*Historia Regum Britanniae*, VIII, xxii) attributes this deed to Uther Pendragon who was repelling Saxon invaders, but Boece's version – which Holinshed followed (*History of Scotland*, 2, 99) – tells the story of Pendragon's brother, Aurelius Ambrosius (see Boswell-Stone, p. 226). The story is also told in Hardyng's *Chronicle* (1543), reprinted H. Ellis, 1812, pp. 120–1.
102 out of hand forthwith (Dent HH1).
103 SD.1 *into the town i.e. through the tiring-house doors.

An alarum; excursions. Enter SIR JOHN FASTOLF *and a* CAPTAIN

CAPTAIN Whither away, Sir John Fastolf, in such haste?

FASTOLF Whither away? To save myself by flight;   105
 We are like to have the overthrow again.

CAPTAIN What, will you fly and leave Lord Talbot?

FASTOLF   Ay,
 All the Talbots in the world to save my life.   *Exit*

CAPTAIN Cowardly knight, ill fortune follow thee.

                                        Exit [into the town]

Retreat; excursions. [LA] PUCELLE, ALENÇON, *and* CHARLES
             [enter from the town and] fly

BEDFORD Now, quiet soul, depart when heaven please,   110
 For I have seen our enemies' overthrow.
 What is the trust or strength of foolish man?
 They that of late were daring with their scoffs
 Are glad, and fain by flight to save themselves.
       Bedford dies, and is carried in by two in his chair

An alarum. Enter TALBOT, BURGUNDY, *and the rest*

TALBOT Lost, and recovered in a day again!   115
 This is a double honour, Burgundy;
 Yet heavens have glory for this victory.

BURGUNDY Warlike and martial Talbot, Burgundy
 Enshrines thee in his heart, and there erects
 Thy noble deeds as valour's monuments.   120

TALBOT Thanks, gentle duke. But where is Pucelle now?

---

103 SD.2 FASTOLF] *Theobald subst.; Falstaffe* F *(throughout)*   104 Sir] F; *omitted Cairncross*   107–8] *Hanmer;*
What?...Talbot? / I,...life. F   109 SD.1 *into the town*] *Dyce; not in* F   109 SD.3 *enter...and*] *Malone; not in* F
114 glad] F; *fled conj. Vaughan*   114 SD.1 *chair*] F *subst.; chair / 3.6 Oxford*   117 Yet] F; *Let Dyce*[2]

---

104 **Sir** Cairncross may be right to omit this, as the word may have been recollected by the compositor from 103 SD.

104 **Fastolf** The name may have been punningly pronounced 'Fast-off'.

106 **have the overthrow** be defeated.

109 SD.2 **Retreat** Sounded by trumpets or drums (Long, p. 20).

110–11 Compare Luke 2.29–30: 'Lord, now lettest thou thy servant depart in peace...For mine eyes have seen thy salvation.'

112 Compare Jer. 17.5: 'Cursed be the man that trusteth in man, and maketh flesh his arm.'

114 **Are...flight** Rejoice and are well pleased to be able to flee.

117 **Yet** Editors since Dyce read 'Let', but F's 'Yet' is more in accord with Ps. 115.1: 'Not unto us [*non nobis*], O Lord, not unto us, but unto thy name give the glory.' Compare Talbot's sentiments in 3.4.10–12.

121 **gentle** noble.

I think her old familiar is asleep.
Now where's the Bastard's braves and Charles his gleeks?
What, all amort? Rouen hangs her head for grief
That such a valiant company are fled.   125
Now will we take some order in the town,
Placing therein some expert officers,
And then depart to Paris to the king,
For there young Henry with his nobles lie.
BURGUNDY What wills Lord Talbot pleaseth Burgundy.   130
TALBOT But yet, before we go, let's not forget
The noble Duke of Bedford, late-deceased,
But see his exequies fulfilled in Rouen.
A braver soldier never couchèd lance,
A gentler heart did never sway in court.   135
But kings and mightiest potentates must die,
For that's the end of human misery.

Exeunt

3.3 *Enter* CHARLES, BASTARD, ALENÇON, [LA] PUCELLE, [*and*
Forces]

PUCELLE Dismay not, princes, at this accident,
Nor grieve that Rouen is so recoverèd:

---

123 gleeks] *Hanmer; glikes* F   Act 3, Scene 3 ·   3.3] *Capell subst.; Scæna Tertia.* F

122 old familiar Customary attendant spirit in animal form (the devil himself?); see Thomas, pp. 530–1.

123 braves boasts.

123 his See 1.2.1 n.

123 gleeks gibes.

124 What...amort A catchphrase (Dent A A6).

124 amort downcast, dispirited.

126 take some order make some necessary arrangements.

127 expert experienced (*OED* sv *adj*[1] 1).

129 Henry...nobles The phrase constitutes a plural subject for the verb 'lie'.

129 lie reside.

133 exequies fulfilled funeral rites performed. Bedford was buried in Rouen Cathedral in September 1435 (Holinshed, p. 184; Hall, p. 178).

134 couchèd levelled, aimed.

135 gentler nobler.

135 sway exercise power.

136–7 Compare the proverb 'Death is the end of all' (Dent D142.1).

137 misery Pronounced with accent on the final syllable to make the rhyme (Cercignani, p. 304).

Act 3, Scene 3

3.3 Burgundy did not desert until 1435, four years after the death of Joan (Holinshed, pp. 183–4; Hall, pp. 177–8). The feud between the houses of Burgundy and Orléans (69–73), resolved only in 1440, is described by Holinshed, pp. 195–6 (Hall, p. 194).

1 Dismay not For this intransitive use of the verb, see *OED* 3.

1 accident unforeseen event (*OED* sv *sb* 1).

Care is no cure, but rather corrosive
For things that are not to be remedied.
Let frantic Talbot triumph for a while   5
And like a peacock sweep along his tail;
We'll pull his plumes and take away his train
If dauphin and the rest will be but ruled.
CHARLES We have been guided by thee hitherto
And of thy cunning had no diffidence;   10
One sudden foil shall never breed distrust.
BASTARD [*To Pucelle*] Search out thy wit for secret policies,
And we will make thee famous through the world.
ALENÇON We'll set thy statue in some holy place
And have thee reverenced like a blessèd saint.   15
Employ thee then, sweet virgin, for our good.
PUCELLE Then thus it must be; this doth Joan devise:
By fair persuasions mixed with sugared words
We will entice the Duke of Burgundy
To leave the Talbot and to follow us.   20
CHARLES Ay, marry, sweeting, if we could do that,
France were no place for Henry's warriors,
Nor should that nation boast it so with us,
But be extirpèd from our provinces.
ALENÇON For ever should they be expulsed from France,   25

---

12 SD] *This edn; not in* F   19 Burgundy] *Rowe;* Burgonie F (*throughout scene*)

---

3 **Care is no cure** Proverbial (Tilley C83).

3 **corrosive** aggravating, wasting – although 'corrosive' medicines were used to draw out festering substances (*OED* sv *adj* 2b); compare the proverb 'Care is a corrosive' (Dent C82.1).

5 **frantic** lunatic, foolish.

6 **peacock** Proverbial for pride (Dent P157).

7 **pull his plumes** Proverbial (Dent P441.1).

7 **pull** pluck.

7 **train** (1) tail, (2) followers.

8 **ruled** guided (by Joan).

10 **cunning** skill (magical power).

10 **diffidence** lack of confidence, distrust.

11 **foil** overthrow (as in wrestling (*OED* sv *sb*² 1, 2)), but here, as at 5.3.23, with a sexual innuendo (*OED* Foil *v*²).

12 Use your abilities to devise unexpected strategies.

14–15 Compare Hall, p. 159: 'the citizens of Orléans had builded in the honour of her an image or an idol . . . she was more to be marvelled at as a false prophetess and seducer of the people than to be honoured or worshipped as a saint sent from God into the realm of France'.

16 **Employ thee** Exert yourself.

18 **sugared** Sugar was still an expensive rarity, so the epithet means 'choice' and not 'deceptive'.

20 **the** Expresses notoriety (Abbott 192).

21 **sweeting** A lover's endearment, which suggests that Joan's 'sugared words' may act as a sexual lure.

23 **boast it so with** lord it over.

24 **extirpèd** rooted out; obsolete form of 'extirpated'. The passage may derive from Hall's account of Charles's speech to Burgundy: 'by your help and aid, we shall expel, clean pull up by the roots, and put out, all the English nation, out of our realms' (p. 177).

25 **expulsed** Obsolete synonym of 'expelled'.

And not have title of an earldom here.
PUCELLE Your honours shall perceive how I will work
To bring this matter to the wishèd end.
           Drum sounds afar off
Hark! By the sound of drum you may perceive
Their powers are marching unto Paris-ward.   30
        Here sound an English march
There goes the Talbot with his colours spread,
And all the troops of English after him.
        French march
Now in the rearward comes the duke and his:
Fortune in favour makes him lag behind.
Summon a parley, we will talk with him.   35
        Trumpets sound a parley
CHARLES A parley with the Duke of Burgundy!

        [*Enter* BURGUNDY *and Forces*]

BURGUNDY Who craves a parley with the Burgundy?
PUCELLE The princely Charles of France, thy countryman.
BURGUNDY What say'st thou, Charles? for I am marching hence.
CHARLES Speak, Pucelle, and enchant him with thy words.   40
PUCELLE Brave Burgundy, undoubted hope of France,
    Stay, let thy humble handmaid speak to thee.
BURGUNDY Speak on, but be not over-tedious.
PUCELLE Look on thy country, look on fertile France,

---

30 SD] F; *Here…march. Enter and pass over at a distance, Talbot and his forces.* / Capell   32 SD] F; *French march. Enter the Duke of Burgundy and forces.* / Capell   36 SD] Capell (*after 35*); not in F

26 **title** A legal term for claim or assertion of right (*OED* sv *sb* 7c).

28–32 It is improbable that, as some editors have suggested, the forces referred to actually made entrances, possibly to 'pass over' the stage. The musical cues provide a kind of theatrical shorthand and are economical of players. If, however, elements of the two armies do appear, Burgundy's forces could break off and stay on stage for the parley instead of entering at 36.

30 **unto Paris-ward** towards Paris.

30 SD *English* The rhythm of an English drum march, notated in the reign of Charles I, is given in Appendix II of Long.

32 SD *French* The French march was, it seems, slower than the English: Dekker wrote of the gentleman who 'comes but slowly on (as if he

trod a French March)' (Dekker, *ND*, II, 51).

31 **colours spread** banners unfurled.

33 **rearward** rearguard (*OED* sv *sb*[1] 1).

33 **his** his men.

34 **in favour** favourably disposed to us.

40 **enchant** Another imputation of witchcraft; compare 58 below.

41 **undoubted** (1) fearless, (2) certain. Sense (1) is not recorded in *OED*, but compare *3H6* 5.7.6.

42 **let…thee** Compare Abigail's words to David, 'let thine handmaid speak to thee' (1 Sam. 25.24). (The Bishops' Bible reads 'in thine audience' (Noble, p. 112)).

44 **Look on** 'In the Biblical sense of "look with pity on" (Wilson).

And see the cities and the towns defaced   45
By wasting ruin of the cruel foe
As looks the mother on her lowly babe
When death doth close his tender-dying eyes.
See, see the pining malady of France;
Behold the wounds, the most unnatural wounds   50
Which thou thyself hast given her woeful breast.
O turn thy edgèd sword another way:
Strike those that hurt and hurt not those that help.
One drop of blood drawn from thy country's bosom
Should grieve thee more than streams of foreign gore.   55
Return thee therefore with a flood of tears,
And wash away thy country's stainèd spots.

BURGUNDY [*Aside*] Either she hath bewitched me with her words,
Or nature makes me suddenly relent.

PUCELLE Besides, all French and France exclaims on thee,   60
Doubting thy birth and lawful progeny.
Who join'st thou with, but with a lordly nation
That will not trust thee but for profit's sake?
When Talbot hath set footing once in France
And fashioned thee that instrument of ill,   65
Who then but English Henry will be lord,
And thou be thrust out like a fugitive?

45–8] As F; 47–8 precede 45–6 / conj. this edn   46 foe] This edn; Foe, F; foe. Pope   47 lowly] F; lovely conj.
Warburton   48 tender-dying] F; tender dying Pope   48 eyes.] F subst.; eyes, Eds.   58 SD] Cairncross; not in F

45 defaced destroyed, laid waste (*OED* Deface *v* 2).

45–8 The difficulty of these lines (see note below) would be eased if 47–8 were placed before 45–6.

*46–8 I follow Sisson (*New Readings*, II, 71) in following substantively the F punctuation rather than dividing the passage into two with a stop after 'foe' and a comma after 'eyes'.

46 ruin devastation (*OED* sv *sb* 9).

47 lowly *OED* cites this as a nonce-use '? Lying low' (*OED* sv *adj* 3b) – but the common meaning 'humble' (*OED* sv *adj* 1) would be appropriate here; compare *WT* 4.4.9. 'Perhaps the poet by "lowly babe" meant the babe lying low in death. "Lowly" answers as well to "towns defaced" and "wasting ruin" as "lovely" [Warburton's conj.] to "fertile"' (Johnson).

48 tender-dying dying young (when only of tender years).

49 pining tormenting.

50 unnatural Because Burgundy has inflicted them on his own people (compare 59 below).

52 edgèd sharpened.

57 stainèd spots Transferred epithet: the country is stained by the spots.

59 nature natural feeling or affection (*OED* sv *sb* 9e).

60 exclaims on loudly accuses (*OED* Exclaim *v* 2b).

61 Casting doubt on your lineage and the legitimacy of your birth ('progeny' = ancestry (*OED* sv 5)).

62 lordly disdainful.

65 fashioned thee turned you into.

66 Hall notes that at the Council of Arras in 1435 Burgundy did not expect 'that the king of England, by the right course of inheritance, took upon him the whole rule and governance, within the realm of France' (p. 176; not in Holinshed).

67 fugitive exile, refugee (*OED* sv *sb* 1c); also deserter (*OED* sv *sb* 1b).

Call we to mind, and mark but this for proof:
Was not the Duke of Orléans thy foe?
And was he not in England prisoner?   70
But when they heard he was thine enemy
They set him free without his ransom paid,
In spite of Burgundy and all his friends.
See then, thou fight'st against thy countrymen,
And join'st with them will be thy slaughtermen.   75
Come, come, return; return, thou wandering lord!
Charles and the rest will take thee in their arms.

BURGUNDY [*Aside*] I am vanquished: these haughty words of hers
Have battered me like roaring cannon-shot
And made me almost yield upon my knees. –   80
Forgive me, country, and sweet countrymen!
And, lords, accept this hearty kind embrace.
My forces and my power of men are yours.
So farewell, Talbot; I'll no longer trust thee.

PUCELLE [*Aside*] Done like a Frenchman: turn and turn again.   85

CHARLES Welcome, brave duke, thy friendship makes us fresh.

BASTARD And doth beget new courage in our breasts.

ALENÇON Pucelle hath bravely played her part in this,
And doth deserve a coronet of gold.

CHARLES Now let us on, my lords, and join our powers,   90
And seek how we may prejudice the foe.

Exeunt

---

78 SD] *Dyce; not in* F   78] *Rowe;* I am vanquished: / These...hers F   85 SD] *Capell; not in* F; *after* Frenchman
Dyce   90] *Rowe;* Now...Lords, / And...Powers, F

69–73 Events are pushed together and distorted. Charles, Duke of Orleans, lay in English captivity from 1415 until 1440, five years after the defection of Burgundy. The English had kept him there to protect Burgundy, whose father had had his father killed (Holinshed, pp. 195–6; Hall, p. 194).

72 without...paid For this grammatical construction, see Abbott 418.

75 slaughtermen executioners.

76 wandering errant, mistaken.

78 haughty (1) high-minded, (*OED* sv *adj* 2), (2) grand (*OED* sv *adj* 1b).

82 kind (1) friendly, (2) kinsman's.

83 power of command over.

***85** The line suggests direct address to the audience. There is, however, no way of telling whether Shakespeare intended Joan to be cynical about all Frenchmen and so to speak the whole

line as an aside, or whether she was mocking just Burgundy's conversion, in which case only the second half of the line is an aside (see Sisson, *New Readings*, 11, 71). Riverside, following Theobald, conjectures that this may be 'an allusion to the conversion, in 1593, of Henry of Navarre to Catholicism after he had long been aided by the English as a Protestant claimant to the throne of France'. If this is so, the line must have been added after what seem to have been performances of the play in 1592 (see p. 36 above). Hall notes (p. 176) that Burgundy 'without long argument or prolonging of time...took a determinate peace'. Moreover the French were, in the English eyes, 'a fickle wavering nation' (4.1.138).

86 fresh ready, eager (*OED* sv *adj* 11).

88 bravely (1) boldly, (2) splendidly.

90 powers forces.

91 prejudice injure (*OED* sv *v* 1b).

3.4 [*Flourish.*] *Enter the* KING, GLOUCESTER, WINCHESTER, [*Richard Plantagenet, now* DUKE OF] YORK, SUFFOLK, SOMERSET, WARWICK, EXETER[, VERNON, BASSET, *and others*]: *to them, with his Soldiers,* TALBOT

TALBOT	My gracious prince, and honourable peers,
	Hearing of your arrival in this realm,
	I have awhile given truce unto my wars
	To do my duty to my sovereign:
	In sign whereof, this arm that hath reclaimed	5
	To your obedience fifty fortresses,
	Twelve cities, and seven walled towns of strength,
	Beside five hundred prisoners of esteem,
	Lets fall his sword before your highness' feet;
	And with submissive loyalty of heart	10
	Ascribes the glory of his conquest got
	First to my God, and next unto your grace. [*Kneels*]
KING HENRY	Is this the Lord Talbot, Uncle Gloucester,
	That hath so long been resident in France?
GLOUCESTER	Yes, if it please your majesty, my liege.	15
KING HENRY	Welcome, brave captain and victorious lord!
	When I was young (as yet I am not old)
	I do remember how my father said
	A stouter champion never handled sword.
	Long since we were resolvèd of your truth,	20
	Your faithful service, and your toil in war;
	Yet never have you tasted our reward,
	Or been reguerdoned with so much as thanks,
	Because till now we never saw your face.
	Therefore stand up; and for these good deserts	25
	We here create you Earl of Shrewbury,

Act 3, Scene 4   3.4] *Capell subst.; Scæna Quarta.* F   0 SD.1 *Flourish*] *Oxford; not in* F   0 SD.3 VERNON...*others*] *Capell; not in* F   12 SD] *Eds.; not in* F   13 the Lord] F; *the Capell*

Act 3, Scene 4

3.4 Talbot's elevation to the earldom of Shrewsbury took place in 1442 (Holinshed, p. 204; Hall, p. 202), while Henry's coronation in Paris took place in 1431 (Holinshed, p. 173; Hall, pp. 160–4).

4 duty feudal homage.

5 reclaimed brought back (*OED* Reclaim *v* 2).

8 esteem account, noble rank (and therefore likely to command a high ransom).

9, 11 his its (referring to 'arm' at 5; see Abbott 228).

17–19 Henry was in fact only nine months old when his father died.

19 stouter champion bolder warrior.

20 resolvèd convinced (*OED* sv *ppl adj* 2).

23 reguerdoned rewarded.

25 deserts deservings.

And in our coronation take your place.

Sennet. Flourish. Exeunt all but Vernon and Basset

VERNON Now, sir, to you that were so hot at sea,
Disgracing of these colours that I wear
In honour of my noble Lord of York,   30
Dar'st thou maintain the former words thou spak'st?

BASSET Yes, sir, as well as you dare patronage
The envious barking of your saucy tongue
Against my lord the Duke of Somerset.

VERNON Sirrah, thy lord I honour as he is.   35

BASSET Why, what is he? As good a man as York!

VERNON Hark ye, not so: in witness, take ye that.

Strikes him

BASSET Villain, thou know'st the law of arms is such
That whoso draws a sword, 'tis present death,
Or else this blow should broach thy dearest blood. 40
But I'll unto his majesty, and crave
I may have liberty to venge this wrong;
When thou shalt see I'll meet thee to thy cost.

VERNON Well, miscreant, I'll be there as soon as you,
And after meet you, sooner than you would.   45

Exeunt

4.1 [*Flourish.*] *Enter* [*the*] KING, GLOUCESTER, WINCHESTER, YORK, SUFFOLK, SOMERSET, WARWICK, TALBOT, *and* GOVERNOR [*of Paris,*] EXETER [*and others*]

---

27 SD *all but*] F2 *subst.; Manet* F 38] *Rowe;* Villaine . . . knowest / The . . . such, F 38 know'st] *Pope;* knowest F 39 whoso] *Rowe;* who so F **Act 4, Scene 1** 4.1] *Capell subst.; Actus Quartus. Scena Prima.* F 0 SD.1 *Flourish*] *Oxford; not in* F

27 SD *Sennet* See 3.1.185 SD n.

28 **hot** angry, fierce.

29 **Disgracing** Speaking slightingly (*OED* Disgrace *v* 6).

29 **these colours** this badge (*OED* Colour *sb* 6).

32 **patronage** defend (compare 3.1.48).

33 **envious** malicious (*OED* sv *adj* 2).

35 **Sirrah** A disrespectful form of address.

38–9 It was a felony to fight within a royal palace – see Blackstone's *Commentaries*, IV, 124. Henry, however, does not allude to this and commands peace between the combatants for reasons of prudence (see 4.1.134 ff.).

40 **broach** tap (as of a barrel).

44 **miscreant** coward.

Act 4, Scene 1

4.1 Those present at the coronation in 1431 are listed in Holinshed (p. 173; Hall, p. 160). 'Historically Talbot, who had been captured at the battle of Patay, was still in French hands; Exeter was dead; and Gloucester was in England' (Sanders, p. 207). The episode of Burgundy's letter of 1435 is narrated in Holinshed (pp. 183–4; Hall, pp. 177–8), and the chroniclers related how Bedford (not Talbot) took Fastolf's Garter badge after his defection at Patay in 1429 (Holinshed, p. 165; Hall, p. 150). The quarrel between Vernon and Basset, continued from 2.4, is fictitious.

The act begins, as always in the play, with an interrupted ceremony.

GLOUCESTER Lord Bishop, set the crown upon his head.
WINCHESTER God save King Henry, of that name the Sixth!
              [*Winchester crowns King Henry*]
GLOUCESTER Now, Governor of Paris, take your oath:
              [*Governor kneels*]
         That you elect no other king but him;
         Esteem none friends but such as are his friends,   5
         And none your foes but such as shall pretend
         Malicious practices against his state.
         This shall ye do, so help you righteous God!

                    Enter FASTOLF

FASTOLF My gracious sovereign, as I rode from Calais
         To haste unto your coronation,   10
         A letter was delivered to my hands,
         Writ to your grace from th'Duke of Burgundy.
TALBOT Shame to the Duke of Burgundy and thee!
         I vowed, base knight, when I did meet thee next
         To tear the Garter from thy craven's leg,   15
              [*Plucks it off*]
         Which I have done, because unworthily
         Thou wast installèd in that high degree. –
         Pardon me, princely Henry, and the rest:
         This dastard, at the battle of Patay,
         When but in all I was six thousand strong   20
         And that the French were almost ten to one,
         Before we met or that a stroke was given,
         Like to a trusty squire did run away;

2 SD] *This edn; not in* F   3 SD] *Capell; not in* F   8 God!] F; God! *Exeunt Gov. and Train / Capell*
9 Calais] *Eds.;* Calice F   14 thee] F2; the F   15 SD] *Capell; not in* F   19 Patay] *Malone, conj. Capell;* Poictiers F

1 **Bishop** Winchester was 'Bishop of Winchester, and cardinal of Saint Eusebie' (Holinshed, p. 166; Hall, p. 152).
    4 **elect** (1) select, (2) accept.
    6 **pretend** intend (Johnson).
    7 **practices** plots (*OED* Practice *sb* 6).
    8 Following Capell, editors have inserted an
exit for the Governor and his train here. This is
unnecessary and muffles the effect of Fastolf's
interruption of the coronation.
    15 **Garter** Badge of the Order of the Garter,
the highest degree of English knighthood.
    15 **craven's** coward's.
    17 **that high degree** i.e. the Order of the
Garter.

17 **degree** dignity, estate (*OED* sv *sb* 4).
    19 ***Patay** The battle of Patay, recorded in
Hall and Holinshed (see 1.1 headnote), took
place near Orléans in 1429. F reads 'Poictiers',
and Poitiers is referred to at 1.1.61 and 4.3.45. As
the battle of Poitiers took place in 1356, there
would seem to be authorial or compositorial
confusion.
    19 **dastard** despicable coward.
    20 **but in all** all told.
    21 **that** when (Abbott 285).
    23 **trusty** Here ironic.

In which assault we lost twelve hundred men;
Myself and divers gentlemen beside   25
Were there surprised and taken prisoners.
Then judge, great lords, if I have done amiss,
Or whether that such cowards ought to wear
This ornament of knighthood – yea or no?

GLOUCESTER To say the truth, this fact was infamous   30
And ill beseeming any common man,
Much more a knight, a captain, and a leader.

TALBOT When first this order was ordained, my lords,
Knights of the Garter were of noble birth,
Valiant and virtuous, full of haughty courage,   35
Such as were grown to credit by the wars;
Not fearing death nor shrinking for distress,
But always resolute in most extremes.
He then that is not furnished in this sort
Doth but usurp the sacred name of knight,   40
Profaning this most honourable order,
And should, if I were worthy to be judge,
Be quite degraded, like a hedge-born swain
That doth presume to boast of gentle blood.

KING HENRY Stain to thy countrymen, thou hear'st thy doom!   45
Be packing therefore, thou that wast a knight;
Henceforth we banish thee on pain of death.

                                        [*Exit Fastolf*]

And now, my lord protector, view the letter
Sent from our uncle, Duke of Burgundy.

GLOUCESTER What means his grace that he hath changed his style?   50
No more but plain and bluntly 'To the king'!

---

38 most] F; worst *Hanmer*   47 SD] *Wilson subst. (after* F2); *not in* F   48 now, my] F2; now F   51 'To the King']
Rowe subst.; (*To the King.*) F

26 **surprised** seized.
30 **fact** evil deed (*OED* sv 1c).
31 **common man** commoner, a man without
rank.
35 **haughty courage** high spirit.
36 **were. . .credit** had achieved honour.
37 **for distress** in the face of adversity (*OED*
Distress *sb* 2).
38 **most extremes** the greatest extremities
(Abbott 17).
39 **furnished. . .sort** possessed of these
abilities (*OED* Furnished *ppl adj* 2c).

43 **quite** completely.
43 **degraded** reduced in rank (*OED* sv *ppl adj*
1).
43 **hedge-born swain** base-born rustic; compare the proverb 'To be born under a hedge'
(Dent H361.1).
44 **gentle** noble.
45 **Stain** Disgrace.
45 **doom** judgement.
46 **packing** off.
50 **style** form of greeting.

Hath he forgot he is his sovereign,
Or doth this churlish superscription
Pretend some alteration in good will?
What's here? [*Reads*] 'I have upon especial cause,   55
Moved with compassion of my country's wrack,
Together with the pitiful complaints
Of such as your oppression feeds upon,
Forsaken your pernicious faction,
And joined with Charles, the rightful King of France.'   60
O monstrous treachery! Can this be so?
That in alliance, amity, and oaths,
There should be found such false dissembling guile?

KING HENRY What? Doth my Uncle Burgundy revolt?

GLOUCESTER He doth, my lord, and is become your foe.   65

KING HENRY Is that the worst this letter doth contain?

GLOUCESTER It is the worst, and all, my lord, he writes.

KING HENRY Why then Lord Talbot there shall talk with him
And give him chastisement for this abuse. –
How say you, my lord, are you not content?   70

TALBOT Content, my liege? Yes. But that I am prevented,
I should have begged I might have been employed.

KING HENRY Then gather strength and march unto him straight;
Let him perceive how ill we brook his treason
And what offence it is to flout his friends.   75

TALBOT I go, my lord, in heart desiring still
You may behold confusion of your foes.   [*Exit*]

Enter VERNON *and* BASSET

VERNON Grant me the combat, gracious sovereign.

BASSET And me, my lord, grant me the combat too.

YORK This is my servant: hear him, noble prince.   80

---

54 Pretend] F; Portend *Rowe*²   55 SD] *Rowe; not in* F   71 liege? Yes.] *Riverside;* Liege? Yes: F; liege? *conj. Capell*
77 SD.1] *Rowe; not in* F

53 **superscription** address.
54 **Pretend** Import, signify.
56 **wrack** destruction.
58 **feeds** preys.
64 **uncle** Henry's uncle the Duke of Bedford had married Burgundy's sister Anne.
64 **revolt** change allegiance (*OED* sv *v* 1c).
69 **abuse** deception, wrong (*OED* sv *sb* 4 and 5).
71 **prevented** forestalled.

73 **strength** a force.
73 **straight** immediately.
74 **brook** tolerate.
75 **flout** insult.
76 **still** always.
77 **confusion** destruction.
78 **the combat** permission to fight a duel.
80 **This** i.e. Vernon.
80 **servant** follower, retainer.

SOMERSET And this is mine: sweet Henry, favour him.

KING HENRY Be patient, lords, and give them leave to speak.
　　　Say, gentlemen, what makes you thus exclaim,
　　　And wherefore crave you combat, or with whom?

VERNON With him, my lord, for he hath done me wrong.　　85

BASSET And I with him, for he hath done me wrong.

KING HENRY What is that wrong whereof you both complain?
　　　First let me know, and then I'll answer you.

BASSET Crossing the sea from England into France,
　　　This fellow here with envious carping tongue　　90
　　　Upbraided me about the rose I wear,
　　　Saying the sanguine colour of the leaves
　　　Did represent my master's blushing cheeks
　　　When stubbornly he did repugn the truth
　　　About a certain question in the law　　95
　　　Argued betwixt the Duke of York and him;
　　　With other vile and ignominious terms:
　　　In confutation of which rude reproach,
　　　And in defence of my lord's worthiness,
　　　I crave the benefit of law of arms.　　100

VERNON And that is my petition, noble lord:
　　　For though he seem with forgèd quaint conceit
　　　To set a gloss upon his bold intent,
　　　Yet know, my lord, I was provoked by him,
　　　And he first took exceptions at this badge,　　105
　　　Pronouncing that the paleness of this flower
　　　Bewrayed the faintness of my master's heart.

YORK Will not this malice, Somerset, be left?

SOMERSET Your private grudge, my Lord of York, will out,
　　　Though ne'er so cunningly you smother it.　　110

KING HENRY Good Lord, what madness rules in brainsick men,
　　　When for so slight and frivolous a cause

---

81 **this** i.e. Basset.
83 **exclaim** cry out.
90 **envious** malicious.
90 **carping** (1) complaining, (2) prattling (*OED* Carp v^1 4).
91 **rose** i.e. the red Lancastrian rose.
92 **sanguine** blood-red.
92 **leaves** petals (*OED* Leaf *sb* 2).
94 **repugn** oppose.
95 **question...law** See 2.4 and 2.5.45; the

'question' presumably involved the matter of York's succession to the throne and the attainder of his father.
100 **benefit** legal privilege (*OED* sv *sb* 3c).
100 **law of arms** trial by combat.
102 **quaint conceit** cunning device.
103 **set...upon** conceal with specious seeming.
105 **took...at** found fault with.
107 **Bewrayed** Revealed.
108 **left** put aside.

Such factious emulations shall arise!
Good cousins both, of York and Somerset,
Quiet yourselves, I pray, and be at peace.   115
YORK Let this dissension first be tried by fight,
And then your highness shall command a peace.
SOMERSET The quarrel toucheth none but us alone:
Betwixt ourselves let us decide it then.
YORK There is my pledge; accept it, Somerset.   120
VERNON Nay, let it rest where it began at first.
BASSET Confirm it so, mine honourable lord.
GLOUCESTER Confirm it so? Confounded be your strife,
And perish ye with your audacious prate!
Presumptuous vassals, are you not ashamed   125
With this immodest clamorous outrage
To trouble and disturb the king and us?
And you, my lords, methinks you do not well
To bear with their perverse objections,
Much less to take occasion from their mouths   130
To raise a mutiny betwixt yourselves.
Let me persuade you take a better course.
EXETER It grieves his highness; good my lords, be friends.
KING HENRY Come hither, you that would be combatants:
Henceforth I charge you, as you love our favour,   135
Quite to forget this quarrel and the cause.
And you, my lords, remember where we are:
In France, amongst a fickle wavering nation;
If they perceive dissension in our looks
And that within ourselves we disagree,   140
How will their grudging stomachs be provoked
To wilful disobedience and rebel!

133] *As Pope;* It...Highnesse, / Good...Friends. F   142 disobedience] *This edn;* Disobedience, F

113 **emulations** jealousies, rivalries.
114 **cousins** kinsmen.
118 **toucheth** concerns.
120 **There...pledge** York would here throw down his gauntlet or glove.
121–2 The lines may both be directed to the king. Alternatively, Vernon's could be taken as an 'overheard aside' and Basset's directed to Somerset.
121 **rest** remain.
124 **audacious** impudent (*OED* sv *adj* 2).
124 **prate** prattle.

125 **vassals** slaves.
126 **immodest** immoderate, arrogant.
129 **objections** accusations (*OED* Objection 1b).
130 **occasion** opportunity.
131 **mutiny** broil, strife.
140 **within** among.
141 **grudging** (1) resentful, (2) exhibiting symptoms of disease (*OED* sv *vbl sb* 2).
141 **stomachs** spirits.
142 **rebel** rebellion (*OED* sv *sb*²).

Beside, what infamy will there arise
When foreign princes shall be certified
That for a toy, a thing of no regard,   145
King Henry's peers and chief nobility
Destroyed themselves, and lost the realm of France?
O think upon the conquest of my father,
My tender years, and let us not forgo
That for a trifle that was bought with blood!   150
Let me be umpire in this doubtful strife.
I see no reason, if I wear this rose, [*Putting on a red rose*]
That any one should therefore be suspicious
I more incline to Somerset than York:
Both are my kinsmen, and I love them both.   155
As well they may upbraid me with my crown
Because, forsooth, the King of Scots is crowned.
But your discretions better can persuade
Than I am able to instruct or teach;
And therefore, as we hither came in peace,   160
So let us still continue peace and love.
Cousin of York, we institute your grace
To be our regent in these parts of France;
And, good my Lord of Somerset, unite
Your troops of horsemen with his bands of foot;   165
And like true subjects, sons of your progenitors,
Go cheerfully together and digest
Your angry choler on your enemies.
Ourself, my lord protector, and the rest,
After some respite will return to Calais;   170
From thence to England, where I hope ere long

---

151 umpire] F3 *subst.* (Umpier); Vmper F   152 SD] *Johnson; not in* F   163 these] F; the *Cairncross*   170 will] F; will straight *conj. this edn*

144 **certified** made certain.
145 **toy** trifle.
145 **regard** consequence.
149 **forgo** forfeit, lose.
151 ***umpire** F's spelling 'Vmper' indicates stress on the first syllable (Cercignani, p. 257).
151 **doubtful** worrying (*OED* sv *adj* 4).
154 **incline to** favour.
157 **King...crowned** There seems no reason to seek out a topical allusion. (James I of Scotland was on the throne at the time of Henry VI's coronation; James VI, who occupied the

throne at the time the play was written, had been crowned in 1567, like Henry VI, as a child.)
158 **discretions** (1) discernment (*OED* sv 3), (2) lordships (*OED* sv 8).
161 **still** ever.
162 **institute** appoint (*OED* sv *v* 2).
163 **these parts** all the regions; York was regent of all France, so the stress is on 'parts'.
167 **digest** dissipate (*OED* sv *v* 1b).
168 **choler** bile (*OED* sv *sb¹* 1); the 'humour' that was the cause of anger.
170 **respite** delay, stay (*OED* sv *sb* 3).

To be presented, by your victories,
With Charles, Alençon, and that traitorous rout.
[*Flourish.*] *Exeunt [all but] York, Warwick, Exeter, Vernon*

WARWICK　My Lord of York, I promise you the king
　　Prettily, methought, did play the orator.　　175
YORK　And so he did, but yet I like it not
　　In that he wears the badge of Somerset.
WARWICK　Tush, that was but his fancy; blame him not:
　　I dare presume, sweet prince, he thought no harm.
YORK　And if I wist he did – but let it rest;　　180
　　Other affairs must now be managèd.

　　　　　　　　　　　　　Exeunt [all but] Exeter

EXETER　Well didst thou, Richard, to suppress thy voice;
　　For, had the passions of thy heart burst out,
　　I fear we should have seen deciphered there
　　More rancorous spite, more furious raging broils,　　185
　　Than yet can be imagined or supposed.
　　But howsoe'er, no simple man that sees
　　This jarring discord of nobility,
　　This shouldering of each other in the court,
　　This factious bandying of their favourites,　　190
　　But sees it doth presage some ill event.
　　'Tis much when sceptres are in children's hands;
　　But more when envy breeds unkind division:
　　There comes the ruin, there begins confusion.　　*Exit*

173 SD *Flourish*] As *Theobald; after 181*, F　173 SD *all but*] F3 *subst.; Manet* F　180 And if I wist he did –] *Capell;* And if I wish he did. F; And if, iwis, he did – *Theobald;* And if – I wish – he did *or perhaps* And if he did, I wish – *conj. Johnson*　181 SD *Exeunt all but*] *Cam.; Exeunt. Flourish. Manet* F　191 sees] *Cairncross, conj.* H. Brooks; that F; at *conj. Vaughan*

173 **rout** rabble.
*173 SD Oxford argues that F's misplacement of '*Flourish*' after '*Exeunt*' suggests that the eight-line dialogue between Warwick and York which follows may be a late addition (Wells and Taylor, *Textual Companion*, p. 223).
174 **promise** assure (*OED* sv v 5).
175 **play the orator** Proverbial (?) (Dent O74.1).
180 ***wist** knew for certain; as this form is not found elsewhere in Shakespeare, Theobald's emendation 'iwis' may be found attractive. (F reads 'wish'.)
181 **managèd** taken in hand (as a horse is trained in the *manège*).
182–94 With this compare Exeter's earlier

prophecy at 3.1.186 ff. and that of the Bishop of Carlisle (*R2* 4.1.114 ff.).
184 **deciphered** discovered.
187 **simple** common (*OED* sv *adj* 4].
189 **shouldering** jostling.
190 **bandying** quarrelling, fighting.
190 **favourites** supporters (*OED* sv *sb* 4).
191 **event** outcome.
192 Compare the proverb 'Woe to the land whose king is a child' (Eccl. 10.16) (Dent W600).
192 **much** serious.
193 **envy** malice.
193 **unkind** unnatural (because between kinsmen).

[4.2] *Enter* TALBOT *with Trump and Drum before Bordeaux*

TALBOT Go to the gates of Bordeaux, trumpeter,
       Summon their general unto the wall.

       [Trumpet] sounds. Enter GENERAL *[and others] aloft*

       English John Talbot, captains, calls you forth,
       Servant in arms to Harry, King of England,
       And thus he would: open your city gates,   5
       Be humble to us, call my sovereign yours,
       And do him homage as obedient subjects,
       And I'll withdraw me and my bloody power.
       But if you frown upon this proffered peace,
       You tempt the fury of my three attendants,   10
       Lean Famine, quartering Steel, and climbing Fire,
       Who, in a moment, even with the earth
       Shall lay your stately and air-braving towers,
       If you forsake the offer of their love.
GENERAL Thou ominous and fearful owl of death,   15
       Our nation's terror and their bloody scourge,
       The period of thy tyranny approacheth.
       On us thou canst not enter but by death;

Act 4, Scene 2   4.2] *Capell subst.; not in* F   2 SD *Trumpet*] *Capell; not in* F   2 SD *and others*] *Malone; not in*
F   3 captains] F; *captain* Oxford   3 calls] F2; *call* F   7 And do] F; *Do conj. this edn*   14 heir] F; *our* Hanmer;
his conj. Wilson   15 SH GENERAL] *Theobald subst.; Cap.* F

Act 4, Scene 2
  *4.2 This attack on Bordeaux is fictitious – the
city actually welcomed Talbot (Holinshed, p. 235;
Hall, p. 228). The sequence that ends with the
death of Talbot in 4.6 is based loosely on the
narrative of his death at Castillon in 1453 (Holinshed, p. 235; Hall, p. 229), 22 years after the
coronation depicted in the last scene.
  0 SD *Trump* Trumpeter.
  0 SD *Drum* Drummer.
  2 SD A parley would be sounded (an example is
provided by Long, p. 271).
  3 captains officers, leaders.
  5 would desires (Abbott 329).
  8 bloody power army ready to shed blood.
  10–11 Compare *H5* 1 Prologue 6–8. Both
passages derive from Henry V's words at the
siege of Rouen with the implication that Talbot,
during this reign, has to play the part of England's
champion: 'The goddess of battle called Bellona
had three handmaidens ever of necessity attend-

ing upon her, as blood, fire, and famine' (Holinshed, p. 104; Hall, p. 85).
  11 quartering dismembering; compare *JC*
3.1.268.
  12 even level.
  13 air-braving defying the air.
  14 forsake refuse (*OED* sv *v* 2).
  14 their There is no need to emend, as editors
have, to 'his' or 'our' as 'their' would seem to
refer back to the attendants, the chroniclers'
'handmaids' (see 10–11 n. above).
  *15 SH F's '*Cap[tain]*' is characteristic of the
inconsistency found in foul papers. A 'captain'
(leader) could in fact hold the rank of general
(*OED* Captain *sb* 3).
  15 owl The owl's screech traditionally pro-
phesied death (see Dent R33).
  16 scourge See 1.2.129 n.
  17 period end.
  17 tyranny cruelty.

For I protest we are well fortified
And strong enough to issue out and fight.　　　　　　20
If thou retire, the dauphin, well appointed,
Stands with the snares of war to tangle thee.
On either hand thee there are squadrons pitched
To wall thee from the liberty of flight;
And no way canst thou turn thee for redress　　　　25
But Death doth front thee with apparent spoil
And pale Destruction meets thee in the face.
Ten thousand French have ta'en the sacrament
To rive their dangerous artillery
Upon no Christian soul but English Talbot.　　　　30
Lo, there thou stand'st, a breathing valiant man
Of an invincible unconquered spirit:
This is the latest glory of thy praise
That I, thy enemy, due thee withal;
For ere the glass, that now begins to run,　　　　35
Finish the process of his sandy hour,
These eyes, that see thee now well colourèd,
Shall see thee withered, bloody, pale, and dead.
　　　　　　　　　Drum afar off
Hark, hark, the dauphin's drum, a warning-bell,
Sings heavy music to thy timorous soul,　　　　40

---

29 rive] F; vyre *Oxford;* drive *conj. Johnson;* rove *conj. Hart*　　34 due] *Theobald;* dew F

19 protest assert.
21 appointed equipped.
22 snares This begins a chain of hunting metaphors that runs through 26, 27, and 45–52.
23 hand thee side of you.
23 pitched in battle array.
24 wall thee hem you in.
25 redress aid (*OED* sv *sb* 2).
26 front face, confront.
26 with apparent spoil promising that you will be slaughtered; 'spoil' (from hunting) means the 'capture of the quarry and division of rewards to the hounds' (Onions).
27 pale The traditional appearance of Death; compare Rev. 6.8: 'I…behold a pale horse, and his name that sat on him was Death.'
28 ta'en the sacrament Swearing of oaths could be reinforced by taking the sacrament.
29 rive…artillery 'fire it so heavily that the cannons would seem to burst' (Onions)? 'Rive' means literally 'split' or 'burst'. Oxford's 'vyre'

(= whirl or throw – taking 'artillery' to mean 'missiles, shot' (*OED* Artillery *sb* 3)) is possible; Hart's conjecture of 'rove' (= aim) must be rejected, as that verb was customarily followed by 'at' (see *OED*).
33 latest last.
34 *due 'endue, deck, grace' (Johnson).
35 Compare the proverb 'His glass is run' (Tilley G132).
35 glass hourglass.
36 Registers by the trickling of its sand that an hour has passed.
37 well colourèd i.e. in good health.
39 dauphin's drum A distinctive drumbeat.
39 warning-bell A bell that warned of fire or invasion (*OED* Warning *vbl sb* 12); or perhaps a reference to the sound of the 'fatal bellman' (*Mac.* 2.2.3) who sounded his bell at midnight before an execution.
40 heavy solemn, doleful.

And mine shall ring thy dire departure out.

Exeunt [General and others aloft]

TALBOT He fables not; I hear the enemy.
Out, some light horsemen, and peruse their wings.

[Exit one or more]

O negligent and heedless discipline!
How are we parked and bounded in a pale,   45
A little herd of England's timorous deer
Mazed with a yelping kennel of French curs!
If we be English deer, be then in blood,
Not rascal-like to fall down with a pinch,
But rather, moody-mad; and, desperate stags,   50
Turn on the bloody hounds with heads of steel
And make the cowards stand aloof at bay:
Sell every man his life as dear as mine,
And they shall find dear deer of us, my friends.
God and Saint George, Talbot and England's right,   55
Prosper our colours in this dangerous fight!

[Exeunt]

[4.3] *Enter a* MESSENGER *that meets York. Enter* YORK *with Trumpet and many Soldiers*

YORK Are not the speedy scouts returned again
That dogged the mighty army of the dauphin?
MESSENGER They are returned, my lord, and give it out

---

41 SD] *Malone subst.; Exit* F   43 SD] *Oxford; not in* F   50 moody-mad; and,] F *subst.;* moody-mad and
Capell   56 SD] F2; *not in* F   Act 4, Scene 3   4.3] *Capell subst.; not in* F

41 **departure** death (*OED* sv 2b).
43 **light** lightly armed.
43 **peruse** reconnoitre.
43 **wings** forces on the flank.
44 **discipline** military training or skill (*OED* sv *sb* 3b).
45 **parked** enclosed.
45 **pale** fenced area.
47 **Mazed** Stupefied, crazed (*OED* sv *ppl adj*).
47 **kennel** pack (*OED* sv *sb*[1] 2).
48 **in blood** (1) in full vigour, (2) in like temper.
49 **rascal-like** (1) like young or lean inferior deer, (2) like rogues.
49 **pinch** slight nip (*OED* sv *sb* 1).
50 **moody-mad** wild with rage.
51 **bloody** cruel, bloodthirsty.
51 **heads of steel** 'continuing the image of the

deer, he supposes their lances to be their horns' (Johnson).

54 **dear** (1) killed at great cost, (2) precious.
56 **colours** standards, banners; but also referring back to the imagery of blood and paleness at 37–8.

Act 4, Scene 3
*4.3 The events in 4.3 and 4.4 are fictitious, but the enmity between York and Somerset in 1435 is described by Holinshed, p. 185 (Hall, p. 179). York was 'so disdained of Edward Duke of Somerset...that by all means possible he sought his hindrance, as one glad of his loss and sorry of his well-doing'.

2 **dogged** tracked (*OED* Dog *v* 1).
3 **give it out** report.

That he is marched to Bordeaux with his power
To fight with Talbot; as he marched along,   5
By your espials were discoverèd
Two mightier troops than that the dauphin led,
Which joined with him and made their march for Bordeaux.

YORK A plague upon that villain Somerset
That thus delays my promisèd supply   10
Of horsemen that were levied for this siege!
Renownèd Talbot doth expect my aid,
And I am louted by a traitor villain
And cannot help the noble chevalier.
God comfort him in this necessity: 15
If he miscarry, farewell wars in France!

Enter another messenger [SIR WILLIAM LUCY]

LUCY Thou princely leader of our English strength,
Never so needful on the earth of France,
Spur to the rescue of the noble Talbot,
Who now is girdled with a waist of iron   20
And hemmed about with grim destruction.
To Bordeaux, warlike duke! To Bordeaux, York!
Else farewell Talbot, France, and England's honour.

YORK O God, that Somerset, who in proud heart
Doth stop my cornets, were in Talbot's place!   25
So should we save a valiant gentleman
By forfeiting a traitor and a coward.
Mad ire and wrathful fury makes me weep
That thus we die, while remiss traitors sleep.

---

5 Talbot;...along,] F2; *Talbot....along.* F   8 Bordeaux] F *subst.*; Bordeaux. *Exit / Cairncross*   13 louted] F; flouted *conj. Johnson*   16 SD SIR...LUCY] *Theobald; not in* F   17 SH LUCY] *Theobald; 2. Mes.* F   20 waist] *Steevens;* waste F

6 espials spies, scouts (*OED sv sb* 2).

9 Henry's attempt at reconciliation (4.1.162–8) has not worked.

10 supply reinforcements (*OED sv sb* 5).

12 expect await (*OED sv v* 2).

13 louted mocked, made a fool of (*OED Lout v³* 1); but Hulme (p. 313) suggests that it means equally 'delayed'.

15 necessity difficulty, deficiency (*OED sv sb* 10).

16 miscarry come to harm.

16 SD *LUCY See collation. In the chronicles there is no mention of a Lucy in France at this time, but the name appears in 43 below. Perhaps Shakespeare introduced him as an obscure compliment to his descendant Sir Thomas Lucy who lived near Stratford at Charlcote – see S. Schoenbaum, *William Shakespeare: A Compact Documentary Life*, 1977, p. 108.

20 waist (1) girdle or belt, (2) waste.

25 cornets cavalry companies (*OED sv sb²* 4); so called because of the shape of their standards.

28 makes For the singular verb with a plural subject see Abbott 336.

29 remiss negligent, idle (*OED sv adj* 2c); accented on the first syllable (Cercignani, p. 34).

LUCY O send some succour to the distressed lord! 30

YORK [*Aside*] He dies, we lose; I break my warlike word;
We mourn, France smiles; we lose, they daily get –
All long of this vile traitor Somerset!

LUCY Then God take mercy on brave Talbot's soul,
And on his son, young John, who two hours since 35
I met in travel toward his warlike father.
This seven years did not Talbot see his son,
And now they meet where both their lives are done.

YORK Alas, what joy shall noble Talbot have
To bid his young son welcome to his grave? 40
Away! Vexation almost stops my breath,
That sundered friends greet in the hour of death.
Lucy, farewell; no more my fortune can
But curse the cause I cannot aid the man.
Maine, Blois, Poitiers, and Tours are won away, 45
Long all of Somerset and his delay.

Exit [*with his Soldiers*]

LUCY Thus while the vulture of sedition
Feeds in the bosom of such great commanders,
Sleeping neglection doth betray to loss
The conquest of our scarce-cold conqueror, 50
That ever-living man of memory,
Henry the Fifth. Whiles they each other cross,
Lives, honours, lauds, and all hurry to loss. [*Exit*]

---

31 SD] *This edn; not in* F   36 travel] *Eds.;* trauaile F   46 SD *with his Soldiers*] *Collier subst.; not in* F   49
loss] *Pope;* losse: F   53 SD] F2; *not in* F

30 **distressed** troubled, straitened; accented
on the first syllable (Cercignani, p. 35).
31–3 These lines seem to constitute a short
soliloquy aside as York realises how he can turn
Somerset's failure to his own political advantage.
He proclaims Somerset's guilt aloud at 46 below
to Lucy – who is unconvinced.
33 **long** because.
35 **who** whom (Abbott 274).
37 **This seven years** For a long time; proverbial and not to be taken literally (see Dent
Y25).
41 **Vexation** Affliction (*ODE* sv 4).
42 **in…death** From the Litany.
43 **no…can** my fortune knows no other skill
(Abbott 307).
44 **the cause** him who brought it about that.
46 **Long all** All because.
47 **vulture of sedition** The metaphor is an
allusion to the stories of Prometheus or Tityus

whose livers were eaten out by birds of prey as
divine punishment.
47 **sedition** factious contest (*OED* sv 1).
48 **bosom** secret thoughts (*OED* sv *sb* 6a).
49 **Sleeping neglection** Negligent disregard.
50 **scarce-cold** Henry V had in fact been dead
for 31 years, but Shakespeare uses him throughout the play as the anti-type of his son.
51 **ever-living…memory** man of ever-living
memory; transferred epithet.
53 **lauds** praises. Most editors have misread F
and printed 'lands'.
53 *SD F does not mark an exit here for Lucy
(or an entrance for him in the following scene),
although the final couplet would seem to suggest
a scene ending. He therefore either remains aside
on stage to be discovered by Somerset and his
men, or enters to them at 9 of the following
scene.

[4.4] *Enter* SOMERSET *with his Army*[*, a* CAPTAIN *of Talbot's with him*]

SOMERSET It is too late, I cannot send them now.
        This expedition was by York and Talbot
        Too rashly plotted. All our general force
        Might with a sally of the very town
        Be buckled with: the over-daring Talbot   5
        Hath sullied all his gloss of former honour
        By this unheedful, desperate, wild adventure.
        York set him on to fight and die in shame
        That, Talbot dead, great York might bear the name.

[Enter SIR WILLIAM LUCY]

CAPTAIN Here is Sir William Lucy, who with me   10
        Set from our o'ermatched forces forth for aid.
SOMERSET How now, Sir William, whither were you sent?
LUCY Whither, my lord? From bought and sold Lord Talbot,
        Who, ringed about with bold adversity,
        Cries out for noble York and Somerset   15
        To beat assailing death from his weak regions;
        And whiles the honourable captain there
        Drops bloody sweat from his war-wearied limbs
        And, in advantage ling'ring, looks for rescue,

Act 4, Scene 4   4.4] *Capell subst.; not in* F   0 SD *a . . . him*] *Capell; not in* F   9 SD] *Capell; not in* F   16
region] F; legions *Rowe (compare 5.3.11)*   19 advantage ling'ring] F; advantage-ling'ring *Wilson;* unadvantaged,
ling'ring *Oxford*

Act 4, Scene 4

*4.4 See 4.3 headnote.

2 expedition Against Bordeaux.

3 rashly hastily (*OED* sv *adv* 1).

3–5 All . . . with The whole of our forces might be joined in close combat if their garrison alone were to come forth.

7 unheedful rash.

10 See 4.3.53 n.

13 Whither, my lord? Lucy scornfully disdains to answer the question put to him, as his concern is for Talbot.

13 bought and sold deceived (Dent B787); perhaps with an allusion to Judas.

14 adversity (1) ill fortune, (2) opposition, i.e. the force of France (*OED* Adversity 1; see Hulme, p. 307).

16 regions parts of the body (*OED* sv 6); compare Talbot's description of his 'weak unable

limbs' at 4.5.4. The allusion is to the way that at death life shrinks to the feet – compare Donne's 'Nocturnal upon Saint Lucy's Day', 7. Rowe's widely followed emendation of F's 'Regions' is supported by a supposedly similar compositorial confusion between MS. 'l' and 'R' at 5.3.11 as well as by a veiled reference to the 'legions of angels' of Matt. 26.53 – which might pick up the Gethsemane allusion in 13.

18 bloody sweat Compare Luke 20.44: 'His sweat was like drops of blood.'

19 in . . . ling'ring Obscure: either 'protracting his resistance by the advantage of a strong post' (Johnson), or 'suffering mortal pain (*OED* Linger *v* 3) even as he enjoys a (temporary) advantage'. Wilson's emendation (see collation) takes 'linger' as a transitive verb. Oxford's 'unadvantaged' is possible and attractive.

You, his false hopes, the trust of England's honour,   20
Keep off aloof with worthless emulation.
Let not your private discord keep away
The levied succours that should lend him aid,
While he, renownèd noble gentleman,
Yield up his life unto a world of odds.   25
Orléans the Bastard, Charles, Burgundy,
Alençon, Reignier compass him about,
And Talbot perisheth by your default.

SOMERSET York set him on: York should have sent him aid.

LUCY And York as fast upon your grace exclaims,   30
    Swearing that you withhold his levied host
    Collected for this expedition.

SOMERSET York lies: he might have sent and had the horse.
    I owe him little duty and less love,
    And take foul scorn to fawn on him by sending.   35

LUCY The fraud of England, not the force of France,
    Hath now entrapped the noble-minded Talbot:
    Never to England shall he bear his life,
    But dies betrayed to fortune by your strife.

SOMERSET Come, go; I will dispatch the horsemen straight: 40
    Within six hours they will be at his aid.

LUCY Too late comes rescue: he is ta'en or slain,
    For fly he could not if he would have fled;
    And fly would Talbot never though he might.

SOMERSET If he be dead, brave Talbot, then adieu!   45

LUCY His fame lives in the world, his shame in you.

Exeunt

---

25 Yield] F; Yields F2   26 Charles,] F; Charles and F2   27 Reignier] *Rowe; Reignard* F   31 host] F *subst.;* horse *Hanmer, conj. Theobald*   41 aid] F *subst.;* side *Cairncross*

20 trust guardian (*OED* sv *sb* 1c).
21 worthless emulation contemptible rivalry.
22 private discord personal quarrel.
23 succours reinforcements (*OED* sv *sb* 3).
25 Yield For the subjunctive use see Abbott 361.
25 a world of immense.
27 compass encircle.
28 default failure, offence (*OED* sv *sb* 5).
29 set him on incited him.
30 upon...exclaims loudly accuses your grace (*OED* Exclaim *v* 2a).
31 his levied host the army mustered for him.

Theobald's conjecture 'horse' is supported by 4.1.165, 4.3.10–11, and 33 below.
33 sent...horse requested and obtained the cavalry.
35 take would regard myself with.
35 to fawn if I were to fawn.
36 fraud faithlessness (*OED* sv *sb* 1).
41 aid Cairncross's emendation 'side' for F's 'ayde' is tempting. 'At his aid' is unidiomatic, is found nowhere else in Shakespeare, is graphically similar to 'syde', and was possibly carried over from the 'ayde' in 11, 23, and 29.

[4.5] *Enter* TALBOT *and* [JOHN] *his son*

TALBOT O young John Talbot, I did send for thee
        To tutor thee in stratagems of war,
        That Talbot's name might be in thee revived
        When sapless age and weak unable limbs
        Should bring thy father to his drooping chair.   5
        But – O malignant and ill-boding stars –
        Now thou art come unto a feast of death,
        A terrible and unavoided danger.
        Therefore, dear boy, mount on my swiftest horse,
        And I'll direct thee how thou shalt escape   10
        By sudden flight. Come, dally not, be gone.
JOHN Is my name Talbot? And am I your son?
        And shall I fly? O, if you love my mother,
        Dishonour not her honourable name
        To make a bastard and a slave of me!   15
        The world will say, he is not Talbot's blood
        That basely fled when noble Talbot stood.
TALBOT Fly, to revenge my death if I be slain.
JOHN He that flies so will ne'er return again.
TALBOT If we both stay, we both are sure to die.   20
JOHN Then let me stay and, father, do you fly.
        Your loss is great, so your regard should be:
        My worth unknown, no loss is known in me.
        Upon my death the French can little boast:
        In yours they will, in you all hopes are lost.   25
        Flight cannot stain the honour you have won:
        But mine it will, that no exploit have done.
        You fled for vantage, every one will swear:
        But if I bow, they'll say it was for fear.
        There is no hope that ever I will stay   30

Act 4, Scene 5   4.5] *Capell subst.; not in* F

Act 4, Scene 5
*4.5 The account of Young Talbot's devotion
to his father at Castillon (not Bordeaux) in 1453
is told in Holinshed (p. 236) and Shakespeare
seems to have been taken by the speeches
composed for the protagonists by Hall (p. 229).
  5 his drooping chair the chair in which he sits
in decline; transferred epithet.
  7 a...death 'a field where death will be

feasted with slaughter' (Johnson).
  8 unavoided unavoidable (*OED* sv *ppl adj* 2a).
  8 danger power (*OED* sv *sb* 1).
  16–55 Compare the couplets in another father
and son scene, *R2* 5.3.
  22 regard 'care of your own safety' (Johnson).
  28 for vantage to gain a tactical advantage.
  29 bow bend, yield.

If the first hour I shrink and run away.
Here, on my knee, I beg mortality
Rather than life preserved with infamy.
TALBOT Shall all thy mother's hopes lie in one tomb?
JOHN Ay, rather than I'll shame my mother's womb.   35
TALBOT Upon my blessing I command thee go.
JOHN To fight I will, but not to fly the foe.
TALBOT Part of thy father may be saved in thee.
JOHN No part of him but will be shame in me.
TALBOT Thou never hadst renown, nor canst not lose it.   40
JOHN Yes, your renownèd name: shall flight abuse it?
TALBOT Thy father's charge shall clear thee from that stain.
JOHN You cannot witness for me, being slain.
If death be so apparent, then both fly.
TALBOT And leave my followers here to fight and die?   45
My age was never tainted with such shame.
JOHN And shall my youth be guilty of such blame?
No more can I be severed from your side
Than can yourself yourself in twain divide.
Stay, go, do what you will, the like do I: 50
For live I will not, if my father die.
TALBOT Then here I take my leave of thee, fair son,
Born to eclipse thy life this afternoon.
Come, side by side, together live and die,
And soul with soul from France to heaven fly.   55

Exeunt

[4.6] *Alarum. Excursions wherein Talbot's son* [JOHN] *is hemmed about,
and* TALBOT *rescues him*

39 shame] F; shamed *Hudson, conj. Walker*   55 SD] F2; *Exit.* F   **Act 4, Scene 6**   4.6] *Capell subst.; not in* F

31 **shrink** yield, give way.
32 **mortality** death (*OED* sv 2c).
39 **shame** Walker's conjecture ('shamed')
seems appropriate to the stichomythia, and F's
reading could be due to an e/d confusion.
41 **abuse** dishonour.
42 **charge** order.
43 **being slain** if you are killed.
44 **apparent** likely (*OED* sv *adj* 5).
46 **age** lifetime.
53 **eclipse** extinguish (*OED* sv *v* 3b) – with a
pun on son/sun.

Act 4, Scene 6
*4.6 The details of the scene are fictitious.
Brockbank notes: 'Shakespeare seems to have
read Hall's more dramatic account of the death
of Talbot and his son (Holinshed omits Talbot's
speech). In consequence, perhaps, he was dis-
satisfied with his own version and rewrote it. Both
scenes may have been accidentally left in the
manuscript. . . and so printed in the Folio, standing in modern texts as 4.6 (the old) and 4.5 (the
new)' (p. 27).

TALBOT Saint George and victory! Fight, soldiers, fight:
       The regent hath with Talbot broke his word
       And left us to the rage of France his sword.
       Where is John Talbot? Pause, and take thy breath;
       I gave thee life and rescued thee from death.   5
JOHN O twice my father, twice am I thy son:
       The life thou gav'st me first was lost and done
       Till with thy warlike sword, despite of fate,
       To my determined time thou gav'st new date.
TALBOT When from the dauphin's crest thy sword struck fire,   10
       It warmed thy father's heart with proud desire
       Of bold-faced victory. Then leaden age,
       Quickened with youthful spleen and warlike rage,
       Beat down Alençon, Orléans, Burgundy,
       And from the pride of Gallia rescued thee.   15
       The ireful Bastard Orléans, that drew blood
       From thee, my boy, and had the maidenhood
       Of thy first fight, I soon encounterèd
       And, interchanging blows, I quickly shed
       Some of his bastard blood, and in disgrace   20
       Bespoke him thus: 'Contaminated, base,
       And misbegotten blood I spill of thine,
       Mean and right poor, for that pure blood of mine
       Which thou didst force from Talbot, my brave boy.'
       Here, purposing the Bastard to destroy,   25
       Came in strong rescue. Speak, thy father's care,
       Art thou not weary, John? How dost thou fare?
       Wilt thou yet leave the battle, boy, and fly,
       Now thou art sealed the son of chivalry?
       Fly, to revenge my death when I am dead;   30

21 him thus: 'Contaminated] F; him: 'This contaminated *conj. Vaughan*   26 Speak,] F4; Speak F

2 **The regent** York (see 4.1.162–3).
2 **word** Pronounced to rhyme with 'sword' (Cercignani, pp. 128–9).
9 **determined** appointed (*OED* sv *ppl adj* 4).
9 **date** limit (*OED* sv *sb*² 5).
10 **crest** helmet (*OED* sv *sb*¹ 4).
13 **Quickened** Enlivened.
13 **spleen** eager courage (*OED* sv *sb* 5).
15 **pride** full power (Schmidt); compare 3.2.40.

15 **Gallia** France.
17–18 **had…fight** first drew blood in your first encounter.
20 **in disgrace** contemptuously (*OED* Disgrace *sb* 4).
24 **brave** fine, courageous.
25 **purposing** while I was intending.
29 **sealed** certified (*OED* sv *ppl adj* 1b).

The help of one stands me in little stead.
O, too much folly is it, well I wot,
To hazard all our lives in one small boat.
If I today die not with Frenchmen's rage,
Tomorrow I shall die with mickle age.   35
By me they nothing gain and, if I stay,
'Tis but the short'ning of my life one day.
In thee thy mother dies, our household's name,
My death's revenge, thy youth, and England's fame:
All these and more we hazard by thy stay;   40
All these are saved if thou wilt fly away.

JOHN The sword of Orléans hath not made me smart;
These words of yours draw life-blood from my heart.
On that advantage, bought with such a shame,
To save a paltry life and slay bright fame,   45
Before young Talbot from old Talbot fly,
The coward horse that bears me fall and die!
And like me to the peasant boys of France,
To be shame's scorn and subject of mischance!
Surely, by all the glory you have won,   50
And if I fly, I am not Talbot's son.
Then talk no more of flight, it is no boot;
If son to Talbot, die at Talbot's foot.

TALBOT Then follow thou thy desp'rate sire of Crete,
Thou Icarus; thy life to me is sweet.   55
If thou wilt fight, fight by thy father's side,
And commendable proved, let's die in pride.

Exeunt

44 on that] F; Out on that *Theobald;* On what *Hanmer*   55 Icarus;] *Capell; Icarus,* F   57 SD] *Rowe; Exit* F

32 **wot** know.
33 Compare the proverb 'Venture not all in one bottom' (Tilley A209).
35 **mickle** great.
38 **our...name** Actually John was a younger son by a second wife.
42 **smart** suffer.
44 **On that advantage** To reap these benefits (see 48–51 below).
48 **like me to** make me resemble.
49 **subject of mischance** victim of ill fortune.
52 **boot** use.

54–5 The allusion is to Icarus, a figure of doomed aspiration or 'over-mounting spirit' (4.7.15) whose death occurred when, attempting to flee from King Minos of Crete, he flew too near the sun so that the wax that held the feathers in his wings melted and he fell into the sea. See *Metamorphoses* VIII, 245 ff.
57 **commendable** Accented on the first syllable (Cercignani, p. 42).
57 **pride** glory (*OED* sv *sb*[1] 8b).

[4.7] *Alarum. Excursions. Enter old* TALBOT *led [by a* SERVANT]

TALBOT	Where is my other life? Mine own is gone.
	O, where's young Talbot, where is valiant John?
	Triumphant Death, smeared with captivity,
	Young Talbot's valour makes me smile at thee.
	When he perceived me shrink and on my knee, 5
	His bloody sword he brandished over me,
	And, like a hungry lion, did commence
	Rough deeds of rage and stern impatience;
	But when my angry guardant stood alone,
	Tend'ring my ruin and assailed of none, 10
	Dizzy-eyed fury and great rage of heart
	Suddenly made him from my side to start
	Into the clust'ring battle of the French;
	And in that sea of blood my boy did drench
	His over-mounting spirit; and there died 15
	My Icarus, my blossom, in his pride.

Enter [Soldiers] with [the body of] JOHN TALBOT *borne*

SERVANT	O my dear lord, lo where your son is borne!
TALBOT	Thou antic Death, which laugh'st us here to scorn,
	Anon from thy insulting tyranny,
	Coupled in bonds of perpetuity, 20

Act 4, Scene 7   **4.7]** *Capell subst.; not in* F   **0** SD *by a servant*] *Cam.; not in* F   **16** SD *Soldiers*] *Capell; not in* F   **16** SD *the body of*] *Capell; not in* F

Act 4, Scene 7

***4.7** The details of the scene are fictitious.

3 Triumphant Riding in a triumph and leading captives after him (compare 1.1.22).

3 smeared with captivity marked with the blood of captives (*OED* Captivity 3); 'that is, death stained and dishonoured with captivity' (Johnson). There is a probable ironical allusion to the Messiah's triumph over death – see Eph. 4.8: 'he led captivity captive'.

8 rage spirited fury (*OED* sv *sb* 9).

8 impatience anger (*OED* sv 1); pronounced with four syllables (Cercignani, p. 294).

9 guardant protector; a term from heraldry.

10 Tend'ring my ruin 'Watching me with tenderness in my fall' (Johnson).

11 Dizzy-eyed Bewildered, with rolling eyes (compare *Ham.* 5.2.113–14: 'to divide him inventorially would dozy [i.e. make dizzy] th'arithmetic of memory').

13 clust'ring battle swarming main body (*OED* Battle *sb* 9).

14–16 For Icarus see 4.6.54–5 n.; the drowning image is appropriate, as Icarus fell into the sea.

14 drench drown (*OED* sv *v* 2).

16 blossom one lovely and full of promise (*OED* sv *sb* 2).

16 pride glory (as at 4.6.57).

18 antic A grotesque, monstrous, grinning figure; Death as a clown appears again in *R2* 3.2.162.

18 laugh'st...scorn Proverbial (Dent LL1).

18 here in this world.

19 Anon Immediately.

19 insulting arrogant, contemptuous (*OED* Insult *v* 1).

Two Talbots, wingèd through the lither sky,
In thy despite shall 'scape mortality –
O thou whose wounds become hard-favoured Death,
Speak to thy father ere thou yield thy breath!
Brave Death by speaking, whether he will or no;   25
Imagine him a Frenchman and thy foe –
Poor boy, he smiles, methinks, as who should say,
'Had Death been French, then Death had died today.'
Come, come, and lay him in his father's arms;
My spirit can no longer bear these harms.   30
Soldiers, adieu! I have what I would have,
Now my old arms are young John Talbot's grave.   *Dies*
                [*Alarums. Exeunt soldiers, leaving the bodies*]

Enter CHARLES, ALENÇON, BURGUNDY, BASTARD,
        and [LA] PUCELLE [*with Forces*]

CHARLES Had York and Somerset brought rescue in,
        We should have found a bloody day of this.
BASTARD How the young whelp of Talbot's, raging-wood,   35
        Did flesh his puny sword in Frenchmen's blood.
PUCELLE Once I encountered him, and thus I said:
        'Thou maiden youth, be vanquished by a maid';
        But with a proud majestical high scorn
        He answered thus: 'Young Talbot was not born   40
        To be the pillage of a giglot wench.'
        So, rushing in the bowels of the French,
        He left me proudly, as unworthy fight.
BURGUNDY Doubtless he would have made a noble knight.

---

25 whether] F3; whither F   32 SD.1 *Dies*] F; *Dies.* / Actus Quintus. Scæna Prima F2   32 SD.2 *Alarums...bodies*]
Capell; not in F   32 SD.3 *with Forces*] Malone; *not in* F   35 Talbot's, raging-wood] *Capell; Talbots raging wood* F

21–2 Talbot seems to proclaim here the apotheosis of his family, and the lines reinforce the suggestion that he embodies the spirit of Henry V. Compare the reference to the latter's apotheosis in 1.1.55–6.
21 wingèd flying (*OED* Wing *v* 2b); a continuation of the Icarus imagery.
21 lither pliant, nimble (*OED* sv *adj* 4); compare *Metamorphoses* VIII, 1027. Probably pronounced with a long *i* as in 'lithe'.
23 become grace, make beautiful (*OED* sv *v* 9c).
23 hard-favoured hard featured, ugly.
25 whether...no Proverbial (Dent w400.1).
27 as who as one who.

30 harms wounds.
35 whelp puppy; introducing a pun on Talbot = hound.
35 wood mad.
36 flesh plunge in for the first time (*OED* sv *v* 3); with a sexual quibble.
36 puny sword sword of an inexperienced ruler (*OED* Puny *adj* 3).
37 encountered A sexual quibble; see *OED* Encounter *sb* 2b.
38 maiden (1) virgin, (2) untried in warfare.
41 giglot 'a wanton or a strumpet' (Johnson).
42 bowels midst.
43 proudly With a quibble on 'proud' = sexually excited (*OED* Proud *adj* 8).

> See where he lies inhearsèd in the arms   45
> Of the most bloody nurser of his harms.
>
> BASTARD Hew them to pieces, hack their bones asunder,
> Whose life was England's glory, Gallia's wonder.
>
> CHARLES O no, forbear! For that which we have fled
> During the life, let us not wrong it dead.   50

Enter LUCY [*attended, the French Herald preceding*]

> LUCY Herald, conduct me to the dauphin's tent,
> To know who hath obtained the glory of the day.
>
> CHARLES On what submissive message art thou sent?
>
> LUCY Submission, dauphin? 'Tis a mere French word:
> We English warriors wot not what it means.   55
> I come to know what prisoners thou hast ta'en
> And to survey the bodies of the dead.
>
> CHARLES For prisoners ask'st thou? Hell our prison is.
> But tell me whom thou seek'st?
>
> LUCY But where's the great Alcides of the field,   60
> Valiant Lord Talbot, Earl of Shrewsbury,
> Created for his rare success in arms
> Great Earl of Washford, Waterford, and Valence,

50 SD *attended...preceding*] *Capell subst.; not in* F   51 LUCY Herald] F; LUCY *Pope*   51–2] *As* F; Herald...
know / Who...day. *Pope*   52 To know who] F; Who *Hanmer*   60 But where's] F; Where is *Rowe*

45 **inhearsèd** laid as in a coffin; see 32 above.
46 **his harms** the injuries he has done us.
51 **Herald** Pope omitted the word and other editors have followed. Oxford conjectures that an original SH 'Herald' may have been changed to Lucy (Wells and Taylor, *Textual Companion*, p. 224). See also 4.3.16 SD n.
51–2 Lucy's lines suggest that he expected an English victory (see 60 n. below).
54 **mere** exclusively.
58 **Hell...is** We have sent all our prisoners to hell.
60 **But where's** The lack of connection with the previous line and the two 'buts' suggest (1) the most likely explanation, that Lucy looks about him before speaking and then delivers his line with some surprise or dismay, (2) that something has been left out, (3) that the compositor caught the second 'But' from the line above (Sisson, *New Readings*, 11, 72), or (4) that it is evidence of Shakespeare revising someone else's draft (Wilson, p. xviii).
60 **Alcides** i.e. Hercules, grandson of Alcaeus.
61–70 The following titles were, it has been claimed, to be read on a tomb erected to Talbot in Falaise (near Caen) and now destroyed. A transcript would have been brought back to England by English soldiers who took the town in 1589. It is likely that his heart and bones, detached from his other mortal remains, were buried separately and soon after his death at Whitchurch in Shropshire. (See G. Lambin, 'Here lyeth John Talbot', *Études Anglaises* 24 (1971), 361–76.) There is no known printed source for this epitaph before Roger Cotton's *Armor of Proofe* (1596). Shakespeare may well have had access to a transcription through his association with Talbot's descendant, Ferdinando, Lord Strange (see p. 37 above).
61 **Shrewsbury** Talbot was created Earl of Salop in 1422 (*DNB*) but always took his title from the city, not the county.
63 **Washford** An old name for Wexford in Ireland; one of the Irish titles to which Talbot succeeded on the death of his niece Ankaret in 1421 (Thomson).
63 **Waterford** In 1446 Talbot was sent to govern Ireland and created Earl of Waterford (Thomson).
63 **Valence** One of Talbot's ancestors was Joan of Valence, sister of Aymer de Valence, last Earl of Pembroke of that line (Thomson).

Lord Talbot of Goodrich and Urchinfield,
Lord Strange of Blackmere, Lord Verdon of Alton,   65
Lord Cromwell of Wingfield, Lord Furnival of Sheffield,
The thrice victorious Lord of Falconbridge,
Knight of the noble order of Saint George,
Worthy Saint Michael, and the Golden Fleece,
Great Marshal to Henry the Sixth   70
Of all his wars within the realm of France?

PUCELLE Here's a silly stately style indeed:
The Turk, that two-and-fifty kingdoms hath,
Writes not so tedious a style as this.
Him that thou magnifi'st with all these titles   75
Stinking and fly-blown lies here at our feet.

LUCY Is Talbot slain, the Frenchmen's only scourge,
Your kingdom's terror and black Nemesis?
O were my mine eye-balls into bullets turned,
That I in rage might shoot them at your faces!   80
O that I could but call these dead to life,
It were enough to fright the realm of France!
Were but his picture left amongst you here
It would amaze the proudest of you all.

---

64 Goodrich] *Oxford;* Goodrig F   69 Worthy…Michael] F *subst.;* – Worthy…Michael – *conj. this edn*   70
Marshal] F; marechal *Capell subst.*   70 to] F; to our King F2

64 *Goodrich Talbot's father was Richard, fourth Baron Talbot, of Goodrich Castle in the Welsh marches.
64 Urchinfield A district in south-east Hertfordshire. Where Shakespeare derived this title from is unknown.
65 Lord Strange of Blackmere Through his mother, Talbot was the sole heir of the last Lord Strange of Blackmere, a place close to Whitchurch in Shropshire (Thomson).
65 Lord Verdon of Alton Talbot held this title through John Furnival, who was the eldest daughter of Theodore de Verdon (d. 1316). Alton or Arelton Castle is in Staffordshire (Thomson).
66 Wingfield In Derbyshire, where Talbot had a manor (Thomson).
66 Lord Furnival of Sheffield Talbot held this title in the right of his first wife, Maud, only daughter of Thomas Neville, who held the title in the right of his wife, Joan Furnival (Thomson).
67 Falconbridge Where Shakespeare derived this title from is unknown.
68 order…George An English order of knighthood.

69 Worthy…Michael As the French chivalric Order of Saint Michael had been instituted only in 1469, it is unlikely that these words could have appeared on Talbot's tomb (he died in 1453). Perhaps, therefore, they could be taken as an aside.
69 Worthy Of the value of (*OED* sv *adj* 1b).
69 Golden Fleece An order of knighthood of the Holy Roman Empire, instituted by Philip III, Duke of Burgundy, in 1429.
70 Great Marshal Commander in chief. 'Marshal' ('martial') could be trisyllabic in the period (Cercignani, p. 347).
72 style form of address.
73 Turk Sultan of Turkey; compare the inflated list of kingdoms subject to Callapine, son of Bajazeth, in Marlowe, *2 Tamburlaine* 3.1.1–7.
77–8 For the Tamburlaine-like imagery compare 1.4.107–8.
77 scourge See 1.2.129 n.
78 Nemesis The Greek goddess who, like the Erinnyes, punished crimes.
84 amaze craze, terrify.
84 the…all Proverbial (Dent P614.1).

Give me their bodies, that I may bear them hence   85
And give them burial as beseems their worth.
PUCELLE I think this upstart is old Talbot's ghost,
He speaks with such a proud commanding spirit.
For God's sake, let him have him; to keep them here,
They would but stink and putrefy the air.   90
CHARLES Go take their bodies hence.
LUCY   I'll bear them hence;
But from their ashes shall be reared
A phoenix that shall make all France afeard.
CHARLES So we be rid of them, do with him what thou wilt.
And now to Paris in this conquering vein: 95
All will be ours, now bloody Talbot's slain.

Exeunt

[**5.1**] *Sennet. Enter* KING, GLOUCESTER, *and* EXETER [*attended*]

KING HENRY Have you perused the letters from the Pope,
The Emperor, and the Earl of Armagnac?
GLOUCESTER I have, my lord, and their intent is this:
They humbly sue unto your excellence
To have a godly peace concluded of   5
Between the realms of England and of France.
KING HENRY How doth your grace affect their motion?

---

85 I may] F; I bear *Collier MS. in Cam.*   89 have him] F; have 'em *Theobald*   91–2] *As Pope; Char. . . . hence. /
Lucy. . . . reard* F   92 ashes] F; ashes, Dauphin *Pope*   94 rid of them] F; rid *Capell*   94 do with him] F; do with
them F2; do *Theobald*   94 thou] F (y^u)   94 wilt.] F; wilt. / *Exeunt Lucy and Attendants bearing out the bodies. / Capell
subst.*   96 SD] *Rowe; Exit.* F   **Act 5, Scene 1**   5.1] *Capell subst.; Scena secunda.* F   0 SD *attended*] *This edn;
not in* F   2, 17 Armagnac] F (Arminack)

87 upstart impertinent fellow; with perhaps a
punning reference to the convention whereby
ghosts emerged from the stage trap.
93 phoenix The fabulous Arabian bird that,
every five hundred years, died in a pyre of its own
making from which its progeny arose again; see
Metamorphoses XV, 432 ff.
95 vein mood.

Act 5, Scene 1
*****5.1** The negotiations for peace, held at Arras
in 1435, are narrated by Holinshed (p. 182; Hall,
p. 175). Proposals for Henry's marriage to the
daughter of the Earl of Armagnac were made in
1442 (Holinshed, p. 205; Hall, pp. 202–3).
Exeter had been dead a year in 1427, which was

historically when Winchester was made a cardinal
(Holinshed, p. 156; Hall, p. 139). In his anger,
Exeter recurs here to Henry V's prophecy that
Winchester would aim to make his 'cardinal's
hat. . .to be egal with princes' (Hall, p. 139;
compare Holinshed, p. 156). Holinshed (pp. 199
ff.) and Hall (pp. 197 ff.) print a second series of
charges against Winchester made by Gloucester
in 1441.
0 SD *Sennet* Sounded on a trumpet to make a
processional entrance (Long, p. 10).
1 Pope Eugenius IV (1431–47).
2 Emperor The Holy Roman Emperor, Sigis-
mund of Luxemburg (1410–38).
7 affect like, incline towards.
7 motion proposal.

GLOUCESTER Well, my good lord, and as the only means
    To stop effusion of our Christian blood,
    And stablish quietness on every side.   10
KING HENRY Ay, marry, uncle, for I always thought
    It was both impious and unnatural
    That such immanity and bloody strife
    Should reign among professors of one faith.
GLOUCESTER Beside, my lord, the sooner to effect   15
    And surer bind this knot of amity,
    The Earl of Armagnac, near knit to Charles,
    A man of great authority in France,
    Proffers his only daughter to your grace
    In marriage, with a large and sumptuous dowry.   20
KING HENRY Marriage, uncle? Alas, my years are young;
    And fitter is my study and my books
    Than wanton dalliance with a paramour.
    Yet call th'ambassadors, and, as you please,
    So let them have their answers every one: 25
                                [Exit Attendant]
    I shall be well content with any choice
    Tends to God's glory and my country's weal.

Enter WINCHESTER *[in cardinal's habit] and three Ambassadors,*
                  [one a PAPAL LEGATE]

EXETER What! Is my Lord of Winchester installed,
    And called unto a cardinal's degree?
    Then I perceive that will be verified   30
    Henry the Fifth did sometime prophesy:

---

17 knit] F; kin *Pope*   25 SD] *This edn; not in* F   27 SD.1 *in cardinal's habit*] *Capell subst.; not in* F   27 SD.2
one...LEGATE] *Kittredge, after Capell; not in* F   28 SH] F; EXETER *[aside] Munro*

9 **effusion** spilling.
13 **immanity** atrocious cruelty.
17 **near knit** closely related.
21 **my...young** As Henry was in fact 21 at
this time, it may be that Shakespeare was
justifying the use of a boy player throughout this
play – see p. 38 n. 9 above. There are similar
references to the king's age at 3.1.71 and 133.
27 **Tends** That tends (Abbott 244).
28–9 Exeter's surprise is not necessarily due to
revision or writing by another hand, as Dover
Wilson surmised (pp. xxii, xxxvii–xxxviii). Winchester appeared as a cardinal in 1.3. Exeter was
not on stage in 1.3, and may be thought of as
responding to the splendour of Winchester's

entry and the richness of his 'grave ornaments'
(54) – Winchester is papal emissary for the first
time. Shakespeare might, though, have forgotten
that he had already brought Winchester on thus
early in the play, and had his attention caught
by the second charges (see headnote) that the
chroniclers list for these years. These begin by
claiming that the elevation was an index of
Winchester's ambition. The moment may also be
accounted for as a continuation in the series of
interrupted ceremonies that have marked the
opening scene of each act of the play.
29 **degree** rank.
31 **sometime** once.

'If once he come to be a cardinal,
He'll make his cap co-equal with the crown.'

KING HENRY My lords ambassadors, your several suits
    Have been considered and debated on;   35
    Your purpose is both good and reasonable:
    And therefore are we certainly resolved
    To draw conditions of a friendly peace
    Which by my Lord of Winchester we mean
    Shall be transported presently to France.   40

GLOUCESTER [*To the Armagnac Ambassador*] And for the proffer of
    my lord your master,
    I have informed his highness so at large
    As, liking of the lady's virtuous gifts,
    Her beauty, and the value of her dower,
    He doth intend she shall be England's queen.   45

KING HENRY In argument and proof of which contract,
    Bear her this jewel, pledge of my affection.
    And so, my lord protector, see them guarded
    And safely brought to Dover where, inshipped,
    Commit them to the fortune of the sea.   50

                  Exeunt [all but Winchester and Legate]

WINCHESTER Stay, my lord legate, you shall first receive
    The sum of money which I promisèd
    Should be delivered to his holiness
    For clothing me in these grave ornaments.

LEGATE I will attend upon your lordship's leisure.   [*Exit*]   55

WINCHESTER Now Winchester will not submit, I trow,
    Or be inferior to the proudest peer.
    Humphrey of Gloucester, thou shalt well perceive
    That neither in birth, or for authority,
    The bishop will be overborne by thee: 60

---

41 SD] *M. Edel (after Capell at 46); not in* F   **49** where, inshipped] F4; wherein ship'd F   **50** SD all...Legate] *Cam., after Capell; not in* F   **55** SD] *Dyce; not in* F   **59** neither...or] F; nor...or *Pope*   **59** in] F; *for conj. Johnson*

33 cap The red hat of a cardinal.
34 several various.
38 draw draw up (*OED* sv v 63).
39 mean intend.
40 presently immediately.
41 master i.e. the Count of Armagnac.
42 at large fully.
43 As That (Abbott 275).
46 argument evidence.
46 contract Accented on the second syllable (Cercignani, p. 31).

49 inshipped once on board.
54 grave ornaments important ecclesiastical robes (*OED* Ornament sb 1b).
59–60 neither...thee 'Thou shalt not rule me, though thy birth is legitimate and thy authority supreme' (Johnson). For an argument that 'neither' represents a modernisation of MS. 'nor' by Compositor B, see Wells and Taylor, *Textual Companion*, p. 224.

I'll either make thee stoop and bend thy knee,
Or sack this country with a mutiny.   *Exit*

[5.2] *Enter* CHARLES, BURGUNDY, ALENÇON, BASTARD,
REIGNIER, *and* JOAN [LA PUCELLE *with Forces*]

CHARLES These news, my lords, may cheer our drooping spirits:
      'Tis said the stout Parisians do revolt
      And turn again unto the warlike French.
ALENÇON Then march to Paris, royal Charles of France,
      And keep not back your powers in dalliance.   5
PUCELLE Peace be amongst them if they turn to us;
      Else ruin combat with their palaces!

Enter SCOUT

SCOUT Success unto our valiant general,
      And happiness to his accomplices!
CHARLES What tidings send our scouts? I prithee speak.   10
SCOUT The English army that divided was
      Into two parties is now conjoined in one,
      And means to give you battle presently.
CHARLES Somewhat too sudden, sirs, the warning is,
      But we will presently provide for them.   15
      I trust the ghost of Talbot is not there.
BURGUNDY Now he is gone, my lord, you need not fear.

---

62 SD] *Dyce; Exeunt* F   **Act 5, Scene 2**   5.2] *Capell subst.; Scæna Tertia.* F   0 SD.2 LA PUCELLE] *Cam.;* Ione
F   0 SD.2 *with Forces*] *Capell; not in* F   7 combat with] F; come within *Cairncross*   12 is now conjoined F; now
conjoins *conj. Cairncross*   16 I] *Sanders; Bur.* I F   17–18] *As Sanders;* PUCELLE Now...fear / Of:...accursed
Oxford subst.   17 BURGUNDY Now] *Sanders;* Now F

62 mutiny rebellion (*OED* sv *sb* 1).

Act 5, Scene 2
  *5.2 Although we were told that Paris had been
lost in 1.1.61 (in '1422'), Henry was crowned
there at the opening of Act 4. The actual revolt of
the Parisians took place in 1436, and is
chronicled by Holinshed (p. 186; Hall, p. 180).
  2 stout valiant.
  3 turn again A characteristic of the French in
this play – compare 3.3.85.
  5 dalliance trifling, idleness.
  7 Else Otherwise.
  7 combat with Cairncross's emendation

'come within' (compare Ps. 122.7: 'Peace be
within thy walls, and prosperity within thy
palaces') is attractive, but F's 'combat with' (=
fight) is possible, as at 1.1.54 (*OED* Combat *v* 1).
Compare also *2H6* 4.1.101–2: 'beggary / Is crept
into the palace of our king'.
  9 accomplices associates (perhaps ironically
= 'partners in incompetence': see *OED* Accom-
plice 2).
  *16 I follow Sanders' reattribution of this line
to Charles; 17 is more likely to be a response than
a second thought of Burgundy's. George Walton
Williams, however, argues that 17–20 should be
given to Pucelle (*S. Sur.* 36 (1983), p. 183).

PUCELLE Of all base passions, fear is most accursed.
     Command the conquest, Charles, it shall be thine:
     Let Henry fret and all the world repine.   20
CHARLES Then on, my lords, and France be fortunate!

                                              Exeunt

[5.3] *Alarum. Excursions. Enter* JOAN [LA] PUCELLE

PUCELLE The regent conquers and the Frenchmen fly.
     Now help, ye charming spells and periapts,
     And ye choice spirits that admonish me,
     And give me signs of future accidents.
                    Thunder
     You speedy helpers, that are substitutes   5
     Under the lordly monarch of the north,
     Appear, and aid me in this enterprise!

                Enter Fiends

     This speed and quick appearance argues proof
     Of your accustomed diligence to me.

Act 5, Scene 3   5.3] *Capell subst.; not in* F   o SD LA] *Rowe; de* F   8 speed and quick] *Dyce;* speedy and quick
F; speedy quick *Pope*

18 **passions** emotions.
20 **repine** complain.
21 **fortunate** favoured by Fortune.

Act 5, Scene 3
 *5.3 Historically Joan was captured in 1430
(Holinshed, p. 170; Hall, p. 157) – not by York,
as in the play, but by a mixed force of English and
Burgundians. Suffolk's capture of Margaret and
their love affair are fictitious although he did, in
1444, arrange the match between her and Henry:
'Suffolk...adventuring somewhat upon his
commission, without the assent of his associates,
imagined, that the next way to come to a perfect
peace was to contrive a marriage between...
Margaret...and...Henry' (Holinshed, p. 206;
Hall, p. 203). Reignier's rapid decision to accept
Suffolk's offer and descend from the walls
(131–45) could be played to satirical effect in the
theatre.
 1 **regent** York, although historically Bedford
was regent at this time; see 4.1.163.
 2 **Now help** Joan resorts to witchcraft only in

despair, This does not prove the English charge
that she was a witch from the first.
 2 **charming** exercising magic power (*OED* sv
ppl adj 1).
 2 **periapts** amulets; worn about the body as a
charm. Reginald Scot, *The Discoverie of Witchcraft* (1584), XII, ix, associates them with popery.
 3 **admonish** warn (*OED* sv *v* 4); see 1.2.68 n.
 4 **accidents** events (*OED* sv *sb* 1).
 5 **substitutes** deputies (*OED* sv *sb* 1).
 6 **monarch of the north** Either Lucifer, as in
Isa. 14.13: 'I will ascend into heaven, and exalt
my throne above beside the stars of God: I will sit
also upon the mount of the congregation in the
sides of the north'; or Zimimar, a devil frequently
invoked by witches and named as King of the
North – see Scot, *Discoverie of Witchcraft*, XV, ii,
iii.
 8 *speed F's 'speedy' is probably dittography
from 5.
 8 **argues** offers.
 9 **diligence** assiduous service (*OED* Diligence[1]
1b).

Now, ye familiar spirits, that are culled   10
Out of the powerful regions under earth,
Help me this once, that France may get the field.
            They walk, and speak not
O hold me not with silence over-long!
Where I was wont to feed you with my blood
I'll lop a member off and give it you   15
In earnest of a further benefit,
So you do condescend to help me now.
            They hang their heads
No hope to have redress? My body shall
Pay recompense if you will grant my suit.
            They shake their heads
Cannot my body nor blood-sacrifice   20
Entreat you to your wonted furtherance?
Then take my soul – my body, soul, and all –
Before that England give the French the foil.
                        They depart
See, they forsake me! Now the time is come
That France must vail her lofty-plumèd crest   25
And let her head fall into England's lap.
My ancient incantations are too weak,
And hell too strong for me to buckle with:

10 culled] F; called *Collier MS.*   11 regions] F; legions *conj. Warburton (compare 4.4.16)*   25 lofty-plumèd] *Capell;* lofty plumed F

10 **familiar spirits** Attendant spirits, often inhabiting the bodies of animals, that could be summoned by a witch. Compare Saul's consultation of the Witch of Endor: 'I pray thee, conjecture unto me by the familiar spirit, and bring me him up whom I shall name unto thee' (1 Sam. 28.8).

10 **culled** chosen.

11 **regions** Warburton's conjectural substitution of 'legions' for F's 'Regions' is attractive; compare 4.4.16 n.

12 **get the field** win the battle.

13–24 With this sequence, where the devils refuse to help their victim before death, compare Dekker, Ford, and Rowley's *The Witch of Edmonton* 5.1.

14 **Where** Whereas (Abbott 134).

14 It was believed that a witch's familiar would feed from a special teat or 'mark' on her body; see

Thomas, p. 530.

15 **member** limb.

16 **In earnest** As an advance payment.

17 **condescend** agree (*OED* sv *v* 5).

18 **redress** aid, help (*OED* sv *sb* 2).

21 **furtherance** assistance.

22 She offers the devils a compact, her soul in return for diabolic power; see Thomas, pp. 528 ff.

23 **give…the foil** defeat the French; from wrestling, where 'foil' = throw your opponent (*OED* Foil *sb²* 1); here with an obscene innuendo (see 3.3.11 n.).

25 **vail** lower.

26 **fall…lap** come under England's power (*OED* Lap *sb¹* 6).

27 **ancient** former (*OED* sv *adj* 1).

28 **buckle** engage (*OED* sv *v* 3; compare 1.2.95 n.).

Now, France, thy glory droopeth to the dust.

Exit [to join the French forces]

Excursions. BURGUNDY *and* YORK *fight hand to hand.*
[The] French fly [leaving La Pucelle in York's power]

YORK Damsel of France, I think I have you fast: 30
  Unchain your spirits now with spelling charms
  And try if they can gain your liberty.
  A goodly prize, fit for the devil's grace! –
  See how the ugly witch doth bend her brows,
  As if, with Circe, she would change my shape!   35
PUCELLE Changed to a worser shape thou canst not be.
YORK O Charles the dauphin is a proper man:
  No shape but his can please your dainty eye.
PUCELLE A plaguing mischief light on Charles and thee!
  And may ye both be suddenly surprised   40
  By bloody hands in sleeping on your beds!
YORK Fell banning hag! Enchantress, hold thy tongue!
PUCELLE I prithee give me leave to curse awhile.
YORK Curse, miscreant, when thou com'st to the stake.

Exeunt

Alarum. Enter SUFFOLK *with* MARGARET *in his hand*

SUFFOLK Be what thou wilt, thou art my prisoner. *Gazes on her* 45
  O fairest beauty, do not fear nor fly,
  For I will touch thee but with reverent hands.

---

29 SD.1 *Exit*] F; *Exit* / 5.4 *Oxford*   29 SD.1 *to...forces*] *This edn; not in* F   29 SD.3 *leaving...power*] *Brooke; not in*
F   44 com'st] F; comest *Rowe*   44 SD *Exeunt*] F; *Exeunt* / 5.5 *Oxford*   47 reverent] *Hanmer;* reverend F

*29 SD.2 No re-entrance is marked for Pucelle
in F, and some editors have conjectured that
'BURGUNDY' is a mistake for 'PUCELLE'. But the
Maid's power, as we have just seen, is spent, and
she is probably a mere spectator at the skirmish.
31 spelling bewitching.
33 the devil's grace his grace the devil
(ironic); compare *1H4* 3.2.119.
34 bend her brows frown, scowl (*OED* Bend *v*
6b).
35 with like (Abbott 195).
35 Circe In Book 9 of the *Odyssey*, Circe turns
Ulysses' companions to swine; compare *Metamorphoses* XIV, 12.
37 proper handsome (*OED* sv *adj* 8).
38 dainty fastidious (*OED* sv *adj* 5).

39 plaguing mischief tormenting disease (*OED*
Mischief *sb* 4; Dent MM14).
40 surprised seized (*OED* Surprise *v* 2b).
41 in while (Abbott 164).
42 Fell Fierce.
42 banning cursing.
43 leave to curse 'the privilege of a loser'
(Wilson).
44 miscreant heretic (*OED* sv *sb* 1).
44 SD.2 There is no need to begin a new scene
here as the capture of Margaret is part of the
same action. In this unhistorical incident Margaret
takes over Pucelle's role as a French 'enchantress'.
44 SD.2 in his hand led by the hand (*OED*
Hand *sb* 29b).
47 *reverent respectful.

I kiss these fingers for eternal peace
And lay them gently on thy tender side.
Who art thou, say, that I may honour thee?   50
MARGARET Margaret my name, and daughter to a king,
    The King of Naples – whosoe'er thou art.
SUFFOLK An earl I am, and Suffolk am I called.
    Be not offended, nature's miracle,
    Thou art allotted to be ta'en by me: 55
    So doth the swan her downy cygnets save,
    Keeping them prisoner underneath her wings.
    Yet if this servile usage once offend,
    Go and be free again as Suffolk's friend.

               She is going

    O stay! [*Aside*] I have no power to let her pass;   60
    My hand would free her, but my heart says no.
    As plays the sun upon the glassy streams
    Twinkling another counterfeited beam,
    So seems this gorgeous beauty to mine eyes.
    Fain would I woo her, yet I dare not speak: 65
    I'll call for pen and ink, and write my mind.
    Fie, de la Pole, disable not thyself!
    Hast not a tongue? Is she not here to hear?
    Wilt thou be daunted at a woman's sight?
    Ay; beauty's princely majesty is such   70
    Confounds the tongue and makes the senses rough.

48–9] *As* F; *49 precedes 48, Capell* 56 her] F; *his Oxford* 57 her] F3; *his* F 60 SD] *Dyce; not in* F 62
streams] F; *stream Singer²* 68 not here to hear] *Oxford; not here* F; *heere thy prisoner* F2; *not prisoner here
Cairncross*

48–9 It is difficult to be sure what gesture accompanies these lines. It may be that Suffolk kisses his own fingers, like Malvolio (*TN* 3.4.32), and places them on Margaret's cheek (see 1.4.74 above) or, more lasciviously, on her crotch (*OED* Side *sb*¹ 1b). Perhaps he kisses her hand only to release it to hang naturally by her body, in token that she may consider herself free. Capell reversed the order of these two lines.
48 for in token of.
52 King of Naples i.e. Reignier.
55 allotted destined (*OED* Allot *v* 4).
55 ta'en (1) captured, (2) made love to.
58 servile usage treatment befitting a slave.
59 friend lover (*OED* *sb* *sb* 4).
62–4 'This comparison made between things which seem sufficiently unlike, is intended to ex-

press the softness and delicacy of Lady Margaret's beauty, which delighted, but did not dazzle; which was bright, but gave no pain by its lustre' (Johnson).
63 Twinkling That shine back.
63 counterfeited i.e. reflected.
67 de la Pole The family name of the Suffolks.
67 disable disparage (*OED* sv *v* 3).
68 *here to hear I accept Oxford's emendation of F's 'here'. (The irregular line encouraged previous editors to insert F2's 'thy prisoner' after 'not'. However, Suffolk has just renounced the role of gaoler.)
69 at...sight at the sight of a woman.
70–1 such Confounds such that it disables.
71 rough agitated (like troubled waters (*OED* Rough *adj* 4a)).

MARGARET Say, Earl of Suffolk – if thy name be so –
          What ransom must I pay before I pass?
          For I perceive I am thy prisoner.

SUFFOLK [*Aside*] How canst thou tell she will deny thy suit,   75
          Before thou make a trial of her love?

MARGARET Why speak'st thou not? What ransom must I pay?

SUFFOLK [*Aside*] She's beautiful, and therefore to be wooed;
          She is a woman, therefore to be won.

MARGARET Wilt thou accept of ransom, yea or no?   80

SUFFOLK [*Aside*] Fond man, remember that thou hast a wife;
          Then how can Margaret be thy paramour?

MARGARET I were best to leave him for he will not hear.

SUFFOLK [*Aside*] There all is marred; there lies a cooling card.

MARGARET He talks at random: sure the man is mad.   85

SUFFOLK [*Aside*] And yet a dispensation may be had.

MARGARET And yet I would that you would answer me.

SUFFOLK [*Aside*] I'll win this Lady Margaret. For whom?
          Why, for my king – tush, that's a wooden thing!

MARGARET He talks of wood: it is some carpenter.   90

SUFFOLK [*Aside*] Yet so my fancy may be satisfied,
          And peace establishèd between these realms.
          But there remains a scruple in that too:
          For though her father be the King of Naples,
          Duke of Anjou and Maine, yet is he poor,   95
          And our nobility will scorn the match.

MARGARET Hear ye, captain? Are you not at leisure?

SUFFOLK [*Aside*] It shall be so, disdain they ne'er so much;
          Henry is youthful and will quickly yield. –
          Madam, I have a secret to reveal.   100

MARGARET [*Aside*] What though I be enthralled, he seems a knight,

75, 78, 81, 88, 91 SD] *Pope; not in* F   83 I were] F; 'Twere *Pope*   84, 86, 98 SD] *Dyce; not in* F
85 random] F3; randon F   101, 104, 107 SD] *Theobald; not in* F

75 **deny** refuse.

79 Compare the proverb 'All women may be won' (Tilley w681).

81 **Fond** Foolish.

82 **paramour** mistress; lady for whom a knight does battle (*OED* sv *sb* 2c).

84 **cooling card** A card that dashes an opponent's hopes; hence an obstacle (Tilley c644).

85 ***at random** recklessly, at great speed (*OED* Random *sb* 3a).

86 **dispensation** annulment (of my marriage).

89 **wooden thing** (1) dull blockish fellow (the king), (2) unlikely undertaking (Steevens).

91 **fancy** amorous inclination, love (*OED* sv *sb* 8b).

93 **scruple** objection, difficulty.

98 **disdain...much** no matter how much contempt they show.

101 **enthralled** (1) made captive, (2) captivated.

And will not any way dishonour me.
SUFFOLK Lady, vouchsafe to listen what I say.
MARGARET [*Aside*] Perhaps I shall be rescued by the French,
    And then I need not crave his courtesy.   105
SUFFOLK Sweet madam, give me hearing in a cause –
MARGARET [*Aside*] Tush, women have been captivate ere now.
SUFFOLK Lady, wherefore talk you so?
MARGARET I cry you mercy, 'tis but *quid* for *quo*.
SUFFOLK Say, gentle princess, would you not suppose   110
    Your bondage happy, to be made a queen?
MARGARET To be a queen in bondage is more vile
    Than is a slave in base servility;
    For princes should be free.
SUFFOLK   And so shall you
    If happy England's royal king be free.   115
MARGARET Why, what concerns his freedom unto me?
SUFFOLK I'll undertake to make thee Henry's queen,
    To put a golden sceptre in thy hand
    And set a precious crown upon thy head,
    If thou wilt condescend to be my –
MARGARET   What?   120
SUFFOLK His love.
MARGARET I am unworthy to be Henry's wife.
SUFFOLK No, gentle madam, I unworthy am
    To woo so fair a dame to be his wife,
    And have no portion in the choice myself.   125
    How say you, madam, are ye so content?
MARGARET And if my father please, I am content.
SUFFOLK Then call our captains and our colours forth!
    And, madam, at your father's castle walls

---

106 cause –] *Capell;* cause. F   **108** Lady] F; Nay, hear me, lady *Capell*   **125**] F; [*Aside*] And...myself *conj.*
Vaughan

107 been captivate (1) been taken prisoner, (2) lost their hearts.
109 *quid* **for** *quo* tit for tat.
112 vile meanly regarded (*OED* sv *adj* 5b).
113 servility slavery.
114 princes men and women of royal blood.
115 happy fortunate.
115 free With a probable suggestion of being 'ready to take liberties', 'licentious', although

OED (sv *adj* 23) records this only from 1635; compare 5.4.82.
120 condescend agree (*OED* sv *v* 5).
120 my – Freud (*The Psychopathology of Everyday Life*, trans. Alan Tyson, 1966, pp. 97–8) discusses Portia's similar slip of the tongue in *MV* 3.2.17.
125 no portion in (1) no share in, (2) nothing to show for.
125 choice (1) choosing, (2) person chosen.

We'll crave a parley, to confer with him.   130

[Enter Captains, Colours, and Trumpeters.] Sound [a parley].
Enter REIGNIER *on the walls*

See, Reignier, see, thy daughter prisoner!
REIGNIER To whom?
SUFFOLK   To me.
REIGNIER   Suffolk, what remedy?
I am a soldier and unapt to weep
Or to exclaim on fortune's fickleness.
SUFFOLK Yes, there is remedy enough, my lord: 135
Consent, and for thy honour give consent,
Thy daughter shall be wedded to my king,
Whom I with pain have wooed and won thereto;
And this her easy-held imprisonment
Hath gained thy daughter princely liberty.   140
REIGNIER Speaks Suffolk as he thinks?
SUFFOLK   Fair Margaret knows
That Suffolk doth not flatter, face, or feign.
REIGNIER Upon thy princely warrant I descend
To give thee answer of thy just demand.

                            [Exit from the walls]
SUFFOLK And here I will expect thy coming.   145

Trumpets sound. Enter REIGNIER *[below]*

REIGNIER Welcome, brave earl, into our territories.
Command in Anjou what your honour pleases.
SUFFOLK Thanks, Reignier, happy for so sweet a child,
Fit to be made companion with a king.
What answer makes your grace unto my suit?   150
REIGNIER Since thou dost deign to woo her little worth

---

130 SD *Enter...Trumpeters*] *Oxford (after 128); not in* F   **130** SD *a parley*] *Capell; not in* F   **136** Consent] F; Assent
Oxford   **136** and for] F; yea, for *conj. this edn*   **144** SD] *Capell; not in* F   **145** SD *below*] *Capell; not in* F

132 remedy help for it.
133 unapt unfitted (*OED* sv *adj* 1).
134 exclaim on accuse, rail at (*OED* Exclaim *v* 2b).
136 The meaning is unclear. Perhaps 'yea, for thy honour' would make better sense.
138 Whom i.e. Margaret.
138 pain much effort.
141 Speaks...thinks? Compare the proverb

'To speak as one thinks' (Tilley s725).
142 face deceive (*OED* sv *v* 1c).
143 warrant assurance (*OED* sv *sb*[1] 4b).
145 expect await (*OED* sv *v* 2).
146 SD The trumpets cover the descent (probably within the tiring-house) of Reignier from the stage balcony.
148 happy for fortunate to have.
151 her...worth her who is so unworthy.

To be the princely bride of such a lord,
Upon condition I may quietly
Enjoy mine own, the country Maine and Anjou,
Free from oppression or the stroke of war,   155
My daughter shall be Henry's, if he please.

SUFFOLK That is her ransom; I deliver her;
And those two counties I will undertake
Your grace shall well and quietly enjoy.

REIGNIER And I again, in Henry's royal name,   160
As deputy unto that gracious king
Give thee her hand for sign of plighted faith.

SUFFOLK Reignier of France, I give thee kingly thanks
Because this is in traffic of a king.
[*Aside*] And yet methinks I could be well content   165
To be mine own attorney in this case. –
I'll over then to England with this news,
And make this marriage to be solemnised.
So farewell, Reignier; set this diamond safe
In golden palaces as it becomes.   170

REIGNIER I do embrace thee, as I would embrace
The Christian prince King Henry were he here.

MARGARET Farewell, my lord; good wishes, praise, and prayers
Shall Suffolk ever have of Margaret.

She is going

SUFFOLK Farewell, sweet madam; but hark you, Margaret,   175
No princely commendations to my king?

MARGARET Such commendations as becomes a maid,
A virgin, and his servant, say to him.

SUFFOLK Words sweetly placed and modestly directed;
But, madam, I must trouble you again: 180
No loving token to his majesty?

---

154 country] F; countries *Capell*   **165** SD] *Rowe; not in* F   **172** here.] F *subst.;* here. *Exit. / conj. anon in Cam.*
175 madam] F; maid *Cairncross*   **179** modestly] F2; modestie F

154 country F's singular suggests that Reignier may be thinking of his two territories as one country – or it may be a mistake (Holinshed has 'duchy of Anjou and...county of Maine' (p. 206; Hall, p. 204)).
158 counties domains of a count (*OED* County[1]).
  160 again in return (*OED* sv *adv* 2).
  161 deputy Suffolk.
  162 plighted faith promise to marry.

164 traffic business (*OED* sv *sb* 3); and, possibly, 'prostitute' (*OED* sv *sb* 4c).
  166 be...attorney act on my own behalf.
  170 as it becomes as is fitting.
  175 madam Anticipates her rank and possibly brands her as a courtesan (*OED* Madam *sb* 3c); compare 164 n.
  176 commendations greetings.
  179 placed arranged.

MARGARET Yes, my good lord; a pure unspotted heart
　　　　　Never yet taint with love, I send the king.
SUFFOLK And this withal.

Kiss her

MARGARET That for thyself: I will not so presume   185
　　　　　To send such peevish tokens to a king.

[Exeunt Reignier and Margaret]

SUFFOLK O wert thou for myself! But, Suffolk, stay;
　　　　Thou mayst not wander in that labyrinth:
　　　　There Minotaurs and ugly treasons lurk.
　　　　Solicit Henry with her wondrous praise;   190
　　　　Bethink thee on her virtues that surmount,
　　　　Mad natural graces that extinguish art;
　　　　Repeat their semblance often on the seas,
　　　　That, when thou com'st to kneel at Henry's feet,
　　　　Thou mayst bereave him of his wits with wonder.   *Exit*   195

[5.4] *Enter* YORK, WARWICK, [a] SHEPHERD, [LA] PUCELLE [*guarded, and others*]

YORK Bring forth that sorceress condemned to burn.
SHEPHERD Ah, Joan, this kills thy father's heart outright!

---

186 SD] Capell; *not in* F   **188, 195** mayst] *Cam.;* mayest F   **190** wondrous] F3; wonderous F   **192** Mad] F; And *Capell;* 'Mid *Collier²;* Maid *conj. Perring in Cam.*   **Act 5, Scene 4   5.4**] *Capell subst.; not in* F   **0** SD guarded] *Capell; not in* F   **0** SD *and others*] *Cam.; not in* F   **1** burn.] F; burn. / *Enter La Pucelle, guarded, and a Shepherd. / Eds. after Capell*

183 taint tainted, tinged (*OED* sv *sb* B1).
186 peevish silly, foolish (*OED* sv *adj* 1).
188–9 labyrinth...Minotaurs Referring to the maze in Crete built by King Minos where lived the Minotaur, the monstrous offspring of the Queen Pasiphaë's intercourse with a bull; compare 4.6.54–5.
190 Solicit Incite, allure (*OED* sv *v* 4).
190 her wondrous praise praise of her wondrous qualities.
191 surmount excel (*OED* sv *v* 2).
192 Mad F's 'Mad' needs no emendation (= wild, extravagant (*OED* sv *adj* 7)). However, editors have tended to emend: 'And' is graphically possible (Sisson, *New Readings*, II, 73) and seems preferable to Collier's ''Mid'.
192 extinguish eclipse (*OED* sv *v* 2b).
193 Repeat their semblance Conjure up the image of them.
195 bereave dispossess.

Act 5, Scene 4

*****5.4** Joan was captured at Compiègne in 1430 and burnt at Rouen in 1431 (Holinshed, pp. 170–1; Hall, pp. 156–9). Shakespeare invented the episode where she denies her father 2–33), but follows Holinshed (p. 171) when she claims she is with child (59–85). The terms of peace announced by Winchester are based on those offered at Arras in 1435 (Holinshed, pp. 182–3; Hall, pp. 175–6; see Appendix 1, p. 200 below). The chroniclers report, however, that these were 'either of frowardness or of disdain on both parts...openly refused' (Holinshed, p. 183). Shakespeare seems therefore to have brought the contest between the two countries to an unhistorical conclusion wherein Henry is triumphant over Charles, the better to highlight Suffolk's treachery.
2 kills...heart discourages me completely (*OED* Kill *v* 7c; Dent KK2).

Have I sought every country far and near,
And, now it is my chance to find thee out,
Must I behold thy timeless cruel death?   5
Ah, Joan, sweet daughter Joan, I'll die with thee!

PUCELLE Decrepit miser, base ignoble wretch!
I am descended of a gentler blood:
Thou art no father nor no friend of mine.

SHEPHERD Out, out! – My lords, and please you, 'tis not so: 10
I did beget her, all the parish knows.
Her mother liveth yet, can testify
She was the first-fruit of my bach'lorship.

WARWICK Graceless, wilt thou deny thy parentage?

YORK This argues what her kind of life hath been,   15
Wicked and vile, and so her death concludes.

SHEPHERD Fie, Joan, that thou wilt be so obstacle!
God knows thou art a collop of my flesh,
And for thy sake have I shed many a tear.
Deny me not, I prithee, gentle Joan.   20

PUCELLE Peasant, avaunt! – You have suborned this man
Of purpose to obscure my noble birth.

SHEPHERD 'Tis true, I gave a noble to the priest
The morn that I was wedded to her mother. –
Kneel down and take my blessing, good my girl.   25
Wilt thou not stoop? Now cursèd be the time
Of thy nativity! I would the milk
Thy mother gave thee when thou suck'dst her breast

---

10 so:] *This edn;* so F; so, F2   28 suck'dst] F2; suck'st F

3 **sought** searched (*OED* Seek *v* 10).
3 **country** district (*OED* sv *sb* 2).
4 **it…chance** I have happened.
5 **timeless** untimely (*OED* sv *adj* 1).
7 **miser** wretch (*OED* sv *sb*¹ 1).
7 **ignoble** of low descent.
8–9 This is a contradiction of her account of her descent at 1.2.72–5.
8 **gentler** nobler.
9 **friend** kinsman (*OEd* sv *sb* 3).
10 **Out, out!** The interjection expresses lamentation or abhorrence (*OED* Out *int* 2).
13 **first-fruit** first-born, and something to be offered to God.
13 **bach'lorship** i.e. she was conceived illegitimately.
14 **Graceless** Unfeeling wretch (*OED* sv *adj* 3).

15 **argues** indicates (*OED* sv *v* 3).
16 **concludes** (1) makes an end, (2) proves the supposition.
17 **obstacle** obstinate, stubborn; a dialect word to suggest rusticity (*OED* sv *adj*).
18 **collop…flesh** Compare the proverb 'It's a dear collop that is taken out of the flesh' (Tilley C517); 'collop' = 'slice'.
20 **Deny** Disown (*OED* sv *v* 4).
21 **suborned…man** procured this man to give false testimony (*OED* Suborn *v* 2).
22 **obscure** conceal.
23 **noble** A gold coin worth about a third of a pound sterling; the same quibble appears at *1H4* 2.4.291.
26 **stoop** humble yourself (*OED* sv *v*¹ 2).

Had been a little ratsbane for thy sake!
Or else, when thou didst keep my lambs a-field,   30
I wish some ravenous wolf had eaten thee!
Dost thou deny thy father, cursèd drab? –
O burn her, burn her: hanging is too good.   *Exit*

YORK Take her away, for she hath lived too long
        To fill the world with vicious qualities.   35

PUCELLE First let me tell you whom you have condemned:
        Not one begotten of a shepherd swain
        But issued from the progeny of kings;
        Virtuous and holy, chosen from above
        By inspiration of celestial grace   40
        To work exceeding miracles on earth.
        I never had to do with wicked spirits;
        But you, that are polluted with your lusts,
        Stained with the guiltless blood of innocents,
        Corrupt and tainted with a thousand vices,   45
        Because you want the grace that others have,
        You judge it straight a thing impossible
        To compass wonders but by help of devils.
        No, misconceivèd! Joan of Arc hath been
        A virgin from her tender infancy,   50
        Chaste, and immaculate in very thought,
        Whose maiden blood, thus rigorously effused,
        Will cry for vengeance at the gates of heaven.

YORK Ay, ay. – Away with her to execution.

---

37 one] *Collier, conj. Malone;* me, F   49 No, misconceivèd!] *Steevens subst.;* No misconceyued F; No, misconceived
F4; No misconceivers *conj. Capell;* Me misconceived *conj. Wilson*   49 Arc] *Rowe;* Aire F   52 maiden blood]
Theobald; Maiden-blood F

29 ratsbane Sublimate of (white) arsenic, used
as a poison.
  30 keep watch over, protect (*OED* sv *v* 14).
  32 drab strumpet.
  35 qualities skills (*OED* Quality *sb* 1b); compare *Ham.* 2.2.432: 'give us a taste of your
quality'.
  37 *one Malone's suggestion for F's 'me'
(Sisson, *New Readings*, II, 74). (For F's one/me
confusion in reverse compare *Shr.* 1.2.166.)
  38 progeny lineage (*OED* sv 5).
  39–53 Joan offers a travesty of the story of the
virgin birth (see Luke 1) and of the way in which
the Pharisees attributed Christ's miracles to
Beelzebub (see Matt. 12.24, 27).
  40 Compare Hall: 'This woman was not

inspired with the Holy Ghost, nor sent from God,
(as the Frenchmen believe), but an enchantress'
(p. 157).
  41 exceeding of surpassing excellence (*OED*
ppl adj 3).
  42 do with With a sexual innuendo.
  43–5 The passage recalls the story of Aholibah
in Ezek. 23.17, 37.
  46 want lack.
  47 straight immediately.
  48 compass accomplish.
  49 *misconceivèd you have misunderstood;
with possibly a taunt at York for alleged bastardy.
Some editors delete F's comma to make the word
an epithet for Joan, meaning 'misbegotten'.
  52 effused spilt.

WARWICK And hark ye, sirs: because she is a maid,   55
    Spare for no faggots; let there be enow.
    Place barrels of pitch upon the fatal stake
    That so her torture may be shortenèd.

PUCELLE Will nothing turn your unrelenting hearts?
    Then, Joan, discover thine infirmity   60
    That warranteth by law to be thy privilege:
    I am with child, ye bloody homicides;
    Murder not then the fruit within my womb,
    Although ye hale me to a violent death.

YORK Now heaven forfend, the holy maid with child?   65

WARWICK [*To La Pucelle*] The greatest miracle that e'er ye wrought!
    Is all your strict preciseness come to this?

YORK She and the dauphin have been juggling.
    I did imagine what would be her refuge.

WARWICK Well, go to; we'll have no bastards live,   70
    Especially since Charles must father it.

PUCELLE You are deceived; my child is none of his:
    It was Alençon that enjoyed my love.

YORK Alençon, that notorious Machiavel?
    It dies, and if it had a thousand lives.   75

PUCELLE O, give me leave, I have deluded you:
    'Twas neither Charles nor yet the duke I named,
    But Reignier, King of Naples, that prevailed.

WARWICK A married man: that's most intolerable!

YORK Why, here's a girl! I think she knows not well   80
    (There were so many) whom she may accuse.

WARWICK It's sign she hath been liberal and free.

---

61 law to be] F; law *Hanmer*   66 SD] *This edn; not in* F   68 juggling] F (iugling); ingling *Oxford*   70 we'll] F;
we will F2   74 Machiavel] *Pope;* Macheuile F

56 **enow** enough.
60 **discover** reveal.
61 **warranteth** guarantees (*OED* Warrant *v* 3).
61 **privilege** The immunity from execution derived from Roman law and granted to pregnant women.
63 **fruit…womb** Compare Ps. 127.3, Gen. 30.2.
64 **hale** drag.
67 **preciseness** morality, puritanical behaviour.
68 **juggling** (1) cheating, (2) fornicating.
69 **imagine** wonder.
69 **refuge** last plea, excuse (*OED* sv *sb* 4c).

74 *****Machiavel** Gentillet's *Contre-Machiavel* (1576) was dedicated to the Duc d'Alençon (later Henri III) who was also the suitor of Elizabeth, and hated because he had taken part in the Massacre of St Bartholomew in 1572. 'Machiavel' was the epithet given in Elizabethan times to any ambitious, greedy, or cruel politician. The Duc d'Alençon who was accused of treason to France was executed in 1476 in Henry's thirty-sixth year – not, as Hall notes, in 1458 (p. 238).
78 **prevailed** Euphemism for 'seduced me'.
82 **liberal** licentious (*OED* sv *adj* 3).
82 **free** generous (ironic).

YORK And yet, forsooth, she is a virgin pure! –
    Strumpet, thy words condemn thy brat and thee.
    Use no entreaty, for it is in vain. 85

PUCELLE Then lead me hence, with whom I leave my curse:
    May never glorious sun reflex his beams
    Upon the country where you make abode;
    But darkness and the gloomy shade of death
    Environ you, till mischief and despair 90
    Drive you to break your necks or hang yourselves!

                                 Exit [guarded]

Enter CARDINAL [BEAUFORT, BISHOP OF WINCHESTER, *attended*]

YORK Break thou in pieces and consume to ashes,
    Thou foul accursèd minister of hell!

WINCHESTER Lord regent, I do greet your excellence
    With letters of commission from the king. 95
    For know, my lords, the states of Christendom,
    Moved with remorse of these outrageous broils,
    Have earnestly implored a general peace
    Betwixt our nation and the aspiring French;
    And here at hand the dauphin and his train 100
    Approacheth, to confer about some matter.

YORK Is all our travail turned to this effect?
    After the slaughter of so many peers,
    So many captains, gentlemen, and soldiers
    That in this quarrel have been overthrown 105
    And sold their bodies for their country's benefit,
    Shall we at last conclude effeminate peace?

---

91 SD.1 *guarded*] Theobald; not in F   **91** SD.2 BEAUFORT…*attended*] Capell subst.; after 93, Pope; not in F   **94** SH WINCHESTER] Eds.; Car. F (Win. / at 123)   **101** some matter] F; the same Cairncross   **102** travail] Steevens; trauell F

84 brat Not necessarily pejorative.
86 whom Refers generally to all those present.
87 reflex cast (*OED* sv *v* 2b).
89 Compare Matt. 4.16: 'The people which sat in darkness…and shadow of death'; and Dent SS5.
  90 mischief misfortune, trouble (*OED* sv *sb* 1).
  91 hang yourselves The conventional end of those driven by despair to suicide; compare *FQ*, I, ix, 50.
  91 SD.2 There seems to be no need to place the cardinal's entrance two lines later as most editors have done. He brings news of peace, and could effectively watch the vindictive raging of York. There is no other example of an anticipated

entrance – a sign of prompt-book copy – in the text.
  92 consume burn away (*OED* sv *v*¹ 6c).
  93 minister servant (*OED* sv *sb* 1).
  95 letters of commision a warrant giving authority (*OED* Letter *sb*¹ 4b).
  96 states rulers (*OED* sv *sb* 26); compare Hall 'the princes…of Christendom' (p. 174).
  97 remorse of pity for (*OED* Remorse *sb* 3).
  97 outrageous violent (*OED* sv *adj* 2).
  99 aspiring ambitious.
  101 matter subject of contention (*OED* sv *sb*¹ 20).
  102 Is this the outcome of all our efforts?
  105 overthrown vanquished.

Have we not lost most part of all the towns,
By treason, falsehood, and by treachery,
Our great progenitors had conquerèd?   110
O Warwick, Warwick, I foresee with grief
The utter loss of all the realm of France!

WARWICK Be patient, York: if we conclude a peace
It shall be with such strict and severe covenants
As little shall the Frenchmen gain thereby.   115

Enter CHARLES, ALENÇON, BASTARD, REIGNIER[, *and others*]

CHARLES Since, lords of England, it is thus agreed
That peaceful truce shall be proclaimed in France,
We come to be informèd by yourselves
What the conditions of that league must be.

YORK Speak, Winchester, for boiling choler chokes   120
The hollow passage of my poisoned voice
By sight of these our baleful enemies.

WINCHESTER Charles and the rest, it is enacted thus:
That, in regard King Henry gives consent
Of mere compassion and of lenity,   125
To ease your country of distressful war
And suffer you to breathe in fruitful peace,
You shall become true liegemen to his crown.
And, Charles, upon condition thou wilt swear
To pay him tribute and submit thyself,   130
Thou shalt be placed as viceroy under him,
And still enjoy thy regal dignity.

ALENÇON Must he be then as shadow of himself?

109–10] *As* F; *110 precedes 109, conj. this edn*   114 severe] F; *several Cairncross, conj. Vaughan*   115 SD *and others*]
Capell; not in F   121 poisoned] F; *prisoned Theobald subst.*   122 baleful] F; *baneful conj. Johnson*

109–10 The sense would emerge more clearly
if the order of the lines were reversed.
114 severe Might be trisyllabic (Cercignani,
p. 34); Vaughan's conjecture 'several' would
mean 'applying to each of the parties'.
114 covenants agreements, conditions.
115 As That (Abbott 109).
119 league covenant (*OED* sv *sb*² 2).
120–2 There may be an allusion here to the
mythical basilisk that killed with a look.
120 choler bile, the humour that caused anger
(*OED* sv *sb*¹ 1); compare *2H6* 5.1.23.

121 poisoned venomous (*OED* sv *ppl adj* 3).
122 baleful malign (*OED* sv *adj* 1).
124 in regard since (*OED* Regard *sb* 15).
125 Of From (Abbot 168).
125 mere pure.
125 lenity mildness.
128 liegemen feudal vassals.
130 submit thyself surrender (*OED* Submit *v*
1c).
133 shadow The opposite of 'substance' in
135.

Adorn his temples with a coronet,
And yet, in substance and authority,   135
Retain but privilege of a private man?
This proffer is absurd and reasonless.

CHARLES 'Tis known already that I am possessed
With more than half the Gallian territories,
And therein reverenced for their lawful king: 140
Shall I, for lucre of the rest unvanquished,
Detract so much from that prerogative
As to be called but viceroy of the whole?
No, lord ambassador, I'll rather keep
That which I have than, coveting for more,   145
Be cast from possibility of all.

YORK Insulting Charles, hast thou by secret means
Used intercession to obtain a league
And, now the matter grows to compromise,
Stand'st thou aloof upon comparison?   150
Either accept the title thou usurp'st,
Of benefit proceeding from our king
And not of any challenge of desert,
Or we will plague thee with incessant wars.

REIGNIER [*Aside to Charles*] My lord, you do not well in obstinacy   155
To cavil in the course of this contract:
If once it be neglected, ten to one
We shall not find like opportunity.

ALENÇON [*Aside to Charles*] To say the truth, it is your policy
To save your subjects from such massacre   160
And ruthless slaughters as are daily seen

149 compromise] *Rowe;* compremize F   155, 159 SD] *Capell; not in* F

134 **coronet** Worn by mere nobles and not monarchs.
139 **Gallian** French.
140 **reverenced for** honoured as.
141 **lucre** gain (*OED* sv *sb* 2).
142 **Detract** Take away.
144–6 **I'll...all** Compare the proverb 'All covet all lose' (Tilley A127).
146 **cast** driven away.
149 **grows to compromise** is about to be resolved.
150 'Do you stand to compare your present state, a state which you have neither right nor power to maintain, with the terms which we offer' (Johnson); compare *Ant.* 3.13.26.
152 **Of benefit** A benefaction; with a legal sense (*OED* Benefit *sb* 2c).
153 **of desert** by rightful claim.
156 **in...contract** while this agreement is being drawn up.
156 **contract** Accented on the second syllable (Cercignani, p. 31).
159 **policy** politic stratagem; an apt piece of advice from a Machiavel (see 74).

By our proceeding in hostility;
And therefore take this compact of a truce
Although you break it when your pleasure serves.
WARWICK How say'st thou, Charles? Shall our condition stand?   165
CHARLES It shall;
    Only reserved you claim no interest
    In any of our towns of garrison.
YORK Then swear allegiance to his majesty:
    As thou art knight, never to disobey   170
    Nor be rebellious to the crown of England,
    Thou, nor thy nobles, to the crown of England.
       [Charles and the rest give tokens of fealty]
    So, now dismiss your army when ye please;
    Hang up your ensigns, let your drums be still,
    For here we entertain a solemn peace.   175

                      Exeunt

[5.5] *Enter* SUFFOLK *in conference with the* KING, GLOUCESTER, *and*
EXETER

KING HENRY Your wondrous rare description, noble earl,
    Of beauteous Margaret hath astonished me:
    Her virtues gracèd with external gifts
    Do breed love's settled passions in my heart,

165] *As Pope;* How...*Charles?* / Shall...*stand?* F   172 SD] *Johnson; not in* F   Act 5, Scene 5   5.5] *Capell subst.; Actus Quintus.* F

163 **compact** agreement.
166–75 Charles's capitulation is quite un-historical (see headnote).
167 **reserved** with the reservation that.
168 **towns of garrison** garrison-towns (*OED* Garrison *sb* 4c).
171, 172 **crown of England** Rather than attributing this repetition to authorial 'puerility' (Wilson) or a 'scribal error' (Cairncross) we might treat it as a cue for an actor playing the part to consider the regal aspirations of York.
173–5 The note of triumph is to be short-lived as Suffolk machinates in the next scene to introduce Margaret to his monarch – Margaret who

will cause such havoc between the countries.
175 **entertain** enter upon (*OED* sv *v* 16).

Act 5, Scene 5
*5.5 Gloucester's opposition in 1444 to the truce arranged by Suffolk at Tours (nine years after the treaty at Arras depicted in the last scene), along with the proposal of marriage to Margaret, is narrated by Holinshed (pp. 206–7; Hall, p. 204).
2 **astonished me** filled me with wonder (*OED* Astonish *v* 4, although no examples are offered from before 1611).
4 **settled** firmly fixed.

And, like as rigour of tempestuous gusts   5
Provokes the mightiest hulk against the tide,
So am I driven by breath of her renown
Either to suffer shipwreck, or arrive
Where I may have fruition of her love.

SUFFOLK Tush, my good lord, this superficial tale   10
Is but a preface of her worthy praise:
The chief perfections of that lovely dame
(Had I sufficient skill to utter them)
Would make a volume of enticing lines,
Able to ravish any dull conceit;   15
And, which is more, she is not so divine,
So full replete with choice of all delights,
But with as humble lowliness of mind
She is content to be at your command –
Command, I mean, of virtuous chaste intents   20
To love and honour Henry as her lord.

KING HENRY And otherwise will Henry ne'er presume. –
Therefore, my lord protector, give consent
That Margaret may be England's royal queen.

GLOUCESTER So should I give consent to flatter sin.   25
You know, my lord, your highness is betrothed
Unto another lady of esteem:
How shall we then dispense with that contract
And not deface your honour with reproach?

SUFFOLK As doth a ruler with unlawful oaths;   30
Or one that, at a triumph, having vowed
To try his strength, forsaketh yet the lists
By reason of his adversary's odds:

11 of] F; t(F2

5–7 'This simile is somewhat obscure; he
seems to mean, that as a ship is driven against
the tide by the wind, so he is driven by love
against the current of his interest' (Johnson).
  5 **rigour** violence (*OED* sv 4).
  6 **Provokes** Impels (*OED* sv *v* 4).
  6 **hulk** ship (*OED* sv *sb²* 1).
  8 **arrive** reach the shore (*OED* sv *v* 2).
  10 **superficial tale** account of her appearance.
  11 **her worthy praise** A latinate construction
for 'the praise of her worth' (Abbott 3).
  15 **conceit** imagination (*OED* sv *sb* 7b).

  17 **full** fully.
  25 **flatter** gloss over, palliate (*OED* sv *v¹* 3).
  27 **another lady** The daughter of the Earl of
Armagnac; see 44 below.
  28 **dispense with** set aside (*OED* Dispense *v*
12).
  28 **contract** Accented on the second syllable
(Cercignani, p. 31).
  29 **deface** blot out (*OED* sv *v* 3b).
  31 **triumph** tournament.
  32 **lists** tournament grounds.

A poor earl's daughter is unequal odds,
And therefore may be broke without offence.   35
GLOUCESTER Why, what, I pray, is Margaret more than that?
Her father is no better than an earl,
Although in glorious titles he excel.
SUFFOLK Yes, my lord; her father is a king,
The King of Naples and Jerusalem,   40
And of such great authority in France
As his alliance will confirm our peace,
And keep the Frenchmen in allegiance.
GLOUCESTER And so the Earl of Armagnac may do,
Because he is near kinsman unto Charles.   45
EXETER Beside, his wealth doth warrant a liberal dower,
Where Reignier sooner will receive than give.
SUFFOLK A dower, my lords! Disgrace not so your king,
That he should be so abject, base, and poor,
To choose for wealth and not for perfect love.   50
Henry is able to enrich his queen,
And not to seek a queen to make him rich:
So worthless peasants bargain for their wives,
As market-men for oxen, sheep, or horse.
Marriage is a matter of more worth   55
Than to be dealt in by attorneyship.
Not whom we will, but whom his grace affects,
Must be companion of his nuptial bed.
And therefore, lords, since he affects her most
Most of all these reasons bindeth us   60
In our opinions she should be preferred.
For what is wedlock forcèd but a hell,

---

35 therefore] F; therefor't *conj. Oxford*   39 my] F; my good F2   46 warrant a] F; warrant F2   55 Marriage] F;
But marriage F2   59 most] *Sisson (New Readings);* most, F   60 Most] F; It most *Rowe;* Which most *Wilson*

---

34 Marrying below one's station brought the dishonour of 'disparagement' (*OED* sv 1). 46 indicates that 'poor' means 'lowly' here – see Lisa Jardine, *Still Harping on Daughters*, 1983, p. 80.

35 And...broke i.e. the pledge of marriage may therefore be broken.

36 I pray The first recorded use of this parenthetical phrase (*OED* Pray *v* 8c).

42 As That (Abbott 109).

42 confirm strengthen (*OED* sv *v* 1).

46 warrant guarantee.

47 Where Whereas.

50 perfect pure (*OED* sv *adj* 5d).

53 So Thus.

56 attorneyship (1) proxy (*OED* sv 1), (2) legal haggling (Sanders).

57 affects desires.

59 since the fact that; the word seems to introduce a noun clause.

62 what...hell Compare the proverb 'Love cannot be compelled' (Tilley L499).

An age of discord and continual strife,
Whereas the contrary bringeth bliss
And is a pattern of celestial peace.   65
Whom should we match with Henry, being a king,
But Margaret, that is daughter to a king?
Her peerless feature, joinèd with her birth,
Approves her fit for none but for a king;
Her valiant courage and undaunted spirit   70
(More than in women commonly is seen)
Will answer our hope in issue of a king;
For Henry, son unto a conqueror,
Is likely to beget more conquerors
If with a lady of so high resolve   75
As is fair Margaret he be linked in love.
Then yield, my lords, and here conclude with me
That Margaret shall be queen, and none but she.
KING HENRY Whether it be through force of your report,
My noble Lord of Suffolk, or for that   80
My tender youth was never yet attaint
With any passion of inflaming love,
I cannot tell; but this I am assured,
I feel such sharp dissension in my breast,
Such fierce alarums both of hope and fear,   85
As I am sick with working of my thoughts.
Take therefore shipping: post, my lord, to France;
Agree to any covenants, and procure
That Lady Margaret do vouchsafe to come
To cross the seas to England and be crowned   90
King Henry's faithful and anointed queen.
For your expenses and sufficient charge,
Among the people gather up a tenth.
Be gone, I say, for till you do return

---

72 Will answer our] F; Answer our *Pope;* Will answer *Hudson, conj. Steevens*   82 love] F2; Ioue F   90 To
cross] F; Across *Hudson, conj. Walker*

64 contrary 'Pronounced as if written "con-
terary"' (Wilson).
65 pattern copy, likeness (*OED sv sb* 4).
68 feature figure (*OED sv sb* 1).
69 Approves Proves.
70 courage sexual energy (*OED sv sb* 3e).
80 for that because.

81 attaint sullied.
87 post hasten.
88 covenants terms.
88 procure contrive (*OED sv v* 4b).
92 sufficient charge to meet your costs.
93 tenth A tax of a tenth part of a profit or
property.

I rest perplexèd with a thousand cares. –   95
And you, good uncle, banish all offence:
If you do censure me by what you were,
Not what you are, I know it will excuse
This sudden execution of my will.
And so conduct me where from company   100
I may revolve and ruminate my grief.   *Exit*
GLOUCESTER Ay, grief, I fear me, both at first and last.

                              Exit Gloucester [with Exeter]
SUFFOLK Thus Suffolk hath prevailed, and thus he goes
As did the youthful Paris once to Greece,
With hope to find the like event in love,   105
But prosper better than the Trojan did.
Margaret shall now be queen, and rule the king:
But I will rule both her, the king, and realm.   *Exit*

FINIS

102 SD *with Exeter*] Hanmer; not in F

95 rest remain.

96 offence feeling of being hurt (*OED* sv *sb* 4b).

97 censure judge (with no connotations of blame).

97 what you were An allusion to Gloucester's infamous first 'marriage' to the Lady Jaquet, wife to John, Duke of Brabant (Hall, pp. 116, 128–9; not in Holinshed).

100 from company alone.

101 revolve consider.

101 grief uneasiness (Johnson); amorous pain (Sanders).

102 grief harm, trouble.

103–6 Suffolk likens himself to Paris who cuckolded Menelaus by stealing his wife Helen from him – the precipitating cause of the Trojan War. Suffolk, however, hopes for fortune in love while avoiding the misfortune of war.

105 event result.

107–8 The lines act as a kind of commercial for the second part of the play.

TEXTUAL ANALYSIS

1 Henry VI was first published in the First Folio edition (F) of Shakespeare's works that appeared in 1623 – that is, some seven years after his death. '*The first Part of Henry the Sixt*'[1] is placed among the history plays after *Henry V*, in the order, that is, of monarchical reign and not the order of composition by Shakespeare. It occupies pp. 96–119 of the volume. The plays had been prepared by John Heminges and Henry Condell, Shakespeare's fellow players, and printed in the workshop of William Jaggard. The texts in the subsequent seventeenth-century Folios (1632, 1664, 1685) are based ultimately on this first edition. Although F2 offers a comparatively large number of metrical regularisations, these represent only conjectures emanating from the printing-house responsible for that text.

The text of a Renaissance play was subject to alteration or corruption at up to seven stages: by the author (or authors) while still in preliminary drafts; by authors or scribes preparing a 'fair copy' for delivery to a company;[2] by an adapter connected with the company by whom it was performed; by the book-holder (who doubled as a prompter)[3] annotating the foul papers[4] or preparing a copy for performance; by an editor preparing copy for the printer;[5] by the compositors; and by the proof-reader. It is logical to look for evidence of changes of these kinds in reverse order and so produce a theory about the nature of the copy used by the compositors who turned the manuscript into the printed texts that survive. A theory of the history of this copy is a prerequisite to the investigation of revision or of authorship: John Dover Wilson, who was a notable 'disintegrator', did not have a theory of the text, and derived his theory of copy from his theory of collaboration and revision.[6]

As a preliminary, we should note that proof-readers did not always check proofs against copy, that their aim was simply to correct typographical inaccuracies or irregularities, and that they might well thereby introduce corruption by correction.[7] In fact there is only one variant in the quires (k, l, m) on which *1 Henry VI* is printed,

---

[1] The entry in the Stationers' Register that covers the seventeen plays first published in the Folio would seem to refer to this play as 'The thirde parte of Henry the Sixt' as *2H6 and 3H6* had already been printed as *1 Contention* and *Richard Duke of York*.

[2] See Fredson Bowers, *On Editing Shakespeare*, 1966.

[3] W.W. Greg, *The Shakespeare First Folio*, 1955, p. 100.

[4] *Ibid.*, p. 109.

[5] These have been studied by S.W. Reid, 'The editing of Folio *Romeo and Juliet*', *SB* 35 (1982), 43–66, and by Eleanor Prosser, *Shakespeare's Anonymous Editors*, 1981. As there is no quarto of *1 Henry VI* we cannot make any inferences about what Edward Knight, Heminges, or Condell (?) may have done to the text.

[6] 'The copy for *1 Henry VI*', Wilson, pp. 102–7.

[7] Charlton Hinman, *The Printing and Proof-Reading of the First Folio of Shakespeare*, 2 vols., 1963, I, 227.

and that simply involved the pushing down of two letters that stood too high in *Enter*, the first word of 2.1.7 SD.[1]

It was established by Charlton Hinman that *1 Henry VI* was, like the remainder of the histories, set by the two compositors, A and B, who, in Jaggard's shop, were responsible for setting most of the Folio.[2] Spelling tests (A preferred the forms 'doe, 'goe, 'here'; B the forms 'do', 'go', 'heere') and the tracing of individual pieces of type allowed Hinman to assign A, working from case x, and B, working from case y, the following stints:[3]

Ax set k2^v–k5a	pp. 96–101a	1.1.1–1.6.31
By set k5b	p. 101b	2.1.1–2.1.44
Ax set k5^v–l3	pp. 102–9	2.1.45–3.4.45
By set l3^v–l4	pp. 110–12	4.1.1–4.5.12
Ax set l5	p. 113	4.5.13–4.7.22
By set l5^v–m2	pp. 114–19	4.7.23–5.5.108

This analysis accounts for spelling inconsistencies that seemed to earlier scholars to point to manuscript copy, either produced by more than one hand or written by more than one author.[4] So we find that A spelt 'Joan' consistently 'Ioane', B spelt 'Ione';[5] A set 'Reigneir', B set 'Reignier'.[6] A used *Talb.* as a SH, B used *Tal.* It also, I believe, accounts for the conspicuously variant spellings of 'Burgundy' and 'Gloucester'.

With regard to the SHs for Burgundy there is absolute consistency in that A always set *Burg.* (12 times) and B, as usual preferring a shorter form, always set *Bur.* (5 times). In the verse, A printed *Burgonie* 13 times, B not at all; B printed *Burgundy* 7 times, A not at all. A printed *Burgundie* twice (TLN 771, 2.2.0 SD; TLN 2185, 4.6.14)[7] and B printed it 3 times (TLN 2090, 4.4.26; TLN 2264, 4.7.32 SD; TLN 2460, 5.3.29 SD). Cairncross surmised that the variant spellings of this name

---

[1] *Ibid.*, I, 274.

[2] *Ibid.*, II, 33–57. Hinman's findings were questioned by Andrew Cairncross who, in an article published after his edition of this play, found traces of Compositor E in it: 'Compositors E and F of the Shakespeare First Folio', *PBSA* 66 (1972), 396–406. His arguments were, however, refuted by Richard Proudfoot, 'Textual studies', *S.Sur.* 27 (1974), 182–3, and by T.H. Howard-Hill, 'Compositors B and E in the Shakespeare First Folio and Some Recent Studies' (privately circulated typescript, 1976).

[3] Further information on the habits of B can be found in two articles by S.W. Reid, 'Justification and spelling in Jaggard's Compositor B', *SB* 27 (1974), 91–111, and 'Some spellings of Compositor B in the Shakespeare First Folio', *SB* 29 (1976), 102–38.

[4] See Wilson, pp. 106–7.

[5] Philip Williams, 'New approaches to textual problems in Shakespeare', *SB* 8 (1956), 3–14, notes that A consistently prints *Puzel* in Act 1 and *Pucell* in Act 3. However, this may have been due to a change in Shakespeare's spelling. He could read *Pusell* consistently in Holinshed (pp. 165, 169, 172), but in Hall *Pucelle* (p. 148) or 'puzell' (pp. 149, 156).

[6] The anomalous spellings 'Reynold' (TLN 105, 1.1.94) and 'Reignard' (TLN 2091, 4.4.27) probably derive from a misreading of 'Veignold' mentioned by Hall (p. 145) as being a companion of the Bastard at the siege of Orléans, and by confusion with the well-known name 'Reynard'. It also appears thus in *The First Part of the Contention* TLN 71.

[7] TLN is a system of numbering that registers all the lines printed on a page of play-text, not just the lines which are spoken.

might go back to the chronicles,[1] but in fact none of the *Burgundie* passages has a direct source.

The case is slightly more difficult with 'Gloucester'. A invariably used *Glost.* as a SH (29 times) or *Glo.* – in two long lines (TLN 1212 and 1369). B invariably printed *Glo.* (13 times). A's preferred spelling was *Gloster* (24 times), although he printed *Gloucester* 3 times (TLN 1051, 1690, 1705) – in the first of these two cases the word is in close proximity to 'Winchester'. He printed *Glocester* once (TLN 1254, 3.1.49) in a passage derived from Holinshed, who prints *Glocester* consistently here[2] – that spelling may therefore be authorial. B's prefered spelling was *Glocester* (4 times) although he printed *Gloster* once (TLN 2393, 5.1.58) and *Gloucester* once (TLN 2857, 5.5.36). The last example is decidedly anomalous: it is a SH, and the long form caused the compositor to run over to another line. It is a key piece of evidence for Cairncross, who thought he had detected the presence of another compositor (E),[3] and, while I cannot explain it, I do not think it carries sufficient weight to conjecture E's hand here or elsewhere in the play. These spelling variants, therefore, tend in my opinion to confirm Hinman's original attribution.

As there is no quarto text of *1 Henry VI*, we cannot form a theory that allows us to emend the text consistently in the light of the compositors' known habits. There is only one piece of possible high-handedness on B's part (see below), and the literals and possible interpolations I have discovered are common to both compositors. There are several almost certain cases of dittography (TLN 480, 942, 986, 1089, 1179, 1380, 1385, 1957) that seem to me to justify emendation, but these could equally derive from manuscript copy.

I believe, however, that one of the textual cruces of the play is probably compositorial in origin. At 2.1.7 we find the following SD: *Enter Talbot, Bedford, and Burgundy; with scaling Ladders: Their Drummes beating a Dead March.* The sounding of drums might not seem to make sense in a scene depicting a surprise attack by night – although it could be here that 'dead' means that the drums were muffled (see 2.1.7 SD n.). Rather than conjecturing that the second part of the stage direction was added by a book-holder who confused the moment with the opening of 2.2,[4] I would suggest that the stage direction may have originally stood at the head of the scene, providing a kind of dumb-show before its opening and, with its image and sound of the dead march, offering a visual quotation of the opening of the play. (The opening of Act 3, set up by A, contains a similar 'dumb-show' – Winchester's tearing of Gloucester's paper, and Act 4 opens with a coronation, an obvious set-piece.) The scene depicts, in other words, Talbot's revenge for Salisbury's death (see 1.4.90 ff.). After the funeral has passed over the stage – now assuming that *Dead March* indicates a funeral procession – the three English lords stand conferring on the stage, unseen by the French above, a simple device for suspense and irony (compare the sequence of actions described at 1.5.0 SD). The dialogue lends

---

[1] Cairncross, p. xv.
[2] Boswell-Stone, pp. 220 ff.
[3] See p. 188 above, n. 2.
[4] See Wilson's note to 2.1.7 SD, p. 138.

weight to this hypothesis: Talbot refers to 'this happy night' (2.1.11), meaning that, having assembled for Salisbury's funeral, they might seize the occasion ('happy' here means 'by good fortune') and mount a surprise attack. The column (k5b) was anomalously set by B, the only setting he did in this quire, and he has been shown elsewhere to be 'unusually prone to take liberties with his copy'[1] when setting stage directions. Hinman has found evidence for the interruption of the normal work sequence at this stage in the printing,[2] and it is tempting to suggest that the two compositors conferred at this point, puzzled by the unusual stage direction, and that B decided it was misplaced and moved it to a position immediately before the dialogue between the Englishmen begins, also undertaking to set up that column. That said, I do not feel that the case I have just made is sufficiently strong to justify an emendation.

The next stage in our investigation must be to decide whether the copy used by the compositors derives from a manuscript used in the playhouse or not. Evidence of theatrical stage directions, added presumably by the book-holder, would suggest that the text passed through such a stage: we must decide whether the copy represented holographic or scribal copy marked up by the book-holder in preparation for the copying out of the prompt-book, or a scribal copy of the prompt-book. As possible book-holder additions are few – indeed there is no mention of important properties like the rose-bush in 2.4 – it is reasonable to assume the former.[3] Dover Wilson argued that 'the copy for F. can never have been used as a prompt-book',[4] although he finds traces of the prompter's hand in the text. Cairncross follows this suggestion[5] and also Wilson's strange argument that *misplaced* stage directions are evidence of prompter annotation. I shall deal with these first.

They both list 2.1.7 SD which I have already conjectured to be compositorially misplaced, and then 4.1.181 'where the *Flourish* should clearly follow the exit of the King at 173'.[6] This is far more likely to be compositorial. Both the SDs in 4.1 contain the formula *Exeunt. Manet*.... So the first probably should have read: *Exeunt. Flourish. Manet Yorke, Warwick, Exeter, Vernon* (TLN 1925); the second: *Exeunt. / Manet Exeter* (TLN 1934). It is easy to see how B's eye could have slipped. The third example both give is 3.2.35 where F reads:

> And then doe execution on the Watch. *Alarum.*
> *An Alarum. Talbot in an Excursion.*   (TLN 1462–3)

Cairncross argues that this 'illustrates the well-known phenomenon of an authorial stage-direction being carried into the margin where it will catch the eye of the

---

[1] Alice Walker, 'The Folio text of *1 Henry IV*', *SB* 6 (1954), 45–59; however, Paul Werstine finds that in *Lear* B's work was much more accurate: 'Folio editors, Folio compositors, and the Folio text of *King Lear*', in G. Taylor and M. Warren (eds.), *The Division of the Kingdoms*, 1983, pp. 248–72.

[2] Hinman, II, 36–41.

[3] The work of a book-holder may be discerned by comparing the stage directions of the quarto editions of *R2*, which derive ultimately from foul papers, with those in the Folio text, which derives from a prompt-book. See A. Gurr (ed.), *R2*, 1984, pp. 176–9.

[4] Wilson, p. 103.

[5] Cairncross, pp. xvi–xviii.

[6] *Ibid.*, p. xvii.

prompter but not deleted in its original position'.[1] Rather I would suggest a sim-
pler solution: Shakespeare intended two alarums, one for the French, one for the
English.

In fact there are examples, listed by neither editor, of marginal stage directions
that might indicate prompter's annotation. These occur at TLN 539–40, 773,
1435, and 2429. The first, second, and fourth of these occur at the bottom of the
columns in which they appear and were therefore, after imperfect casting-off,
probably placed in the margin to save space. The third, *Knock* (TLN 1435, 3.2.12),
could well have been authorial – like that at TLN 2628, 5.3.184 *Kisse her.*

There is one possible example of an anticipatory entrance (TLN 2732, 5.4.91). I
do not think it necessary to amend here as York's vindictive exclamation and
Winchester's entrance bearing news of peace could be effectively witnessed simul-
taneously by the audience.[2] My analysis suggests, therefore, that there is no compelling evidence for annotation by the book-holder.

One of the distinctive features of the stage directions is, in Act 1, the number
that begin with *Here*. None marks an entrance. There are ten: TLN 216, 306, 425,
441, 539, 569, 578, 587, 600, 629. There is one example in Act 3 at TLN 1617.
Dover Wilson pointed out that this convention can also be found in Nashe's
Summer's Last Will and Testament and used it as evidence for Nashe's hand in the
play.[3] However, the usage, although uncommon, is found in *The Merchant of
Venice* TLN 1406, 3.2.62 SD: *Here Musicke*. This text seems to derive from prompt-
book copy. There are examples in *King John* (2.1.299 SD) and *Coriolanus* (1.8.13
SD), both foul-paper texts, and in the Folio text of *King Lear* (2.4.125), possibly a
reported text. It also occurs in *2 Henry VI*, TLN 2964, 4.10.57 SD, *3 Henry VI* TLN
230, 1.1.205 SD, and TLN 2850, 5.2.50 SD. As these examples derive from foul
papers, prompt-books, and reports, the evidence cannot be used for textual
provenance or authorship. Again they might be compositorial: Philip Williams
points out that they all, along with the two examples from *3 Henry VI*, occur in
stints set by Compositor A.[4]

One of the most vexing problems of the text is its division into acts and scenes.
As is common, only the act division and first scene are marked in Acts 1 and 2, but
Act 3 is fully divided.[5] Act 4 would seem to run from its beginning through to the
end of 5.4 where we find the anomalous *Actus Quintus* standing as a heading for the
last scene of the play (5.5). *Scena secunda* and *Scœna Tertia* stand as headings to 5.1
and 5.2 respectively. Various explanations have been offered. Pollard, followed by
Alexander, suggested that Scene 2 is Scene 2 not of Act 4 but of Act 5, Scene 1

---

[1] *Ibid.*, p. xvii. Compare Greg, *First Folio*, who points out that in fact duplication of stage directions is
rare (pp. 138–9).
[2] Greg, *First Folio*, p. 183, concluded that such entrances are not necessarily evidence of prompt-book
copy.
[3] Wilson, p. 105; Gary Taylor, 'Shakespeare and others', also uses it in his argument over authorship.
[4] Philip Williams, 'New approaches', p. 8.
[5] I cannot agree with Williams that the scene division in Act 3 indicates a change in manuscript copy.
Rather it would seem to be the result of imperfect casting-off. Pages 107–9 are conspicuously
uncrowded and use scene headings to fill out the page.

having been excised along with the Act 5 heading, and that the *Actus Quintus* head-ing is an error for *Scena Quinta*. He points out that there is a similar error in *King John* where *Actus Secundus* stands for *Scena Secunda*.[1] Cairncross, following a suggestion of Harold Brooks, suggests that some 'agent' preparing the text for the printer was confused by the large number of entrances and exits marked by alarums and excursions and woke up to the need for divisions in the action when the scene moved from France to England or vice versa.[2]

A third explanation could again be compositorial interference. B had set up the first part of Act 4 (13^v–14^v, the inmost sheet of the quire), and then A set 15^r. Returning to the task at 15^v, B set from copy from which the heading *Actus Quintus. Scena Prima* was missing or inconspicuous (a simple marginal numeral?). He must have assumed that it appeared in the copy for 15^r. When he came to the opening of 5.1, a moment where the action reverts to England after the death of Talbot in France, he registered a break, marked *Scena secunda*, and, having cast off imper-fectly and to fill out the column, displayed *SENNET*, anomalously, on a single line. His *Scæna Tertia* marks the return to France. By the time he reached $m1^r$, im-perfect casting-off brought about a crowding of the page (folios 1 and 6 of a quire were generally set up last). Entrances are unspaced here, and, to save more space, he omitted a heading *Scæna quarta*. The heading *Actus Quintus* accordingly has two explanations. Either it is an error for *Scæna Quinta* (the manuscript reading merely 'v' or '5')[3] or, more probably, it marks B's awareness that no Act 5 heading had been set and his impulsive decision to set one before the copy for the play ran out.[4]

My argument so far supports the hypothesis that the copy for *1 Henry VI* was holographic or a scribal copy of a holographic manuscript that might have been lightly annotated by a book-holder. The principal textual cruces, the misplaced SDs in 2.1 and the confusion over act and scene numbering, may well be due to compositorial interference. It is now necessary to decide whether it is possible to discover whether the compositors were working from a holographic fair copy or from a scribal transcript. Cairncross argued that a scribal presence might be detected.[5] His evidence falls under five headings. His first is his assumption that the scribe transposed words and phrases, generally destroying inversion or

---

[1] Cited by Cairncross, p. xxv.

[2] Cairncross, p. xxvi; Taylor notes that the divisions are literary rather than theatrical and that the confusion derived from multiple authorship (Wells and Taylor, *Textual Companion*, p. 218).

[3] Errors of this kind could easily occur because, as Hinman points out (I, 179), act and scene headings were often not distributed. A compositor could easily therefore pick up the wrong line of type.

[4] There are analogies with the even more confused act and scene numberings in *John*. Honigmann suggests that 'the compositor read certain numbers at the head of the scenes and interpreted these unmethodically, confusing acts and scenes. Thus "II" or "2" (for Act II?) he made *Scæna Secunda*; "2" (for Act II, Sc. ii?) he made *Actus Secundus*' (Honigmann (ed.), *John*, 1954, p. xxxviii). By analogy with *1H6* it may be that the reduplication of *Actus Quartus* that occurs in *John* was due to Compositor C taking over the setting of b3^v – Compositor B having set the first *Actus Quartus* on b1. For a list of other plays where act and scene divisions seem to be the result of compositorial error see Gary Taylor in *The Division of the Kingdoms*, p. 417.

[5] Cairncross, pp. xviii–xxiv; Cairncross is followed by Sanders (pp. 240–1) and by Fredson Bowers (although no evidence is given) – *On Editing Shakespeare*, 1966, p. 114.

chiasmus. He conjectures, for example, that at 2.4.41 F's 'The fewest Roses are cropt from the Tree' should read '. . . from the tree are cropt'. He lists at least ten examples. However, there is no way of proving that Shakespeare was incapable of writing like this,[1] and Alice Walker has shown[2] that transposition was a habit of both compositors, A and B. His second examples are of interpolations to supply an ellipsis or fill out a title. Again Walker showed this to be a compositorial habit.[3] Thirdly, he give examples of dittography. But to these, compositors are obviously as prone as scribes. His fourth and fifth categories, of errors in meaning rather than form (substitutions) and of omissions, are those for which B has become notorious, especially the second.[4] It seems, therefore, that we should wield Occam's razor and argue that there is no evidence for the text having been set up from a scribal copy of foul papers.[5] Cairncross's turn of mind was Augustan and his desire for metrical regularity and rhetorical order led him to postulate the existence of this scribe. Even if we agree that emendation is necessary, this will be because of compositorial rather than scribal corruption.

We must now look to the text to see whether it presents positive signs of authorial copy[6] to support further our hypothesis. It does. First, we find descriptive stage directions. The opening SD of the play, which contains the information that Bedford is Regent of France, is one example of this. At TLN 217 we find the note that the French are driven back *with great losse*.[7] At TLN 392 we find a description of dress: Winchester's men are *in Tawney Coates*. We find a permissive SD at TLN 488–9 when Salisbury and Talbot enter *with others*.[8] At TLN 720 we find *The French leape ore the walles in their shirts*, a sentence taken almost verbatim from Hall's chronicle.[9] A property, the porter's bunch of keys, is mentioned at TLN 870.[10] At TLN 1949 we find a location *before Burdeaux*. The scene with the fiends (TLN 2433) contains descriptions of attitudes and gestures. (There are in addition many examples of missing stage directions (see 1.1.81, 161 SDs, etc.) which point to authorial copy.)

There are also examples of 'ghost' characters – that is, characters who enter but do not speak.[11] It would be expected that a book-holder, seeking to accommodate a large number of characters to a small number of players, would have cut these as much as possible. But neither Warwick nor Somerset speaks in 1.1, Suffolk is

---

[1] Compare Gary Taylor in *The Division of the Kingdoms*, p. 409.
[2] Walker, 'Folio text', p. 53; Walker's article should be read in conjuntion with Paul Werstine, 'Compositor B of the Shakespeare First Folio', *Analytic and Enumerative Bibliography* 2 (1978), 241–63.
[3] Walker, 'Folio text', pp. 50–1.
[4] *Ibid.*, pp. 49–50.
[5] Gary Taylor believes that a scribe would have obscured many of the orthographical and linguistic features which distinguish the authorial shares he distinguished (Wells and Taylor, p. 217).
[6] Greg, *First Folio*, pp. 124 ff.
[7] Further examples are to be found at TLN 1298, 1614, 1989, 2169–70, 2820.
[8] Further examples are to be found in TLN 927, 1560, 2009.
[9] Hall, p. 143.
[10] Compare TLN 1423.
[11] Greg, *First Folio*, p. 112.

silent in 3.1 and 4.1, and in 3.4 Shakespeare assembles all the lords for a short ceremonial scene in which only Gloucester speaks (compare 5.2). Alençon is silent in 4.7.

There are examples of inconsistency in speech headings. In 1.2 *Charles* becomes *Dolphin* at 47, an example of the well-known phenomenon of a character's name being replaced by that of his role.[1] At 2.5.35 *York(e)* becomes *Rich.* – both examples occur immediately after the alternative designation has occurred in the dialogue.[2] Joan/Pucelle, Cardinal/Winchester, Pole/Suffolk, General/Captain are further examples of these alternations.

Cairncross, who followed Greg[3] and postulated annotation of the manuscript by a book-holder, thought that the missing entrances for Reignier and Alençon at 3.2.17 and 40 indicated an attempt to amalgamate the two parts in order to reduce the size of the 'cast'.[4] His argument, however, is vitiated by a failure to make a distinction between *characters* and *players*. Elizabethan companies could not perform the large-cast plays without doubling,[5] and reducing the number of characters in one or two scenes does not reduce the number of actors necessary for a performance of the play. To have done this, moreover, would have reduced the French court to only three nobles, an unviable number. As there is no further sign of interference with regard to these characters, I prefer to think that this is an example of authorial omission,[6] parallel to the missing entrances of Glansdale and Gargrave at 1.4.21, of Vernon and Basset at 3.4.0, and of the Captain at 4.4.0.

Strangely, Cairncross argues that the same editorial hand sought to replace Sir William Lucy by a Messenger and a Herald, which would serve to *increase* the number of characters. Lucy appears in 4.3 where, at his entrance, he is designated *another Messenger*, and the speech headings are *2.Mes.* then *Mes.* York's address to him at 43, however, refers to him as 'Lucy'. He remains on stage through 4.4 (in some ways a continuation of the previous scene)[7] where he is given the speech heading *Lu(c)*. In 4.7 he again appears, and to Pope and succeeding editors his opening lines seemed hypermetric:

> Herald, conduct me to the Dolphins Tent,
> To know who hath obtain'd the glory of the day.   (4.7.51–2)

It is tempting to suggest that originally this small part was assigned to the actor playing Lucy, then re-assigned by the book-holder to a bit-part actor as a herald. This is Cairncross's suggestion: he surmises that 'Herald' was written over the

---

[1] *Ibid.*, p. 113–14.

[2] *Rich.* is used in 3.1, the scene of his investiture as Duke of York, and *York* is used for the remainder of the play.

[3] Greg, *First Folio*, p. 187; Taylor explains this sort of anomaly 'by the fact that the foul papers were in this instance collaborative' (Wells and Taylor, *Textual Companion*, p. 217).

[4] Cairncross, p. xvii.

[5] See Stanley Wells and Gary Taylor, *Modernizing Shakespeare's Spelling with Three Studies in the Text of Henry V*, 1979, pp. 72–123.

[6] Greg, *First Folio*, p. 112.

[7] See 4.3.53 SD n.

original speech heading, but that the compositor printed both.[1] Rather I would suggest that Shakespeare replaced the unnecessary English herald by the character which had evolved during his writing of 4.3 and 4.4 – Lucy did not figure in the sources.[2] This conjecture, however, does not seem to me to justify the omission of 'Herald' and the consequent relineation.

My review of the textual problem, therefore, leads me to conclude that there is some evidence of compositorial interference, but no real evidence for the intervention of a scribe or methodical annotations of a book-holder in the transmission of the manuscript to the printer. The conclusion is that the text was set up from holographic fair copy.

[1] Cairncross, p. xviii.
[2] See the note in the List of Characters.

APPENDIX 1

Examples from Shakespeare's sources

Longer extracts from these texts are to be found in Bullough and Boswell-Stone

1. Henry V

This Henry was a king whom life was immaculate and his living without spot. This king was a prince whom all men loved and of none disdained. This prince was a captain against whom fortune never frowned nor mischance once spurned. This captain was a shepherd whom his flock loved and lovingly obeyed...He had such knowledge in ordering and guiding an army and such a grace in encouraging his people that the Frenchmen said he could not be vanquished in battle...What policy he had in finding sudden remedies for present mischiefs, and what practice he used in saving himself and his people in sudden distresses, except by his acts they did plainly appear, I think it were almost a thing incredible...What should I say, he was the blazing comet and apparent lantern in his days, he was the mirror of Christendom and the glory of his country, he was the flower of kings past and a glass to them that should succeed...No prince had less of his subjects and never king conquered more: whose fame by his death as lively flourisheth as his acts in his life were seen and remembered. When his death was published among the common people, incontinent their hearts were appalled and their courages abated; their dolour so much increased and their wits were so much troubled that they, like madmen, rent their garments and tore their hair, accusing and blaming fortune which had taken away from them so precious a jewel, so noble an ornament, and so sure a defence; for no doubt as much hope as was taken away from the Englishmen for the getting of France by his sudden death, so much trust was increased in the stomachs of the French nation, hoping to recover their ancient liberty and parentage. (Hall, pp. 112–13)

2. The loss of Paris in 1436 (see 1.1.69–73)

Although the Duke of York was worthy (both for birth and courage) of this honour and preferment [to the regency of France], yet so disdained of Edmund Duke of Somerset (being cousin to the king) that by all means possible he sought his hindrance, as one glad of his loss and sorry of his well doing. By reason whereof, ere the Duke of York could get his dispatch, Paris and diverse other of the chiefest places in France were gotten by the French king. The Duke of York, perceiving his evil will, openly dissembled that which he inwardly minded, either of them working things to the other's displeasure, till through malice and division between them, at length by mortal war they were both consumed with almost all their whole lives and offspring.

The Normans of the country of Caux, being heartened by the death of the Duke of Bedford, began a new rebellion, slew diverse Englishmen, robbed many towns that were under the English obeisance, and took the town of Harfleur by assault and diverse other towns...

But here is one chief point to be noted: that either the disdain amongst the chief peers of the realm of England (as ye have heard), or the negligence of the king's council (which did not foresee dangers to come) was the loss of the whole dominion of France, between the rivers of Saône and Marne, and, in especial, of the noble city of Paris. For where before there were sent over thousands for defence of the holds and fortresses, now were sent hundreds, yea, and scores, some rascals, and some not able to draw a bow or carry a bill; for the Lord Willoughby and the Bishop of Terwin which had the governance of the great city of Paris had in their company not two thousand Englishmen.

(Holinshed, p. 185; compare Hall, p. 179)

3. Joan of Arc

(a) From the beginning of Hall's account

For as he [Jean Bouchet] and other say, there came to him being at Chinon a maid of the age of twenty years and in man's apparel, named Joan, born in Bourgogne in a town called Domremy beside Vaucouleurs, which was a great space a chamberlain in a common hostry, and was a ramp of such boldness that she would course horses and ride them to water, and do things that other young maidens both abhorred and were ashamed to do; yet, as some say, whether it were because of her foul face that no man would desire it, either [or] she had made a vow to live chaste, she kept her maidenhead and preserved her virginity. She (as a monster) was sent to the Dauphin by Sir Robert Baudricour, captain of Vaucouleurs, to whom she declared that she was sent from God, both to aid the miserable city of Orléans and also to remit him to the possession of his realm out of the which he was expulsed and overcome; rehearsing to him visions, trances, and fables full of blasphemy, superstition, and hypocrisy that I marvel much that wise men did believe her and learned clerks would write such fantasies. What should I rehearse, how they say, she knew and called him her king whom she never saw before. What should I speak, how she had by revelation a sword, to her appointed in the church of Saint Catherine, of Fierbois in Touraine, where she had never been. What should I write, how she declared such privy messages from God, Our Lady, and other saints to the Dauphin, that she made the tears run down from his eyes. So was he deluded, so was he blinded, and so was he deceived by the devil's means which suffered her to begin her race, and in conclusion rewarded her with a shameful fall. But in the mean season such credit was given to her that she was honoured as a saint of the religious, and believed as one sent from God of the temporality, in so much that she, armed at all points, rode from Poitiers to Blois and there found men of war, victual, and munitions ready to be conveyed to Orléans.

(Hall, p. 148)

(b) From the beginning of Holinshed's account

In time of this siege at Orléans, French stories say, the first week of March 1428, unto Charles the Dauphin, at Chinon as he was in very great care and study how to wrestle against the English nation, by one Peter [*sic*] Baudricourt...was carried a young wench of an eighteen years old, called Ione Are [*sic*; in margin: *Ione de Are, Pusell de dieu*], by name of her father, a sorry shepherd, James of Are, and Isabel her mother; brought up poorly in their trade of keeping cattle; born at Domprin (therefore reported by Bale, Joan Domprin) upon Meuse in Lorraine within the diocese of Toul. Of favour was she counted likesome, of person strongly made and manly, of courage great, hardy, and stout withal, an understander of counsels though she were not at them, great semblance of chastity both of body and behaviour, the name of Jesus in her mouth about all her businesses, humble, obedient, and fasting diverse days in the week. A person (as their books make her) raised up by power divine only for succour to the French estate then deeply in distress; in whom, for planting a credit the rather, first the company that toward the Dauphin did conduct her, through places all dangerous as holden by the English, where she never was alone, all the way and by nightertale, safely did she lead. Then at the Dauphin's sending by her assignment, from Saint Catherine's church of Fierbois in Touraine (where she never had been and knew not), in a secret place there among old iron, appointed she her sword to be sought out and brought her, that with five fleur-de-lis was graven on both sides, wherewith she fought and did many slaughters by her own hands. On warfare rode she in armour cap-à-pie and mustered as a man; before her an ensign all white wherein was Jesus Christ painted with a fleur-de-lis in his hand.

Unto the Dauphin into his gallery when first she was brought, and he shadowing himself behind, setting other gay lords before him to try her cunning from all the company, with a salutation...she picked him out alone, who thereupon had her to the end of the gallery, where she held him an hour in secret and private talk, that of his privy chamber was thought very long, and therefore would have broken it off, but he made them a sign to let her say on. In which (among other) as likely it was, she set out unto him the singular feats (forsooth), given her to understand by revelation divine, that in virtue of that sword she should achieve, which were, how with honour and victory she would raise the siege at Orléans, set him in state of the crown of France, and drive the English out of the country, thereby he to enjoy the kingdom alone. Hereupon he heartened at full, appointed her a sufficient army with absolute power to lead them, and they obediently to do as she bade them. Then fell she to work, and first defeated indeed the siege at Orléans, by and by encouraged him to crown himself king of France at Rheims, that a little before him the English she had won. Thus after pursued she many bold enterprises to our great displeasure a year or two together, for the time she kept in state until she were taken and for heresy and witchery burned: as in particularities hereafter followeth. But in her prime time she, armed at all points like a jolly captain, rode from Poitiers to Blois, and there found men of war, victuals, and munition ready to be conveyed to Orléans...   (Holinshed, pp. 163–4)

4. The Parliament of Bats (see 3.1)

[Fabyan notes that the parliament which witnessed the reconciliation of Winchester and Gloucester] was cleped of the common people the Parliament of Bats: the cause was, for proclamations were made that men should leave their swords and other weapons in their inns [dwellings], the people took great bats and staves in their necks, and so followed their lords and masters unto the parliament. And when that weapon was inhibited them, then they took stones and plummets of lead and trussed them secretly in their sleeves and bosoms.   (Fabyan, p. 596)

5. Talbot and Young Talbot (see 4.5)

This conflict continued in doubtful judgement of victory two long hours, during which fight the lords of Montamban and Humadayre with a great company of Frenchmen entered the battle and began a new field, and suddenly the gunners, perceiving the Englishmen to approach near, discharged their ordnance and slew three hundred persons near to the earl who, perceiving the imminent jeopardy and subtle labyrinth in which he and his people were enclosed and illaqueate [ensnared], despising his own safeguard and desiring the life of his entirely and well-beloved son the Lord Lisle, willed, advertised, and counselled him to depart out of the field and to save himself. But when the son had answered that it was neither honest nor natural for him to leave his father in the extreme jeopardy of his life, and that he would taste of that draught which his father and parent should assay and begin, the noble earl and comfortable captain said to him, 'O son, son, I thy father, which only hath been the terror and scourge of the French people so many years, which hath subverted so many towns, and profligate [vanquished] and discomfited [defeated] so many of them in open battle and martial conflict, neither can here die for the honour of my country without great laud and perpetual fame, nor fly or depart without perpetual shame and continual infamy. But because this is thy first journey and enterprise, neither thy flying shall redound to thy shame nor thy death to thy glory: for as hardy a man wisely flieth as a temerarious person foolishly abideth. Therefore the fleeing of me shall be the dishonour not only of me and my progeny but also a discomfiture [rout] of all my company. Thy departure shall save thy life and make thee able another time, if I be slain, to revenge my death and to do honour to thy prince and profit to his realm.' But nature so wrought in the son that neither desire of life nor thought of security could withdraw or pluck him from his natural father who, considering the constancy of his child and the great danger that they stood in, comforted his soldiers, cheered his captains, and valiantly set on his enemies and slew of them more in number than he had in his company. But his enemies, having a greater company of men and more abundance of ordnance than before had been seen in a battle, first shot him through the thigh with a hand-gun, and slew his horse, and cowardly killed him lying on the ground (whom they never durst look in the face while he stood on his feet); and with him there died manfully his son the Lord Lisle, his bastard son Henry Talbot, and Sir Edward Hull, elect to the noble Order of the Garter, and thirty valiant personages of the English nation. . .   (Hall, p. 229)

6. The terms at Arras (compare 5.4)

Upon the day of the first session, the Cardinal of St Cross declared to the three parties the innumerable mischiefs that had followed to the whole state of the Christian commonwealth by their continual dissension and daily discord, exhorting them for the honour of God and for the love which they ought to bear towards the advancement of his faith and true religion, to conform themselves to reason and to lay aside all rancour, malice, and displeasure, so that in concluding a godly peace they might receive profit and quietness here in this world and of God an everlasting reward in heaven. After this admonition and diverse days of communication, every party brought in their demands which were most contrary and far from any likelihood of coming to a good conclusion.

The Englishmen would that King Charles should have nothing but what it pleased the king of England, and that not as duty but as a benefit by him of his mere liberality given and distributed. The Frenchmen, on the other part, would that King Charles should have the kingdom frankly and freely, and that the king of England should leave the name, arms, and title of the king of France and be content with the dukedoms of Aquitaine and Normandy, and to forsake Paris and all the towns which they possessed in France between the rivers of Somme and Loire being no parcel of the Duchy of Normandy. To be brief, the demands of all parts were between them so far out of square, as hope of concord there was none at all.

The cardinals, seeing them so far in sunder, minded not to dispute their titles, but offered them reasonable conditions of truce and peace for a season, which notwithstanding, either of frowardness or of disdain on both parts, were openly refused. Insomuch that the Englishmen in great displeasure departed to Calais and so into England.   (Holinshed, pp. 182–3 (Hall, p. 175))

APPENDIX 2
Genealogical tables

Edward III m. Philippa of Hainault
1312–*1327*–*1377*

Edward, the Black
Prince
1330–76

William
of Hatfield

Lionel, Duke of
Clarence
1338–68

Blanche of m. John of Gaunt m. Cathe
Lancaster   1340–99   Swyr

Richard II
1367–*1377*–*1399*–1400

Henry IV
(Bullingbrook)
1367–*1399*–*1413*

THOMAS, DUKI
OF EXETER
d. 1427

Charles VI of France

Charles VII
1403–*1422*–*1461*
(THE DAUPHIN)

Katherine m. Henry V
1387–*1413*
–*1422*

Thomas, Duke of
Clarence
1388?–1421

JOHN, DUKE OF
BEDFORD
1389–1435

HUMPHREY, DUKE OF
GLOUCESTER
1391–1447

HENRY VI m. MARGARET
1421–*1422*–   OF ANJOU
1461–1471   1430–*1445*–*1482*

Edward, Prince
of Wales
1453–71

Names of those in the play appear in capitals.
Italicised dates are those of reigns.
*See Notes to List of Characters, p. 63 above.

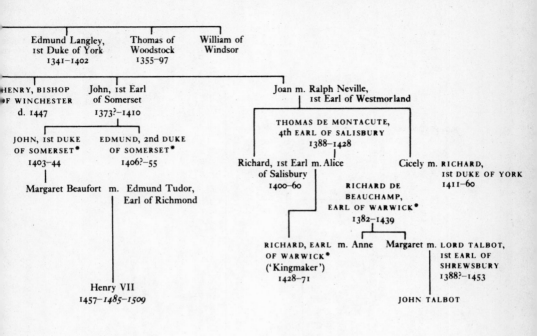

Table 1
THE HOUSE OF LANCASTER

Edward III m. Philippa of Hainault
1312–1327–1377

Edward, the Black Prince
1330–76

Richard II
1367–1377–1399–1400

William of Hatfield

Lionel, Duke of Clarence
1338–68

Philippa m. Edmund Mortimer, 3rd Earl of March

Elizabeth m. Henry Percy (Hotspur)
1364–1403

John, 7th m. Elizabeth
Lord Clifford

John, 12th Baron Clifford (Old Clifford)
1414–55

John, 13th Baron Clifford (Young Clifford)
1435?–1461

Roger Mortimer, 4th Earl of March
1374–98

Sir Edmund Mortimer
1376–1409?

EDMUND MORTIMER, 5th EARL OF MARCH
1391–1425

Anne m. Richard, Earl of Cambridge d. 1415

John of Gaunt, Duke of Lancaster
1340–99

Edmund Langley, 1st Duke of York
1341–1402

Edward of Norwich, 2nd Duke of York
1373?–1415

Constance

Isabella m. RICHARD DE BEAUCHAMP, EARL OF WARWICK*
1382–1439

RICHARD PLANTAGENET, m. Cicely Neville
3rd DUKE OF YORK
1411–60

Edward IV m. Elizabeth Woodville (Lady Grey)
1442–1461–1483   *1437?–1492*

Edward V
1470–1483

Richard
1472–1483

Elizabeth m. Henry VII (Richmond)
1465–1503   *1457–1485–1509*

Edmund, Earl of Rutland
1443–60

George, Duke m. Isabella of Clarence   Neville
1449–78

Richard III (Duke of Gloucester)
1452–1483–1485

Thomas of Woodstock
1355–97

William of Windsor

Names of those in the play appear in capitals.
Italicised dates are those of reigns.
*See Notes to List of Characters, p. 63 above.

Table 2 THE HOUSES OF YORK AND MORTIMER

APPENDIX 3
The Rose theatre

Illustrations 3, 5 and 8, showing possible methods of staging *Henry VI*, were drawn in 1987. They are necessarily conjectural in certain respects (for example, the structure and decoration of the castle-like stage-house) but the scale of the stage itself and the theatre surrounding it are derived from good documentary evidence about the shapes and sizes of certain public-theatre stages of Elizabethan London. These appear generally to have been large: three we have evidence for measured 40 × 27 feet, 39 × 25 feet, and 40 × 30 feet respectively. But in February 1989 an archaeological excavation on Bankside in Southwark revealed the actual remains of the Elizabethan Rose theatre. This is the first and only existing physical evidence of such a theatre ever to be seen, and it has immediately confounded much conjecture by being smaller, with a much smaller stage, than has from the earlier evidence been generally supposed. Therefore, as the Rose was the very theatre on whose stage a play of *Henry VI* (presumably Shakespeare's) was first acted in public (on 3 March 1591/2), it is clearly useful and proper to include here a tentative representation of the conditions and scale of that theatre, for comparison with – and perhaps as a corrective to – my earlier drawings.

It should be stated that my reconstructive sketch in illustration 17 has been made at an early date of the archaeological find. Many questions arising from that have yet to be resolved. Also, there is much more material still to be unearthed and analysed at the site. This drawing is therefore offered for the time being only, as a schematic simplification from some of the present facts. The plan dimensions I give here are approximate, and may possibly need adjusting (if by only a little) after further excavation and study. The vertical dimensions of the main gallery building are those known for certain from another theatre (the Fortune) built and owned by the same proprietor as the Rose. The shape of the stage is as found at the Rose, but the decoration of it is as imagined by me, to make it reasonably comparable with my previous drawings. It will immediately be seen that the staging of *Henry VI* at the Rose must have been more limited in scope than at any of the larger playhouses where at other times the cycle of *Henry VI* plays is likely also to have been performed.

C. Walter Hodges

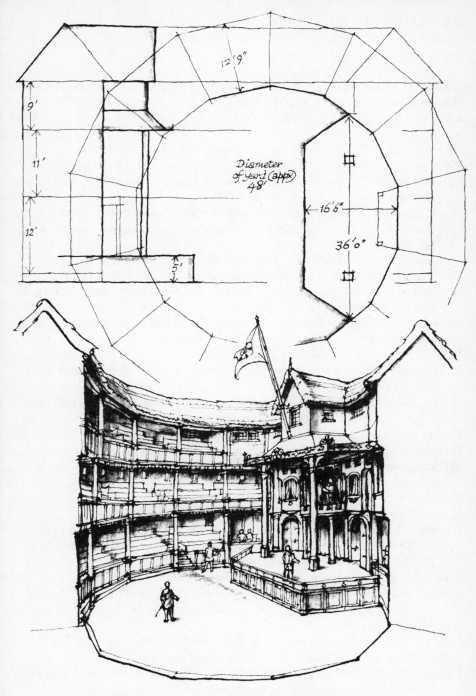

17   The Rose theatre: a conjectural reconstruction by C. Walter Hodges

READING LIST

A selection of critical texts central to the study of the play is listed here. The list also includes relevant works of reference, as well as some books and articles which might be found useful for further study.

Alexander, Peter. *Shakespeare's 'Henry VI' and 'Richard III'*, 1929

Baldwin, T. W. *Shakspere's 'Small Latine & Lesse Greeke'*, 2 vols., 1944

Berman, Ronald S. 'Fathers and sons in the *Henry VI* plays', *SQ* 13 (1962), 487–97

Berry, Edward. 'Twentieth-century Shakespeare criticism: the histories', in Stanley Wells (ed.), *The Cambridge Companion to Shakespeare Studies*, 1986, pp. 249–56

    Patterns of Decay: Shakespeare's Early Histories, 1975

Bevington, David. 'The domineering female in *1 Henry VI*', *S.St.* 2 (1966), 51–8

Blanpied, J. W. ' "Art and baleful sorcery": the counterconsciousness of *Henry VI Part 1*', *SEL* 15 (1975), 213–27

Boswell-Stone, W. G. *Shakespeare's Holinshed: The Chronicle and the Historical Plays Compared*, 1896

Bristol, Michael D. *Carnival and Theater*, 1985

Brockbank, J. P. 'The frame of disorder – *Henry VI*', in J. R. Brown and B. Harris (eds.), *Early Shakespeare*, 1961

Brooke, Nicholas. 'Marlowe as provocative agent in Shakespeare's early plays', *S.Sur.* 14 (1961), 34–44

Brownlow, F. W. *Two Shakespearean Sequences*, 1977

Bullough, G. *Narrative and Dramatic Sources of Shakespeare*, III, 1960

Bulman, James C. *The Heroic Idiom of Shakespearean Tragedy*, 1985

    'Shakespeare's Georgic histories', *S.Sur.* 38 (1985), 37–47

Burckhardt, S. *Shakespearean Meanings*, 1968

Burke, Peter. *The Renaissance Sense of the Past*, 1969

Campbell, Lily B. *Shakespeare's 'Histories': Mirrors of Elizabethan Policy*, 1947

Carroll, D. Allen. 'Greene's "vpstart crow" passage: a survey of commentary', *Research Opportunities in Renaissance Drama* 28 (1985), 111–27

Champion, L. *Perspective in Shakespeare's English Histories*, 1980

Clemen, Wolfgang. 'Some aspects of style in the *Henry VI* plays', in P. Edwards, I-S. Ewbank, G. K. Hunter (eds.), *Shakespeare's Styles: Essays in Honour of Kenneth Muir*, 1980, pp. 9–24

Colman, E. A. M. *The Dramatic Use of Bawdy in Shakespeare*, 1974

Cox, John D. *Shakespeare and the Dramaturgy of Power*, 1989

Dean, P. 'Shakespeare's Henry VI trilogy and Elizabethan "romance" histories: the origins of a genre', *SQ* 33 (1982), 34–48

Dent, R. W. *Shakespeare's Proverbial Language: An Index*, 1981

Dessen, Alan C. *Elizabethan Stage Conventions and Modern Interpreters*, 1984

Eccleshall, Robert. *Order and Reason in Politics: Theories of Absolute and Limited Monarchy in Early Modern England*, 1978

Edmond, Mary. 'Pembroke's Men', *RES* 25 (1974), 129–36

Elton, G. R. *England Under the Tudors*, 1974

Fiedler, L. A. *The Stranger in Shakespeare*, 1972

Fleischer, Martha Hester. *The Iconography of the English History Play*, 1974

French, A. L. 'Joan of Arc and *Henry VI*', *English Studies* 49 (1968), 425–9

George, D. 'Shakespeare and Pembroke's Men', *SQ* 32 (1981), 305–23

Goy-Blanquet, D. 'Images de la monarchie dans le théâtre historique de Shakespeare', in E. Konigson (ed.), *Les Voies de la création théâtrale, VIII: théâtre, histoire, modèles*, 1980

Le Roi mis à nu: l'histoire d'Henri VI de Hall à Shakespeare, 1986

Griffiths, Ralph. *The Reign of King Henry VI*, 1981

Hammond, A. C. *The Early Shakespeare*, 1967

Harlow, C. G. 'A source for Nashe's *Terrors of the Night* and the authorship of *1 Henry VI*', *SEL* 5 (1965), 31–47 and 269–81

Hattaway, Michael. *Elizabethan Popular Theatre*, 1982

Hinchcliffe, Judith. *King Henry VI, Parts 1, 2, and 3*, Garland Shakespeare Bibliographies, 1986

Hinman, Charlton. *The Printing and Proof-Reading of the First Folio of Shakespeare*, 2 vols., 1963

Hodgdon, B. 'Shakespeare's directorial eye: a look at the early history plays', in S. Homan (ed.), *Shakespeare's 'More than Words can Witness'*, 1980, pp. 115–29

Honigmann, E. A. J. *Shakespeare: The 'Lost Years'*, 1985

Shakespeare's Impact on his Contemporaries, 1982

Howard-Hill, T. H. (ed.). *1 Henry VI: A Concordance to the Text of the First Folio*, 1970

Jackson, Sir Barry. 'On producing *Henry VI*', *S.Sur.* 6 (1953), 49–52

Jackson, Gabriele Bernhard. 'Topical ideology: witches, Amazons, and Shakespeare's Joan of Arc', *ELR* 18 (1988), 40–65

Jones, Emrys. *The Origins of Shakespeare*, 1977

Scenic Form in Shakespeare, 1971

Kastan, David Scott. 'Proud majesty made a subject: Shakespeare and the spectacle of rule', *SQ* 37 (1986), 459–75

Kay, C. McG. 'Traps, slaughters, and chaos: a study of Shakespeare's *Henry VI* plays', *Studies in the Literary Imagination* 5 (1972), 1–26

Kelly, F. L. 'Oaths in Shakespeare's *Henry VI* plays', *SQ* 24 (1973), 357–71

Kelly, H. A. *Divine Providence in the England of Shakespeare's Histories*, 1970

Leggatt, Alexander. *Shakespeare's Political Drama*, 1988

Long, J. H. *Shakespeare's Use of Music: The Histories and the Tragedies*, 1972

McCanles, Michael. *Dialectical Criticism and Renaissance Literature*, 1975

McFarlane, K. B. *England in the Fifteenth Century*, 1982

McMillin, Scott. 'Casting for Pembroke's Men: the *Henry VI* quartos and *The*

Taming of A Shrew', *SQ* 23 (1972), 141–59

Manheim, M. *The Weak King Dilemma in the Shakespearean History Play*, 1973

Mincoff, Marco. 'The composition of *Henry VI, Part 1*', *SQ* 16 (1965), 279–87

Price, Hereward T. *Construction in Shakespeare, University of Michigan Contributions in Modern Philology* 17, 1951

Reese, M. M. *The Cease of Majesty*, 1961

Rhodes, E. L. *Henslowe's Rose: The Stage and Staging*, 1976

Ribner, Irving. *The English History Play in the Age of Shakespeare*, rev. edn, 1965

Riddell, J. A. 'Talbot and the Countess of Auvergne', *SQ* 28 (1977), 51–7

Riggs, D. *Shakespeare's Heroical Histories: 'Henry VI' and its Literary Tradition*, 1971

Saccio, Peter. *Shakespeare's English Kings: History, Chronicle, and Drama*, 1977

Shepherd, Simon. *Marlowe and the Politics of Elizabethan Theatre*, 1986

Siegel, Paul N. *Shakespeare's English and Roman History Plays: A Marxist Approach*, 1986

Smidt, K. *Unconformities in Shakespeare's History Plays*, 1982

Sprague, A. C. *Shakespeare's Histories: Plays for the Stage*, 1964

Talbert, E. W. *Elizabethan Drama and Shakespeare's Early Plays: An Essay in Historical Criticism*, 1963

Taylor, Gary. 'Shakespeare and others: the authorship of *1 Henry VI*', *Medieval and Renaissance Drama in England* (forthcoming)

Tennenhouse, Leonard. *Power on Display: The Politics of Shakespeare's Genres*, 1986

Thomas, Keith. *Religion and the Decline of Magic*, 1971

Tillyard, E. M. W. *Shakespeare's History Plays*, 1944

Warren, Roger. '"Contrarieties agree": an aspect of dramatic technique in *Henry VI*', *S.Sur.* 37 (1984), 75–83

Wells, Stanley, and Taylor, Gary. *William Shakespeare: A Textual Companion*, 1987

Wilders, John. *The Lost Garden: A View of Shakespeare's English and Roman History Plays*, 1978

Williams, Penry. *The Tudor Regime*, 1979

Williamson, Marilyn L. '"When men are rul'd by women": Shakespeare's first tetralogy', *S.St.* 19 (1987), 41–60

Winny J. *The Player King: A Theme of Shakespeare's Histories*, 1968

Yates, Frances. *Astraea: The Imperial Theme in the Sixteenth Century*, 1975